"In the Open"

"In the Open"

Jewish Women Writers and British Culture

Edited by
Claire M. Tylee

DELAWARE

Newark: University of Delaware Press

Associated University Presses
2010 Eastpark Boulevard
Cranbury, NJ 08512

The paper used in this publication meets the requirements of the American National Standard for Permanence of Paper for Printed Library Materials Z39.48–1984.

Library of Congress-Cataloging-in-Publication Data

In the open : Jewish women writers and British culture / edited by Claire M. Tylee.
    p. cm.
Includes bibliographical references and index.
ISBN 13: 978-0-87413-933-4
ISBN 10: 0-87413-933-3
1. English literature—Jewish authors—History and criticism.
2. English literature—Women authors—History and criticism.
3. English literature—20th century—History and criticism. 4. Judaism and literature—Great Britain—History—20th century.
5. Women and literature—Great Britain—History—20th century.
6. Jewish women—Great Britain—Intellectual life—20th century.
7. Holocaust, Jewish (1939–1945), in literature. 8. Jews in literature.
I. Tylee, Claire M., 1946–
PR120.J48152   2006
820.9′9287089924—dc22

                                                        2005037717

PRINTED IN THE UNITED STATES OF AMERICA

Contents

Part III: Multicultural Literature

Part IV: Post-Holocaust Writing

Acknowledgments

Editor's Note and Acknowledgments

Because there is no one standard transliteration of Hebrew or Yiddish into English (e.g., "Hasidic" and "Chassidic"), I have left the varying spellings adopted by the contributors. Similarly, I have respected their wishes as to where to use capitalization in, for instance, H/holocaust, antis/Semitism, and whether to adopt the more generally recognizable term of "Holocaust" in place of "Shoah." I wish to acknowledge the inspiration, help and support I received from Phyllis Lassner, Jane Marcus, and Elaine Turner in devising this collection, and from my indefatigable research assistant, Anne Hoyle, in bringing it together. At all times, especially when the going got tough, I kept in mind my loving Jewish sister-in-law and her three children.

Publishers' Acknowledgments

The publishers acknowledge with thanks the kind permission granted by Roger L. Conover, literary executor to the estate of Mina Loy, to publish extracts from "Three Moments in Paris," "Anglo-Mongrels and the Rose," and "To You," and extracts from unpublished manuscript material held in the Mina Loy Papers, Yale Collection of American Literature, Beinecke Rare Book and Manuscript Library, Yale University, in the essay by Alex Goody.

"In the Open"

Introduction: The Visibility and Distinctiveness of Jewish Women's Writing in Britain

Claire M. Tylee

This collection of essays on British-Jewish women writers has been modelled on an earlier collection on Jewish American women writers edited by Jay L. Halio and Ben Siegel: *Daughters of Valor* (1997).[1] Despite the planned similarities, the results are significantly different. The contrast between the two collections not only emphasizes the differences between British and American literature; it helps to make plain the distinct environment of the Jewish women writers considered here. From this we can begin to understand their writing as both a reaction against "overweening Englishness" as well as a contribution to multicultural British literature and to the international Jewish collective.

The contrast is not due solely to the sizes of the Jewish population in the two countries: over six million in the United States, less than half a million in the United Kingdom.[2] It has more to do with the visibility of that population. Whereas Halio and Siegel could confidently jump off from the springboard of the established critical reputation of Jewish male authors who are prominent not only in American culture, but globally—writers such as Saul Bellow, Philip Roth, Bernard Malamud, Chaim Potok—no such apparatus presents itself to a British editor. There might be a few British Jewish male novelists to merit the esteem deserved by Roth et al. (the jury is still out);[3] there are certainly dramatists who do. Harold Pinter is the most obvious, encircled by Arnold Wesker, Tom Stoppard, Bernard Kops, Jack Rosenthal, Stephen Berkoff, Ronald Harwood, Stephen Poliakoff, Frederic Raphael, Anthony Shaffer, Peter Barnes, Ben Elton—the list seems endless. However, they are seldom treated as *Jewish* writers (not even Wesker, who so notably brought Jewish-British history to the stage with *Chicken Soup with Barley* in 1959). As Bryan Cheyette ruefully revealed in 1998, in the preface to his anthology *Contemporary Jewish Writing in Britain and Ireland,* despite the fact that he had been researching and publishing on British-Jewish literature for nearly twenty years: "As Jewish writers are thought not to exist in Britain, the common reaction to my eccentric enthusiasm has been . . . incredulity" (xi). The disbelief was shared, surprisingly, not only by literary journalists but by academic critics. They should have known better.

If the Jewish background of male writers in Britain is a "guilty secret" (Cheyette 1998, xi), then there has been an even guiltier effort to shield the modesty of women writers in Britain. Some of these are award-winning authors who have helped to define the character of twentieth-century English literature and are read worldwide.[4] They include novelists such as Muriel Spark (James Tait Prize 1965),[5] Eva Figes (*Guardian* prize 1967), Bernice Rubens (Booker Prize 1970), Leila Berg (Eleanor Farjeon medal 1973), Ruth Prawer Jhabvala (Booker Prize 1975), Anita Brookner (Booker Prize 1984), Linda Grant (Orange Prize 2000), and Elaine Feinstein (who was made fellow of the Royal Society of Literature in 1980), none of whom is reticent about the significance to their writing of their Jewish heritage; to take but one example, in *Sexing the Millennium* (1993) Linda Grant made this avowal of what it meant to her to be Jewish:

> I grew up in Liverpool, my parents the newly middle-class children of working-class Jewish immigrants. Judaism, with its emphasis on justice and the redemptive quality of social action, framed my moral world. To the Americans, being an English Jew is a contradiction. Jews eat pastrami and run Hollywood; Brits talk like John Cleese and drink tea. Hence English Jews aren't "real" Jews. But my parents were well aware that if the German army had crossed the Channel, they would have joined their cousins in the death camps. Haunted by the past, we had no choice but to believe in the future. (14)

British-Jewish women writers have persistently "outed" themselves.[6] Yet, as Louise Sylvester has demonstrated, this has not informed readings of their work.[7] This essay collection is firstly intended to be an acknowledgment of their avowals, attempting to keep their Jewish identity out in the open in order to see what follows for the analysis of their writing.

The essays are also part of an enterprise that has been gaining momentum since the 1970s: the enterprise of challenging the conservative canon of English literature that had been promoted by the older universities in Britain. This canon was notoriously thin on women writers until new histories were delineated by American critics such as Elaine Showalter, Sandra Gilbert, and Jane Marcus, aided by British editors like Michelene Wandor and publishing houses such as Virago and the Women's Press. It was a canon that also abetted a vision of Britain as culturally and ethnically homogeneous. If the syllabus at the Open University from the 1970s recognized working-class culture and the relevance of Scotland, Ireland, and Wales as well as England, then the New Universities, translated from the former polytechnics in the 1980s and often located in the inner cities, recognized the ethnic diversity of urban Britain. As the Afro-Caribbean novelist Caryl Phillips argued in his anthology *Extravagant Strangers*, "English literature was never 'pure,' untainted by influence . . . [it] has for at least 200 years, been shaped and influenced by outsiders [to Britain]" (1997, xiii). His examples demonstrate how this social heterogeneity has in fact invigorated British writing.

As was to be expected, the majority of his thirty-seven extracts witness the effects of the British Empire in bringing to the metropolitan center writers who were, or were descended from, immigrants from such places as Africa, the Indian subcontinent, Australasia, the Caribbean, or even Hong Kong (he does not include Ireland but he does include the United States). Yet not all held British passports. Four of the writers were of foreign nationality, Jewish asylum seekers: two were men who arrived postwar, George Szirtes (from Hungary) and Christopher Hope (from South Africa), and two were women, Ruth Prawer Jhabvala and Eva Figes, who were both prewar refugees from Nazi Germany. They are arranged, in Phillips's new configuration, among other foreign-born writers such as William Thackeray, T. S. Eliot, Joseph Conrad, Katherine Mansfield, and Salman Rushdie. Figes and Jhabvala also figure in Cheyette's anthology, *Contemporary Jewish Writing in Britain and Ireland,* along with native-born Jewish women writers Rubens, Feinstein, Brookner, and Wandor, and the American-born Ruth Fainlight, in among George Steiner, Harold Pinter, and Dan Jacobson.

Placed against such other collective works as those edited by Halio and Siegel, Cheyette, and Phillips,[8] this set of essays will aid readers to appreciate the significance of Jewish contributions to British culture, right across the British Isles and all through the twentieth century, as British literature energetically forged its way into the new millennium. There is no question that, just as in the nineteenth century and just as in the United States, Jewish women in twentieth-century Britain were prominent creators of prose and poetry, fiction and nonfiction, even if they have been less productive in the field of drama. Focusing primarily on women writers, these essays help reveal patterns among them and will enable scholars to relate these to specifically gynocritical concerns, such as tracing lines of influence between female authors, and the development of female-oriented genres and themes like romantic fiction, the Woman's Novel, lesbianism, and the mother-daughter bond. Unexpectedly, since feminist criticism has concentrated so strongly on relationships between women, and since Judaism is perceived as a religion that grants particular importance to domestic space and to mothers, autobiographical writing by these authors tends to reveal the powerful effect of the father-daughter bond,[9] and their fiction is much concerned with male characters and heterosexual relations.[10]

This is not entirely the case, and the effect of such a collection should be to dispel any tendency toward stereotyping the writers or straightjacketing the analysis of their writing. Like the volume by Halio and Siegel, one aim of this collection has been to be as inclusive and wide-ranging as possible, in order to demonstrate the diversity of Jewish writing in Britain.[11] Authors studied cover the whole twentieth century, from those born during the reign of Queen Victoria such as Naomi Jacob, Lily Tobias, and Mina Loy, to those writing at the start of the new millennium, such as Linda Grant and Anita Brookner, and they have been chosen to represent the cosmopolitan nature of British literature. Whilst the majority publish in London, only two were born there and few, unlike Anita Brookner, concern themselves mainly with metropolitan life. Most notably the novelists Bernice Rubens and Lily Tobias were Welsh-born and much of their work is set in Wales, while Betty Miller was educated in Ireland, Sweden, London, and France, all prominent locations for her writing; the dramatists Julia Pascal and Diane Samuels stem from the North of England; and the poet and novelist Elaine Feinstein was raised in the English Midlands. Other writers are incomers or outgoers. Ellen Galford, who now lives and writes in Scotland, was born in New Jersey, Deborah Levy is an exile from South Africa, and Silvia Rodgers, Karen Gershon, and Anita Lasker-Wallfisch were refugees from Germany. By contrast, the poets Mina Loy and Denise Levertov, who are generally thought of as American, were actually born in England and only emigrated as adults; their poetry is shown to be indebted to their British upbringing.

These writers are all here discussed in relation to Jewish identity, although their own Jewish connections are as diverse as their origins. Despite the fact that Levertov's father converted to Anglicanism, she writes out of the Hasidic heritage he brought from Russia. Betty Miller was born in Cork, Ireland, where her Lithuanian father was a magistrate and secretary to the local synagogue. Through Loy's poetry we recapture her father's Hungarian-Jewish origin. Feinstein's grandfather had been a *tsaddik* in Russia and her father was president of the orthodox synagogue in Leicester. Lily Tobias, the daughter of Polish-Jewish immigrants to Wales who created their own *minyan*, wrote ardently from her Welsh nationalist, Zionist, and pacifist convictions, eventually immigrating to Palestine. Lynne Reid Banks, a militant Zionist, married a Jewish sculptor and wrote from her experience of living for eight years on a kibbutz in Galilee where her Israeli sons were born before she returned to England. Silvia Rodgers was the socialist daughter of atheist Communists, expelled from Poland for their political beliefs. Linda Grant, whose grandparents had immigrated to Liverpool from Poland and Russia, has looked outward to both Palestine and United States in her novels. Similarly, Bernice Rubens, whose father immigrated to Cardiff from Lithuania, has set novels in Palestine, Indonesia, and Russia, as well as Germany, Wales, and England. With a German-Jewish father (like Naomi Jacob), Anita Brookner has written about the translated culture of Central European Jewry, raising dilemmas over assimilation.

The holocaust is an anxious presence[12] in the work of many of these writers, some of whom, such as the playwrights Julia Pascal, Deborah Levy, and Diane Samuels, were not born until after the war. On the other hand, the cellist Anita Lasker-Wallfisch immigrated to Britain after an adolescence spent in Belsen and Auschwitz. Her one book, recovering that experience for her grandchildren, can be considered alongside the self-writing of other refugees from Nazi Europe, including the children's books by Judith Kerr, the *When Hitler Stole Pink Rabbit* trilogy, the collective memoirs of child refugees, *We Came As Children,* edited by Karen Gershon, and *I Came Alone,* edited by Bertha Leverton and Schmuel Lowensohn, novels by Gershon, *A Lesser Child,* and Lore Segal, *Other People's Houses,* and other autobiographies such as Eva Figes's *Little Eden* and *Tales of Innocence and Experience.*[13] (Clearly the number of Jewish women writers in Britain far exceeds those covered by this collection.) The inclusion of nonobservant, secular, or even 'disaffected Jews'[14] such as Silvia Rodgers reminds us again how difficult it is not only to define either 'Jewishness' or what constitutes "Jewish literature" but also how strongly the position of secularity has been attested to by Jewish scholars such as David Cesarani and Susie Orbach.[15] Yet one feature that unites these various writers is their participation in the Jewish custom of retelling the past and inserting themselves into that communal history of Jewish persecution.

The earlier writers such as Naomi Jacob and Betty Miller are perhaps less well known now, and less read, than many of our contemporaries such as Anita Brookner or Ruth Prawer Jhabvala, although their Jewishness may have been more outspoken. However, it will be seen that they contribute coherently to the consistent, overall picture of prejudice, persecution, diaspora, and exile, and to the central themes of identity, alienation, and assimilation that are typical of Jewish writers.[16] Above all they manifest the continuing concern with history and with living the past in the present that marks Jewish culture. This collection also justifies the frequent assertion by critics that the Holocaust casts its shadow more darkly over Jewish writers than over other writers in Britain.[17] To that extent, this study contributes a particular strand to the recent analysis of the multicultural nature of twentieth-century British literature. It is typical of ethnic minority literature in Britain (Irish, South Asian, Caribbean, or Chinese) that it will show signs of exile, alienation and "unbelonging." One of the distinctive features of Jewish writing in Britain is how strongly it relates this sense of alienation and exile to the international literature of the Holocaust and to women's interest in traumatic testimony.

Other notable themes identified by these essays are the Jewish family and Israel/Palestine. In the 1970s and 1980s, both of these proved to be so contentious that they caused rifts in the British Women's Liberation Movement. Leaders were accused of ignoring ethnic difference in ways that not only promoted an implicit white Protestant universalism but were also actively racist and antisemitic. Especially after the invasion of Lebanon in June 1982 and the massacres of Palestinian women and children in the refugee camps of Sabra and Shatilla, there were angry arguments in the feminist journal *Spare Rib*. Although there was no overall agreement among Jewish feminists, in *Outwrite* the Jewish Feminist Group accused other feminists of being antisemitic for assuming that Judaism and Zionism were synonymous. Juliet Pope argued that the debate over Zionism "posed the most serious challenge to the movement to date" (1986).[18] The movement had already been challenged over its failure to recognize ethnic differences with regard to the family.[19] (This is still apparent in Michelene Wandor's history of the BWLM, *Once a Feminist* [1990], which commences with the historic Women's History Workshop conference in Oxford in 1970 and includes Jewish voices, but takes a socialist-feminist stance and omits ethnic dissent.)

As commentators like Adrienne Baker have demonstrated, "the family is central to Judaism, not simply because dispersion strengthened the need for family stability, but because Judaism became a 'domestic religion' to resist public anti-Semitism (1993, 123–25).[20] The Jewish family plays a special role in the transmission of Jewish identity, especially through the cultural and religious ritual that women preserve in the home. It is unsurprising, then, that the family should figure prominently in Jewish women's writing in Britain as well as America. The Jewish family is not only a scene of conflict between the generations, "a battleground" as Michael Woolf has called it (1995, 133–35), as in novels by Jacob, Brookner, and Rubens, or drama by Samuels, but also a source of happily contemplated continuation, as in the poetry of Elaine Feinstein. Either way, Jewish writers do not take the existence of the Jewish family for granted as a secure background.

One of the major differences between United States and United Kingdom as writing environments for Jewish authors is the far longer, more intimate association between Britain and the Middle East. In popular history this is epitomized through the romantic figure of Lawrence of Arabia. Political analysis points more coldly to the "carve up" of that region between France and Britain at the end of the First World War. There had been a particular connection between the United Kingdom and Palestine since the mid-nineteenth century when it was still a neglected part of the Turkish Empire and wealthy British-Jews helped finance the emigration there of poorer families to escape pogroms in Russia. Britain, of course, took over responsibility for Palestine after the peace settlement following World War I, hoping in some double-minded way to provide a "Homeland" for Jews in accordance with the Balfour Declaration of 1917 while simultaneously recognizing the rights of indigenous Arabs according to a secret treaty of 1915, and undertaking the mandate to bring the Palestinians to eventual self-government. The international debates over Zionism, over the need for a place of secure refuge from persecution, over invasion by and of surrounding states, over settlement and control of the West Bank and the Gaza Strip, over nuclear arms in the region, have been anxiously regarded in Britain as a continuing responsibility, part of the legacy of empire. British-Jewish writers have taken prominent part in the debates.[21] One of the most powerful scholarly arguments for the importance of literary analysis to our understanding of the arenas of political conflict such as Palestine/Israel is Jacqueline Rose's *States of Fantasy* (1996). Palestine and Israel have featured imaginatively in British-Jewish women's fiction, especially concerning the difficult times toward the end of the Mandate when certain groups of Zionist terrorists targeted British soldiers.[22] Two essays in this collection analyze novels by Lily Tobias and Lynne Reid Banks set, respectively, in Palestine and Israel before and after the Declaration of the State of Israel in 1948.[23]

Contents of This Collection of Essays

To try to put the essays in chronological order, either by date of birth of the authors discussed or by date of composition of their works, would be misleading. This is mainly because some of the authors only began writing late in life. It is more illuminating to place the essays in clusters according to themes. Then we can begin to see how topics thread across the generations. We can also see how different authors respond differently to shared issues, both in their writing and in their own lives. Yet personal and community experiences have resulted in a collective literature, that identifies both an overbearing middle-class, Protestant Englishness (Cheyette 1998, xiii) and a stifling Jewishness (Kenyon 1991, 36) that the writers escape, transform and celebrate, contributing to a new Anglo-Jewish/Jewish-British culture that is sustaining and inspiring.

The collection begins with three essays on the most easily accessible writing, examining authors who used popular fiction genres for political purposes and who foregrounded the norms of gender and sexuality that underpin racism and intolerance. Naomi Jacob wrote best sellers, particularly family sagas, for a working-class readership, combating the antisemitism of the 1930s. Although forgotten now, she was a celebrity in her own lifetime, transgressing codes of femininity, class respectability, and racial segregation with great good humor. Behind her generous laughter is a serious purpose. *Barren Metal* is one of her works of romantic fiction that deserves renewed recognition. Lynne Reid Banks is best known for two works of fiction that were made into highly successful films: *The L-Shaped Room* and *The Indian in the Cupboard*. Deborah Philips has chosen to concentrate on disregarded aspects of her writings: the constructions in her romantic fiction of connections between the new State of Israel and the Jewish New Man and Woman. Despite the criticism of Israel's foreign policies now prevalent in Britain, Banks has written admiringly of the self-confident Israeli state and the new courageous Israeli manhood forged in war; she represents British society as insipid and complacent by contrast. Ellen Galford is perhaps the most fantastically imaginative of all the writers included here. Paulina Palmer demonstrates how, drawing on tropes from Jewish folklore and transatlantic cinema, Galford created a lesbian dybbuk who haunts contemporary London with memories of pre-Holocaust Eastern Europe. The contributors of this group of three essays have used a range of cultural theory to demonstrate the political design beneath the entertaining surface of the texts, and to make manifest their constructions of gender, race, and sexuality. In the process, Philips reveals the anti-Arab racism latent in Banks's works, and Palmer and Tylee reveal the traumatic memories of antisemitic persecution, hidden deep in British culture.

The second group of essays builds on research that has identified the genre of "the Woman's Novel," fiction concerned with domestic life, written by well-educated women for a well-educated, bourgeois readership.[24] The novelists considered here, Betty Miller, Bernice Rubens, and Anita Brookner, all take the family as their major subject, particularly the expectations forced on children by their parents and the destructive love-hate relationships that result. Themselves the daughters of European Jewish immigrants, they all assimilated successfully into British culture. Their ambivalence about this gives ironic depth to their writing. Not all their writing deals with Jewish characters. The essay contributors, Sarah Sceats, Arancha Usandizaga, and David Brauner, have focused on novels that do, foregrounding issues of the push to success, the costs of assimilation and the search for roots. What is uncovered is the desperate sense of insecurity that lies behind the pressure to conform and to achieve. The underlying links thus revealed between the discreet calm of Miller and Brookner and the Gothic monstrosities of Rubens come as some surprise.

Brauner stresses the productive inspiration Rubens gained from Kafka, and the "anxiety of influence" that besets British writers such as Bernice Rubens and Linda Grant as they glance over their shoulders at male American novelists like Philip Roth and Saul Bellow. In fact, the international perspective is one of the features Jewish-British writers have in common. That is not to say that the rest of British literature is insular or parochial, but it has been dominated by English interests and has traditionally looked toward parts of the world affected by British imperialism, such as Ireland, India, and Africa. The interest in Middle and Eastern Europe, in Yiddish, and in exile and migration that is shared by Jewish writers gives their writing a different perspective from the norm. It also colors their language—the idioms, rhythms, and allusions by which poets in particular create their literary art. There are three poets discussed in this collection: Mina Loy, Denise Levertov, and Elaine Feinstein. But I have not grouped them together.

Instead I have put essays on Loy and Levertov by Alex Goody and David Fulton with one by Jasmine Donahaye on the Welsh novelist and short story writer Lily Tobias. These three writers were all the daughters of immigrants to Britain and themselves emigrated as adults and their commentators stress the sense of alienation to be found in their writing. Their works are cross-cultural, fertilized by the conflicts raised between Judaism and Anglicization and the diverse literary, religious, and political traditions the authors inherited. Loy and Levertov tend to be treated as American poets[25] so the discussion of the importance of their

British roots is illuminating. Tobias is hardly known at all; she is a Welsh-Zionist who immigrated to Palestine yet continued to publish in London, so her radicalism faded from view in Wales, England, *and* Israel (but it is well worth comparing her attitudes to Palestinian Arabs with those of Lynne Reid Banks). As the essays demonstrate, out of a sense of cultural hybridity, these writers helped to create new hybrid cultures.[26]

The last section groups together essays by Sue Vice, Susanne Greenhalgh, and Rose Atfield that deal with explicitly post-Holocaust writing. Holocaust literature is now widely researched and studied but English examples have until now been largely ignored by the canon. Mainly produced by inexperienced writers, they are often more of social interest than literary merit. However, Vice has selected three memoirs by German-Jewish refugees who all achieved renown in British society: Silvia Rodgers, wife to an MP who became a peer; the cellist Anita Lasker-Wallfisch, who helped found the British Chamber Orchestra; and the poet and novelist Karen Gershon. These three memoirists were all born in Germany before the Second World War and had lived in Britain for over fifty years before they published their memoirs, yet they engage with both Protestant Englishness and Nazi Germanness from the position of outsiders, alienated even from their mother tongue of German. Vice argues that their works constitute part of a collective "memoir of exile," their personal stories being representative of the common experience of refugees from Nazism and also standing as a memorial for those who did not escape. By contrast, Diane Samuels, Deborah Levy, and Julia Pascal, the three British playwrights discussed as Holocaust dramatists by Susanne Greenhalgh, were all born in Britain after the war and did not write out of personal experiences. Nevertheless, Greenhalgh argues that they too contribute to a collective memory of the Holocaust. Furthermore, the production of their plays is also a ritual of memorialization.

The final essay concerns the poetry of Elaine Feinstein. The grandchild of Jewish immigrants, she was born in England before World War II. She became novelist, translator, and poet as well as wife and mother. Herself raised as an Orthodox Jew and ensuring that her own children observe the rituals of Judaism, hers is perhaps the most Orthodox voice considered in this volume. Atfield displays some of the themes that Feinstein has in common with the other writers considered here, an awareness of the

Jewish heritage of dispossession, persecution, and abjection in particular. It is this that gives her work its political gravitas and marks her poetry out from that of her contemporaries in the Movement. Feinstein has spoken of the significance of the Holocaust to her sense of her own identity as a Jew. Atfield argues that feeling the pressure of that inheritance and the fortuitousness of her survival is precisely what gives Feinstein the relish for life which she celebrates in her poetry.

NOTES

1. Jay L. Halio and Ben Siegel, eds. *Daughters of Valor: Contemporary Jewish American Women Writers* (Newark: University of Delaware Press, 1997).

2. It is notoriously difficult to calculate the number of Jews in United Kingdom, partly because of the problems over defining what a Jew is. Figures quoted are usually dependent on the National Census or on synagogue attendance, both of which rely on religious definitions of Jewishness and therefore exclude many people who might identify themselves as secular or nonobservant Jews. For a discussion of these issues, see for instance, Paul Johnson, *A History of the Jews* (London: Weidenfeld and Nicholson, 1987), 538–39, 565, and David Graham "So How Many Jews Are There in the UK?: The 2001 UK Census and the Size of the Jewish Population," *J(ewish) P(olicy) R(esearch) News* Spring 2003.

3. David Brauner argues that the only two British-Jewish novelists to survive comparison with Philip Roth are Howard Jacobson and Clive Sinclair. *Post-War Jewish Fiction: Ambivalence, Self-Explanation and Transatlantic Connections* (London: Palgrave, 2001), 170; Michael Woolf makes out a case for Bernard Kops as well as Jacobson and Sinclair; see Michael Woolf, "Negotiating the Self: Jewish Fiction in Britain since 1945," in *Other Britain, Other British: Contemporary Multicultural Fiction,* ed. A Robert Lee, (London: Pluto, 1995).

4. It has not been the aim of this collection to study the rise of writing by British-Jewish women during the nineteenth century, such as Grace Aguilar, Amy Levy, or Julia Frankau. That has already been thoroughly investigated in works by Michael Galchinsky, *The Origin of the Modern Jewish Woman Writer: Romance and Reform in Victorian England* (Detroit: Wayne State University Press, 1996) and Linda Gertner Zatlin, *The Nineteenth-Century Anglo-Jewish Novel* (Boston: Twayne, 1981). We commence after World War I.

5. Spark was made a DBE in 1993. She was the only British woman writer included by Emanuel Litvinoff in his collection *The Penguin Book of Jewish Short Stories* (Harmondsworth: Penguin, 1979), and her work has recently been reassessed from a Jewish viewpoint by Bryan Cheyette, *Muriel Spark* (Devon: Northcote House, 2000).

6. See for instance Brookner in interview with John Haffenden, in John Haffenden, *Writers in Interview* (London: Faber, 1985), 67; Spark interviewed by Sara Frankel, *Partisan Review* 54 no. 3, (1987): 448–49; Rubens in conversation

with Rosemary Hartill "Bernice Rubens: Our Father," in *Writers Revealed* (London: BBC, 1989), 32; and autobiographical writing by Grant, *Remind Me Who I Am, Again* (London: Granta, 1998); Feinstein in Jeni Couzyn, ed., *The Bloodaxe Book of Contemporary Women Poets: Eleven British Writers* (Newcastle upon Tyne. Bloodaxe, 1985), 114–15, and in conversation with Peter Lawson, "Way Out in the Centre," *Jewish Quarterly* 181 (Spring 2001), 65–69; Betty Miller, "Notes for an Unwritten Autobiography," in *Modern Reading* 13 (1945): 39–46; Julia Pascal, "Prima Ballerina Assoluta," in *Truth, Dare or Promise: Girls Growing Up in the Fifties,* ed. Liz Heron 27–43; (London: Virago 1985); Deborah Levy, "Placing Ourselves," in *So Very English,* ed. Marsha Rowe, 228–37; (London: Serpent's Tail, 1991); and Leila Berg, *Flickerbook: An Autobiography* (London: Granta, 1997).

7. Louise Sylvester, "Troping the Other: Anita Brookner's Jews," *English,* 50, no. 196 (Spring 2001): 47–58.

8. Other recent anthologies besides Bryan Cheyette's *Contemporary Jewish Writing in Britain and Ireland* (London: Peter Halban, 1998), Caryl Phillips's *Extravagant Strangers: A Literature of Belonging* (London: Faber, 1997) and Emanuel Litvinoff's *The Penguin Book of Jewish Short Stories* (Harmondsworth: Penguin, 1979) have included British-Jewish women writers. See for instance: *The Slow Mirror and Other Stories: New Fiction by Jewish Writers,* ed. Sonja Lyndon and Sylvia Paskin (Nottingham: Five Leaves, 1996), which includes stories by Feinstein, Galford, and Wandor, and *Passionate Renewal: Jewish Poetry in Britain since 1945,* ed. Peter Lawson (Nottingham: Five Leaves, 2001), which includes poetry by Feinstein and Gershon. *The Babel Guide to Jewish Fiction* (London: Boulevard, 1998) edited by Roy Keenoy and Saskia Brown includes Brookner and Rubens; *Mordechai's First Brush with Love: Stories by Jewish Women in Britain,* edited by Laura Phillips and Marion Baraitser (London: Loki, 2004) contains work by new writers.

9. See for instance, Elaine Feinstein "A Legendary Hero," in *Fathers: Reflections by Daughters,* ed. Ursula Owen, 159–68 (London: Virago, 1983); Olga Kenyon identified and discussed the magical "father-enchanters" at the heart of Feinstein's fiction, in *Writing Women: Contemporary Women Novelists* (London: Pluto, 1991), 39–50.

10. See, for instance, Bernice Rubens, *The Elected Member* (1970) and *Brothers* (1983), Anita Brookner, *Latecomers* (1988) and *The Next Big Thing* (2002), and Linda Grant, *Still Here* (2002), and the discussions below by Brauner, Donahaye, Philips, Sceats, and Usandizaga.

11. Even so, many interesting Jewish-British women writers have had to be omitted, for instance: Caryl Brahms, G. B. Stern, Judith Kerr, Claire Rayner, Julia Neuberger, Jenny Diski, Anne Karpf, and Lisa Appignanesi, among others.

12. In his classic statement about the relevance of the Holocaust to his own identity as a Jew, in an essay first published in 1966, "On the Necessity and Impossibility of Being a Jew," the Austrian Auschwitz survivor Jean Améry quotes from the French philosopher Robert Misraeli in *La condition refléxive de l'homme juif:* "The Nazi Holocaust is henceforth the absolute and radical reference point for the existence of every Jew," in *At the Mind's Limits: Contemplations by a Survivor on Auschwitz and Its Realities* (translated from the

German *Jenseits von Schuld und Sühne* by Sidney and Stella B. Rosenfeld [Bloomezten: Indiana University Press, 1980; London: Granta 1999], 82).

13. The contributions to such collective *Kindertransport* memoirs include a letter by Sir Richard Attenborough, whose family fostered two *kinder* as sisters to himself and his brothers, that attests to the relationship of Jews to the national British family and its long-term effects. See Bertha Leverton and Schmuel Lowensohn, eds., *I Came Alone: The Stories of the Kindertransports* (Sussex: Book Guild, 1990), 22–23; reprinted with additions in Jonathan Mark Harris and Deborah Oppenheimer, eds., *Into the Arms of Strangers: Stories of the Kindertransport* (London: Bloomsbury, 2000), xi–xiii.

14. "Disaffected Jews" is a term coined by Gillian Rose in *Love's Work* to express "the energetic alienation from traditional Judaism which so forms the modern Jew" (London: Chatto and Windus, 1995), 43. She is the author of *Judiasm and Modernity.*

15. By the term "secular Jew" I refer to the fact that although the British National Census treats Jewish identity as a religious category, many Britons identify themselves as Jewish yet do not belong to a synagogue or observe Jewish rituals and they may not belong to Jewish political organizations or community groups. There is some resentment of attempts by political and religious leaders to impose a definition of Jewish identity that "de-judaizes" such individuals. See Julia Bard, "Face to Face with the Community," in *A Word in Edgeways* (London: J. F. Publications, 1988), 3–7; David Cesarani, "The Alternative Jewish Community" *European Judaism* 1985/6: 50–54; Adrienne Baker, *The Jewish Woman in Contemporary Society: Transitions and Traditions* (London: Macmillan, 1993), 92–95. See also Susie Orbach, who claimed, "as a second generation secular Jew, part of the nine per cent of British and American Jewry who have no religious affiliation and practise none of the fundamental pietistic precepts associated with Judaism" that "for the generation raised in the wake of the Holocaust, there is an imperative to claim that ethnicity and that history; to not deny that aspect of one's personal and family heritage" in preface to Baker (1993, ix).

16. See David Brauner (2001), for a discussion of these phenomena in novels by male British and American writers.

17. For instance, Olga Kenyon claims: "The Holocaust casts a stronger shadow on Jewish writers than on [other] British ones. The need to survive the horrifying behaviour of fellow men has shaped Jewish personality—and writing . . . In Jewish and black novels the figure of the survivor occurs more than in [other] British fiction." Olga Kenyon, *Writing Women*, 53. (My parenthetical insertions.)

18. For a further account and discussion of these debates see Juliet J. Pope, "Anti-racism, anti-Zionism and anti-Semitism: Debates in the British Women's Movement," *Patterns of Prejudice* 20, no. 3 (July 1986); Jenny Bourne, "Homelands of the Mind: Jewish Feminism and Identity Politics," *Race and Class* 29, no. 1 (Summer 1987): 1–24; Baker, (1993, 209–11).

19. See Roszika Parker on the distinctive character of the Jewish family in "Being Jewish: Anti-Semitism and Jewish Women," *Spare Rib* 79 (Feb. 1974). This was ignored by Michelene Wandor when she edited *Once a Feminist: Stories of the 1970's Generation* (London: Virago, 1990).

20. Baker (1993) cites many other authors in support of this standard analysis.

21. British television documentaries broadcast to mark the Jewish new year in August-September 2002 included John Pilger's ("Palestine Is Still the Issue: a Special Report" ITV, September 16, 2002) in answer to those by Jewish intellectual leaders such as Jacqueline Rose, Professor of English Literature at the University of London ("Dangerous Liaisons: Israel and America" Channel 4, August 28, 2002), and the Labour MP, Gerald Kaufman ("Kaufman: The End of the Affair?" BBC2, September 7, 2002). In December 2002 another leading Jewish intellectual, the British playwright Harold Pinter, was a signatory to the Cairo Declaration against Globalisation and War. Alongside other prominent cultural figures including Tariq Ali, Professor Hilary Rose, Ken Loach, and Paul Foot, he declared himself "against US hegemony and war on Iraq and in solidarity with Palestine." Pinter spoke forcibly on a platform shared with Michael Foot, Tony Benn, and Mo Mowlem at the antiwar demonstration in Hyde Park, February 15, 2003, again denouncing U.S. government policy. Against this background of straight commentary we should place the quizzical humor of the play about a visit to Israel and the occupied territories by another cultural leader who boasts a Jewish wife, David Hare's *Via Dolorosa,* performed both in London and American theaters as well as on British television in 1998. Jacqueline Rose has now published *The Question of Zion* (Princeton: Princeton University Press, 2005).

22. See introduction to Jacqueline Rose, *States of Fantasy* (Oxford: Oxford University Press, 1996). There was not room to include discussion here of the recent novels by Linda Grant, *When I Lived in Modern Times* (2000), and Bernice Rubens, *The Soldiers' Tale* (2003), that focus on that transitional period. It would be interesting to compare them with much earlier fiction like Arthur Koestler's *Thieves in the Night* (1946), Olivia Manning's *School for Love* (1952), and Amos Oz, *The Hill of Evil Counsel* (1976).

23. A discussion of Zionism and the State of Israel with particular regard to women's equality, comparing the aspirations, myths, and social reality, is given by Judith Plaskow, *Standing Again at Sinai: Judaism from a Feminist Perspective* (San Francisco: HarperCollins, 1990). In chapter 3, "Israel: Toward a New Concept of Community," she gives extensive references to historical and sociological research by women, including Natalie Rein's *Daughters of Rachel: Women in Israel* (Harmondsworth: Penguin, 1979).

24. The critical construction of this category of fiction was originated by Nicola Beauman, *A Very Great Profession: The Woman's Novel 1914–39* (London: Virago, 1983); and developed by works such as Olga Kenyon, *Women Novelists Today: A Survey of English Writing in the Seventies and Eighties* (Brighton: Harvester, 1988) and Clare Hanson, *Hysterical Fictions: The "Woman's Novel" in the Twentieth Century* (Basingstake: Macmillan, 2000). Anita Brookner has become recognized as central to the genre; Rubens is peripheral.

25. See for instance Rachel Blau DuPlessis's essay on Levertov in *Writing Beyond the Ending: Narrative Strategies of Twentieth-Century Women Writers* (Bloomington: Indiana University Press, 1985, chapter 8).

26. I have chosen the word "hybridity" for its implications of cultural synergy, bearing in mind the disputes over its use in the area of postcolonial theory; see especially Homi K. Bhabha, *The Location of Culture* (London: Routledge, 1995) and Robert J. C. Young, *Colonial Desire: Hybridity in Theory, Culture and Race* (London: Routledge, 1995).

I
Popular Fiction

"Ticketing oneself a Yid": Generic Fiction, Anti-Semitism, and the Response to Nazi Atrocities in Naomi Jacob's *Barren Metal*

Claire M. Tylee

As FEMINIST CRITICS HAVE DEMONSTRATED, THERE WAS A LARGE body of women's writing entirely disregarded by standard histories of nineteen-thirties British literature before the 1990s.[1] In particular, the overemphasis on Auden and the Spanish Civil War by influential critics like Samuel Hynes and Valentine Cunningham overlooked the ways in which female authors had addressed the rise of Nazism.[2] However, while gynocentric revisionist studies have been a corrective to the high evaluation of Modernism at the expense of the Woman's Novel, they still tend to ignore popular fiction in generic forms such as the family saga and women's romantic fiction. On the other hand, cultural critics such as Tony Kushner and Bryan Cheyette have paid particular attention to the prevalence of anti-Semitic attitudes in both "High Art" and popular fiction by male and female authors. Yet they have offered insufficient analysis of the so-called "apologist" writing by Jewish authors such as Louis Golding and Naomi Jacob that specifically attempted to challenge anti-Semitism (Kushner 1994, 156).[3] As Raymond Williams so cogently argued in *Marxism and Literature*, while any hegemony is by definition always dominant, "it is never either total or exclusive"; hegemony is always in process. Ethnic or racial hegemony is no exception: "It has continually to be renewed, recreated, defended and modified. It is also continually resisted, limited, altered, challenged by pressures not at all its own" (Williams 1977, 112). He claims that works of art are some of our most important evidence of this complex process at work. The openness of many works of art which may require, or at least enable, variable responses, is especially significant (113).

29

I intend here to take issue with the low regard in which critics of 1930s literature have held Naomi Jacob, even feminist critics specifically discussing women writers or Jewish critics analyzing Jewish writing and anti-Semitism. In particular, I shall argue that Jacob merits greater attention than she receives in Barbara Brothers's pioneering study of how British women wrote the story of the Nazis. What Williams calls "the significant openness" of Jacob's writing is important if we are to understand how British culture varied from continental cultures in its response to fascism.

I also intend to counter the misogyny and intellectual snobbery in Paul Bailey's biography of Naomi Jacob in *Three Queer Lives* (2001) echoed by Miranda Seymour's judgement that Naomi Jacob was "a truly dreadful and irrepressibly prolific writer."[4] Prolific, yes; dreadful, no. A committed socialist and feminist, she wrote for the kind of people whose children she had taught in the back streets of Middlesborough. Knowing that "they came from ugly, dirty homes and they ached for brightness, light, sunshine and a little laughter,"[5] that is what she gave them in order to introduce them to new ideas. One of her best novels, *Barren Metal*,[6] is a good example of her ability to identify with despised people and their temptations to hopelessness. It concerns a working-class Jewish woman, Rachel, who marries a successful businessman but becomes disoriented by his repudiation of their Jewish identity. As Rachel grows in confidence, she finds a way to take her own, independent political stand against Nazism. Naomi Jacob understood despair and found ways of suggesting positive activity, without being patronizing.

This particular novel was clearly designed to confront the persecution of Jews in Nazi Germany and to oppose the weaker anti-Semitism of British society. Written in 1935–36, in Merano, North Italy, the book was presumably prompted by the anti-Semitic riots and violence against Jews that erupted in Nazi Germany in the summer of 1935 and made headline news in British newspapers. The orchestrated riots were followed by the institution of the Nuremberg Laws in November 1935 which, among other rules, proscribed Jewish/Aryan miscegenation. *Barren Metal* is the only example given by Brothers of the fact that between the wars "so prevalent was the prejudice against Jews that it spurred a number of novelists of Jewish heritage to use their vocation to change the hearts and minds of the British." Nevertheless, she stigmatizes this one example as "a repetitious, oversimplified presentation of Jewish life and character in the thirties" (Brothers 1993, 258). Bailey also condemns *Barren Metal* for lacking subtlety (2001, 156). He claims it is shallow in dealing with the situation of "the Eastern Jews" and that it trivialises "what would soon be the fate of millions" (161). However we need to remember that Betty Miller's sophisticated, modernist attempt at the same political project, *Farewell Leicester Square,* had been rejected by Victor Gollancz in 1935 and was not published until 1941.[7] The efforts to ironize genteel anti-Semitism by other modernist novelists such as Virginia Woolf and Elizabeth Bowen (in *The Years* [1938] and *The House in Paris* [1935]) were so oblique that they risked actually reinforcing it.[8] Jacob used her best-selling status to tackle the issues head on. That is not to say that she lacked finesse.

Naomi Jacob was one of the most successful writers of popular fiction in the 1930s. Born in 1884, she did not take up writing until she was in her forties. Her first novel, *Jacob Ussher,* was published in 1926. This was about an elderly Jew, an adaptation of a theatrical play by Henry Esmond, *Birds of a Feather.* She was at that time working on the stage as a comic actress in light drama. Resurgence of tuberculosis a few years later meant that she needed to find other means of support in order to live in a dry climate. From 1929 she lived in Italy by producing two to six books a year. (During the next thirty-year period she published over eighty books.) These were mainly light fiction but she became a celebrity through her stream of nonfictional works about her own life and opinions, commencing with *Me: A Chronicle about Other People* (1933). After the war she developed her celebrity status with talks on the BBC radio program, *Woman's Hour.*

Her undoubted popularity clearly stems from just that characteristic that alienates her biographer, Paul Bailey; she was boldly transgressive in the three major area of social control: gender, class, and race. She often dressed in trousers in an era when this was most unusual for women and she openly lived a lesbian life, sharing her house with two other women. Although she was discreet about sexuality, in life and in her books, there was nothing ladylike about her behavior, which could best be described as hearty. Her maternal grandfather was a North Country publican and she was at home in the public-house culture of drinking, jokes, and loud talk. Erratically educated but widely read, she left school at fifteen to train as an elementary-school teacher in a church school in Middlesborough's slums. She was often short of money at this time, and in constant conflict with the narrow-minded, disciplinarian regime at the school. Her own teaching was imaginative and inspiring. After six years she abandoned the teaching profession to work as secretary/companion to a music hall singer, Marguerite Broadfoote, with whom she was in love. Jacob claimed that their seven years together, 1905–12, were the happiest of her life.

Her personal courage is most evident with regard to racism. Her mother's family had roots in Yorkshire going back centuries; her father was a Jewish immigrant, with a German mother, and a father who had fled from a pogrom in Poland in which both of his parents were slaughtered.[9] Naomi's father had converted to Christianity and worked in an Anglican school. He despised Jewish culture but she was much attached to her Yiddish-speaking paternal grandfather, a tailor, who, although not Orthodox, still maintained Judaic traditions. Her parents' marriage broke up when Naomi was only eight, due to her father's promiscuity and marital abuse. Nevertheless, unlike her mother, Naomi Jacob never changed her name, adopting neither a stage name nor a pen name. In a period of shameless anti-Semitic prejudice, she proudly drew attention to her Jewishness. Her alertness to racism, well before the age of political correctness, is one of the most significant features of her writing. As she aged, her fictional work grew increasingly slapdash, oiled by her drinking habit and driven by the need to be popular and make money; her prose is seldom innovative and it lacks decorum, the dialogue veering disconcertingly between high oratory and low slang; she is not given to self-criticism and her plots nourish wishfulfillment in ways that often seem adolescent.[10]

However, *Barren Metal*, written in 1936 at the height of her writing career, is far from lackadaisical in construction. It is a novel she obviously planned with great care in order to engage directly with anti-Semitism in Britain and apathy toward the current political situation in Germany. No idiot, she knew that nothing makes an audience switch off more quickly than preaching or polemics; this novel is not a political tract. Nevertheless it is genre fiction consciously designed for ideological purposes and aimed at a particular readership. Jacob drew on the entertainment skills she had imbibed from music hall culture, using pathos, melodrama, romance, and comic dialogue to amuse her readers and sugar the effort of imagination she required of them. Her success is evident from the reprints of this novel, even after the war. The novel draws attention to its own position within the pleasures of a self-fashioning culture. It refers to music, clothes design, interior decoration, filmmaking, music hall artists and songs, to music appreciation and to novel reading. (This was typical of mass fiction of that period, which often encouraged its readers, likely to be early school-leavers, in the enterprise of self-education.)

Barren Metal's own construction draws heavily on the one art it does not describe: the theater, especially the melodrama and broad comedy typical of music hall playlets. Her adoption of the theatrical conventions of her period includes the use of emphatic "curtain moments" at the end of sections or chapters, where a resounding, summarizing statement or noise is followed by silence, a brief tableau and then the blank of a scene change, leaving the audience/reader to contemplate. For instance: Rachel's voice, "filled with emotion" ordering her son: "Now—please go!" at the end of book 3, chapter 2; or the conclusion of a scene of marital discord: "He did not answer; the door between their rooms closed" (1936a, 117); or Albert Bromel's curtain speech denouncing capitalist greed and the worship of the Golden Calf, at the close of book 2 (165–66). In fact Bromel functions as the *raisonneur*, the "right-thinking figure who guides audience response in the well-made Society Drama" (Chothia 1998, xv). Bromel functions as a moral guide not only for Rachel but for the reader.

Further aspects of Jacob's method, such as her attention to clothes, objets d'art, and furnishings, but the absence of descriptions of such matters as places, weather, or crowds, imply that she thinks in terms of costumes, props, and stage sets. Other theatrical conventions include confrontations between characters where powerful emotional states are acted out in large gestures aimed to be seen from the back rows; for instance, when Rachel forgives Meyer, "he made a sudden movement, slipped to the floor and, lifting the hem of her skirt, pressed it to his lips" (1936a, 191). A more modern convention is the achievement of dramatic suspense through a phone call where the audience/reader can only hear one side of the conversation (285). All of these features, which may strike the reader of highbrow literature as histrionic, are typical of literature written for an audience used to having its imagination prompted by pointed physical enactment.

Her writing is at the opposite pole from the cool, detached, minimalist approach of modernism, with its development of complex motivation, absence of authorial comment, and use of stream-of-consciousness narrative. There are moments of silent reflection and of unspoken comment in *Barren Metal*, particularly when Rachel's dissenting thoughts are relayed to us. But Jacob's characters are not intellectual or complicated and the object of the novel is only occasionally to reveal their consciousness; the main point lies in what they say and do in the public world rather than in what they think in the privacy of their own minds. When emotions, beliefs and memories are kept secret it is for good reason and their revelation is always a high moment of the narrative.

The other major theatrical convention that Bailey finds particularly irritating in Jacob's writing is her playful use of different voices, especially the strong cockney of the servant, Sarah. Bailey mocks the "generous sprinkling of apostrophes and deliberate misspellings" by which Jacob represents the accents or dialects of her speakers, "by having them drop aitches, elongate their vowels, substitute 'v's' for 'w's' and vice versa. There are nightmarish pages in the novel *Barren Metal* when a Yiddish-speaking Jew, a cockney and a Yorkshireman are conversing in what [Jacob] believes to be idiomatic English. The apostrophes come at the hapless reader like shrapnel" (2001, 135). Unfortunately, readers of popular fiction are seldom conversant with phonetic transcription.

Sarah is an example of the character type that Jacob herself frequently acted, and probably overacted, on the stage to the delight of the gallery. That is, the female version of the "allowed fool" who opens her mouth and speaks her mind when a refined lady would keep politely quiet. Hers is the voice of common assumptions, the taken-for-granted ideology of everyday life that Jacob's readers would identify with but that the book often gently prompts them to disengage from. She means no offense: "Theer'll ondly be Yids theer, won't theer? Wot a gime, eh?" she retorts when she is to be the only gentile at Meyer's wedding. But Sarah is bonded to Rachel and openly tells her what she thinks, performing a releasing function that encourages Rachel to disregard bourgeois values. That cross-race bonding is itself subversive and binds Rachel into the wider culture. The figure of the loud-mouthed, working-class woman, frequently a charwoman, was stock in the theater of Jacob's time and is found, for instance, in G. B. Shaw's suffrage farce, *Press Cuttings* (1911), and Elizabeth Robins's *Votes for Women!* (1907). It continued into film and television with the parts played by actresses like Gracie Fields, Dora Bryant, and Barbara Windsor. It would be hard to convey to Bailey the pleasures of hearing in the mind's ear the familiar sound of voices and language frowned on in dominant culture. For anyone born and bred in London, as I was, there is a glee in seeing colloquial words such as *"schlemozzle"* in print, acting as a bridge between Sarah's cockney and the less familiar Yiddish expressions of the older generation, that Rachel and Meyer still fondly use between themselves: "What's *chiddush?"* (Any News?). Jacob represents the two idioms as having absorbed each other in the voices of the next generation, the young East End Jewish women who "screamed and chattered" in the Pardo workshops.

It is by such writing that we can trace the links in British lower-class culture from the Edwardian music hall, through Ealing Comedies, Carry On films, and Theatre Workshop, to the pubs and television soap operas of the twenty-first century. The constructed bonhomie of that world may also help to indicate why fascist extremism did not take hold in Britain, despite an upper-class leadership that did so little to counter racial prejudice. Of course it is easy to succumb to false nostalgia and to sentimentalize and romanticize that working-class culture, but it certainly promoted broadmindedness and it ridiculed self-flattery or bigotry. It is more generous than the alternative tradition of football hooliganism and the BNP.

Jacob wrote a series of novels based on her mother's Yorkshire background, but her series known as the *Gollantz Saga*[11] is what really made her name and is what reference works continue to list. For instance, Margaret Ashby judges that "while all her novels are characterised by a warmth and a tolerance of human nature, the Gollantz Saga books, written during the Nazi era, make a contribution to a concept of the brotherhood of men, and are probably her most lasting work" (1989, 349). Paul Bailey suggests that "from her vast output of fiction, only the novels concerned with the Gollantz family can be recommended with any confidence," though he immediately qualifies this recommendation by saying that "these books—whatever their obvious stylistic failings—do contain some interesting and unusual detail" (2001, 240–41). Such detail could not have been all that recommended them to their original readers. More likely they enjoyed the fast pace of the narrative, the exoticism of a family of Continental Jewish antique-dealers, and the piquancy of their interface with the British upper class, as well as what Ashby calls their "warmth and tolerance." A family saga, these books enabled their female readers to identify vicariously with the activities of the male protagonists while secure in the cocoon that protected the female members of the family.

The Gollantz Saga fulfils the criteria by which genre fiction becomes successful, as identified by John G. Cawelti in his discussion of the "dialectic between formulaic literature and the culture that produces and enjoys it" (1976, 55–56).[12] Like other popular fiction, it diverts readers from the stress of their own lives, it enables them to contemplate gradual changes to the status quo in an unthreatening way, and it offers certain pleasures as well as the satisfactions to be gained from the stable values of the genre. These include the reinforcement of moral certainties by the containment of evil and the reward of happiness to the good. Jacob's saga reassures its gentile readers that, although there are Jewish bounders and parasites, the majority of Jews are respectable, decent, honest people with firm family values and strong community connections that do not exclude gentiles. There is successful intermarriage. Britain is shown as right to provide a haven to such immigrants who will certainly contribute to the economy, encouraging a sound business ethic while not disturbing the moral fabric of society. In return for their confidence in Jacob's storytelling, readers are indulged with the pleasures of fantasizing about a rich way of life, rich in the sense of sumptuous possessions, rich in the sense of eventful and varied lives, and also rich in the sense of powerfully emotional relationships.

This is a very different picture from, for example, Trollope's portrayal of a wealthy Jewish embezzler in *The Way We Live Now*, or the sinister Jewish financier who lies behind international conflict in John Buchan's *39 Steps* (or of course, T. S. Eliot's Jews), not to mention Shylock, Fagin, or Svengali. Nor does it idealize Judaism as, for instance, George Eliot does in *Daniel Deronda*. Rather, Jacob normalizes Jewish people and their customs, integrating them into British society. In the 1930s, when

Britain was still recovering from the xenophobia of the First World War, undergoing the Depression that followed the 1929 crash, and suffering from the loss of imperial confidence of late Victorianism, Jacob's series of novels about family continuity and social integration, with the luxury and prosperity of an antiques business, provided just the hope and reassurance people needed from the drug of light fiction.

Barren Metal told a different, bleaker story and was Jacob's effort to adapt popular cultural conventions in the direction of social realism. Although it commences like a family saga as her established readership might have expected, the novel quickly develops into the closely allied genre of women's romantic fiction. Jacob proceeds to subvert the ideology of both genres. Instead of her previous peddling of permanence and security, with women as baggage to be comfortably carried by their male relatives—fathers, husbands, and sons—this new novel focuses on change and on the ability of a middle-aged, working-class Jewish woman to break tradition, to escape domesticity, and to take responsibility for her own life. In this novel Jacob expresses the socialist feminism of the WSPU campaign for women's suffrage to which she was committed before World War I.[13] More originally, she enables her heroine to play her own small part in opposing Nazism. Thus, in *Barren Metal,* Jacob finds a way to convert popular fiction into an unthreatening vehicle for her radical politics of class, gender, and race. At the end, Jacob fulfils her contract with the reader by providing the expected happy ending, with a lasting love relation; as Cawelti puts it, "the moral fantasy of the romance is that of love triumphant and permanent, overcoming all obstacle and difficulties" (1976, 41). Yet even this ending is subversive in *Barren Metal.* It not only condones adultery but breaks other taboos. Overcoming the obstacles of age and race, Rachel finally finds permanent love with a man younger than herself, who is a gentile.[14]

Barren Metal appears at first to follow the format of a "rags-to-riches" story, typical of the romance genre, telling of a poor Cinderella figure who captures the heart of a wealthy man, marries him, and lives happily ever after. This is the staple plot-backbone of love stories from *Mansfield Park* and *Jane Eyre* onward to the best sellers of Catherine Cookson and Denise Robins. However, *Barren Metal* does not address the middle-class miss who was the target of Jane Austen and Charlotte Brontë. Rather, its readership is assumed to be working-class women, the new mass-fiction market that later novelists like Cookson also wrote for. This makes it insensitive of Paul Bailey to castigate Jacob as one of the "lazy novelists who wrote for equally lazy readers" (2001, 183). Cookson, born on Tyneside in 1906, the illegitimate daughter of an alcoholic barmaid, drew on her own background of early hardship when she commenced writing in 1950. Jacob's novel is similarly grounded in the experience of her own life, although she is more given to a desire to make people laugh than Cookson (a tendency that clearly irritated Bailey). Apart from the social realism of back-street sweatshop life for women in the clothing industry, *Barren Metal* offers particular interest to contemporary feminist critics. Courtship and wedding are dealt with in the first quarter of the novel, which is divided into four books. The final three books, the majority of the novel, concern marriage and widowhood. In the second half, the heroine is in her early forties, with her sons grown up and a faltering relationship with her husband, and faced with the prospect of beginning again. This is a most unusual narrative pattern and had no classical models. (It is as if *Hamlet* were to be told from the point of view of Gertrude, a Gertrude who decides after the funeral of Hamlet's father to leave Elsinore and work for a landmines charity in Africa, while married to an Arab playboy.)

Barren Metal begins in 1880 with the arrival in Whitechapel of a poor Jewish immigrant family from Hamburg. Leah and Israel Pardo, with their small son, Meyer, come to live with Leah's crippled brother, Benjamin Lazarus. The Pardos are less religious than Benjamin is, but the family's week is structured around the joy of the Friday evening ritual, with its special food and ceremonial meal. (Among Leah's meager baggage are the necessary brass candlesticks.) Living all together in two rooms, they survive as "*schniders*," tailors who do outwork in their home (Leah does the buttonholing). Meyer is the only child and he is encouraged to work hard at school and to be ambitious. By borrowing and by inheriting some money when Benjamin dies, he sets up a workshop and employs young female seamstresses, "swarthy young Jewish girls" (1936a, 18), first to make decorations for Victoria's Jubilee celebrations, then to make uniforms for the Boer War. Eventually he makes a fortune providing uniforms during World War I. By this time his parents are dead and he has been encouraged by his housekeeper, Sarah, to develop a personal life. At the age of twenty-eight, he courts and marries Rachel Jacob, a beautiful, orphaned, Jewish waitress he encounters in a cheap kosher restaurant. Meyer is physically unprepossessing. His nose is "too heavy and inclined to be fleshy" and he "could never have passed for anything but a German or Polish Jew" (12). Ten years younger, Rachel sees him as "a queer little Jewboy" (38) but she is moved by him and loves him for his qualities with a passionate yet somewhat maternal attachment. Although they are not orthodox and their wedding takes place in a registry office, without a *chuppah*,[15] they retain their Jewish friends, kosher diet, and Yiddish turns of speech. Rachel says she has had no time to be "*froom*" (strictly observant) but "Mind you, I'm always glad to be a Jew" (28). Meyer announces that Rachel will not wear the *shaitel* (ritual wig) of the Orthodox wife because she will be respected without it; she is his Rose of Sharon, and his chief desire is to work to make her happy.

Book 1 is told mainly from his point of view. Between chapters 4 and 5, the point of view changes to Rachel. She has twin sons who are sent away to boarding school. The family moves to a large house in Maida Vale and Meyer forbids his sons to use Yiddish expressions. (Sarah moves with the family as Rachel's personal maid.) As Rachel warns Meyer, his ambitiousness has turned to selfish determination and the business swallows him up (60). The change in their relationship is depicted for us by the first big dinner party Meyer throws in a hotel for his rich business associates, inviting a goy (gentile) newspaper magnate, Sir Henry Yardley, and his wife as well as several Jews, including Marcus Rosenbaum and Percy Levinson.[16] Rachel has no idea how to be a hostess, but takes advice from the man who is to become her Jewish fairy godfather, Albert Bromel. (He says later that he would never have taken his wife, Marion, to mix with such men [163].) Rachel and Albert talk happily together and agree not to eat the oysters (Jacob does not labor this point but, of course, oysters are not kosher). Meanwhile we overhear Rosenbaum and Levinson's view that Rachel is "pure Ghetto" and that Meyer will "have to drag her up after him" (68). In fact, Rosenbaum, Levinson, and Yardley drag Meyer down to prison with them by involving him in their business fraud.

In book 2, we see the results of Meyer's determination to move on in the world, and Rachel's efforts to retrieve him from the "money-machine" and save her marriage. As she says, every ring he has given her is a sign that he has been unfaithful to her, not with women but with "trench-coats, artificial silk and rising stocks" (91). But it is too late. Meyer has adopted the values of Rosenbaum and Levinson. Swearing ("*Shetus!*"), he begins to abuse her, physically and psychologically, claiming: "You were born in the Ghetto, and you don't take no trouble to climb out of it. You want to bring Whitechapel and everything about it, up to the West End. You let everyone know you're a Jewess, you can't forget it, you won't let other people forget it. All right! Cut off your hair, wear a *sheitel* and go to *shool*, [synagogue] live *kosher*— I don't care. Only you damn well do it without me!" (136–37).

While one son, David, plans to train as a film director in Germany, the other, Ike, had inherited Meyer's capitalist values and aims to become a gentleman's tailor in Savile Row. To that end he acquires a rich fiancée, the intolerably affected heiress Helen Neubauer. On marrying, they change their names to George and Henrietta Samson. Asking his mother not to call him Ike or use Yiddish words, Ike points out that many people have "a prejudice against the Ghetto"—and "people don't care about ticketing themselves—Yids, these days" (144, 156). It is Helen who mentions the new German movement against the Jews: "Dreadful, but one must remember that many of the Eastern Jews have brought it on themselves."[17] Her own family has "almost forgotten we evah had Jewish blood in the family" (137). As Sarah comments acerbically to Rachel afterwards, "'Er mother must have been passhionately fond o' kids to bring 'er up" (161).[18] Rachel can only reply to Helen, "But we *are* Jews." She does not understand the reference to Nazism or Eastern Jews. Having left school at the age of twelve, she is practically illiterate and does not read the newspapers. She just looks at the pictures. (Ashamed of her handwriting, she can barely express herself on paper but she has been trying to educate herself by reading novels.) From now on she struggles with the *Daily Mail* and eventually learns more directly about what is going on from David, on his return from Germany.

David mocks Ike, suggesting he call himself "Micky Pardo"[19] so he can pass as an Irishman. He hates Ike's hypocrisy and snobbery, insisting that, although life is too short and too full for "fasts or feasts and ceremonies and all the rest of it," nevertheless: "I'm David Pardo, I'm a Jew, and I'm not going to pretend to be anything else to please Ike or the King of England . . . Orthodox, Liberal, Reformed—it doesn't matter, we're a nation, and unless we're damned unpatriotic we stick to our nationality" (147). This is the major ethic transmitted down through the generations in *The Gollantz Saga* and repeated in Jacob's own nonfiction: not to deny one's own ethnicity. David is here speaking in Naomi Jacob's voice to outface any anti-Semitic reader.

However, this new novel deliberately sabotages the ideology of women's self-sacrifice to family and domestic happiness that informs both the genres of the family saga and romantic fiction. In *Barren Metal* passion dies and the family disintegrates, nearly destroyed by Meyer's determination to eradicate his Jewish roots. Jacob challenges the reader by David's remarks to Rachel before he leaves for Germany: "We aren't a family, we're a number of separate interests. We don't overlap anywhere. We're dreadfully self-sufficient . . . I often wonder how much real interest you have in any of us, Mother?" (120). She wants to discuss her unhappiness over his father but he sidesteps her, saying that relationships don't count for much, either between children and parents or between married couples. There is a limit to what Rachel can do to counteract Meyer's pernicious example. The family breaks up. When Meyer is imprisoned for embezzlement, Ike disowns him and so Rachel disowns Ike; David does not return from Germany to help his mother during the trial. Neither son offers her financial support. (Fortunately the Bromels do not let her down.)

Yet Rachel stands by Meyer, visiting him in prison and making a home for him on his release, even though there is no passionate love left in their relationship. While he is in prison she starts up a small workshop again in order to pay off his debts, with Cohen and Levy, two of his Jewish associates whom he had ruined. (Rachel may be no good with words but she seems to be good at mental arithmetic.) It is this enterprise that marks an innovative step for women's fiction. Drawing on Jacob's experience as the women's supervisor in a First World War munitions factory, and on what she knew about her grandfather's small tailoring business, this section of the novel portrays life in a sweatshop convincingly, especially the quarrels among the Jewish women who work there. The other original aspect from a feminist perspective is that the novel argues for the right of a woman over forty to have a sex life, even an adulterous one. While Meyer is in prison Rachel commences a physical relationship with

Sholto Falk, a gentile friend of the Morels, and she marries him after Meyer dies. In this way Jacob quietly opposes the Nazi laws forbidding such miscegenation.[20]

Thus the novel subverts dominant cultural ideologies of race, class, and sexuality,[21] by drawing the reader to empathize with a working-class Jewish woman who demands a life of her own, with passion, once her sons are grown up. And while challenging the stigma attached to prison and adultery, Jacob slips in an indication of the importance of love between women. In a telling exchange between Rachel and Sarah, Rachel remonstrates that she herself is no better than her employees; she was working class, has a husband in jail and has not been faithful to him:

> "Sarah, you mustn't have one rule for me and another for other people! It's not fair."
> "Ain't it? It's what everyone 'as, I reckon—one rule for the people they love an' another fur the ones they don't. Wot's fair don't come inter it." (258)

The affection between these two women, gentile and Jew, is one of the moral strengths of the novel.[22] Once again it issues a quiet challenge to Nazism and anti-Semitism.

The novel is also innovative in telling the story of the background to Jewish immigration and in relating Rachel's tale of her refugee mother at the end of the nineteenth century to the contemporary situation of Jewish refugees from Nazi Germany. Jacob is aware of how little her readers may want to hear distressing tales and she works artfully to evade their resistance. This is indicated by David's inability to get his newspaper articles about Nazi Germany published when he returns to Britain in about 1934.[23] Rachel warns that he might only break his heart trying. (By this time, worried about David being in Germany, she has made the effort to read in the *Daily Mail* about Jews whose business had been closed down, either being driven out or committing suicide.) Yet David has insisted that "all England, the world, ought to know—know it all. Work, money, education— even a clean decent death is denied us! Everyone must know— they shall, because I shall tell them!" (231). Rachel says, "You may tell them . . . They will listen, they may even listen with kindness, but in their hearts they will say that you have—imagined these things, or that they are too dreadful to hear, or that it is—unwise to speak them" (231). And indeed he finds that "they won't look at it, or listen to me. One man told me that the Jews had ceased to be an item of news" (232). This we can believe, since we know how people now become numb to television news reports about atrocities, especially when they feel powerless to help. (Kushner refers to people's response of distancing themselves in order to avoid 'empathic distress' (1994, 275).)[24] So Jacob does not labor the point; she certainly does not devote her whole novel to detailing the situation in Germany as did other novelists discussed by Barbara Brothers (such as Phyllis Bottome in *The Mortal Storm*).[25]

Instead she offers us Rachel's counsel to David not to become bitter over his sense of powerlessness: "The moment you rage and burn to no purpose, you are wasting the power that is yours" (233). Only in his early twenties, he already has "a burden of hatred laid on his shoulders, with recollections and memories which would remain all through his life" (234). Rachel's advice is presumably Jacob's: to recognize the limitations of one's power "to reorganise a whole state" and instead to help in whatever small way one can. In Rachel's case, she is employing a woman refugee from Germany. Bromel has taken on twelve refugee men. Of course, this novel is Jacob's own "small way" of helping.

Rachel herself was an immigrant from Germany with a family history of anti-Jewish atrocities. As she talks to David she recalls her own mother speaking to her when she was a little girl, telling her about what had been done to *her* when *she* was a little girl, and her mother's reply when she asked what she had done to deserve it: "Me—vot hed I done already? I hed committet der c-crime of b-being b-born a Jew—von of der Ch-Chosen race" (231). In fact the reader already knows this story, because Rachel had earlier confided it to Sholto Falk in one of the intimate conversations by which lovers reveal themselves to each other. Her mother had been born in Russia in a small town with a nice park that was not for Jews, who had to dress differently from other people. One day, as a little girl, she had been playing in the park while her pregnant mother was resting. Suddenly a soldier slapped her and ordered her out: "It was for clean Christians, not Jews who made the air stink. If Jews had been anywhere, he said, decent people could not breathe, the smell was so bad" (131). The soldiers followed her home and kicked her father to death; as a result her mother miscarried and she and her baby also died. A pogrom followed but Rachel's mother and uncle escaped to Germany with her great uncle. Rachel says she never tells this story, but "one must not forget" (132). (Although the details are different, Jacob based this story on what she knew of her grandfather's experiences.) That instance of unmerited violence is repeated in Meyer's unprovoked attack on Rachel for being a "Ghetto Jew." Thus, without arguing, Jacob has illustrated the irrational rage that British liberals found so hard to credit as influencing events on the Continent.

The Russian's prejudice against Jews as smelly and dirty must be what lies behind Jacob's frequent mention of bathing. Meyer was too poor ever to have had a proper bath before he was an adult, when he could afford to go to the municipal baths for the first time. The pleasures of that experience are lovingly rendered. The first thing he asks for when he gets out of prison is to have a hot bath—with bath salts. Sarah runs hot baths for Rachel, to comfort her. And there is toward the end of the novel some discussion of how a sweatshop actually is a place in which people working get hot and sweat. Sarah implies that Rachel has fainted due to the girls' smell: "Thet kid o' yours 'ul stand a fine charnce, young Esther—if yer 'ouse smells anythink like wot you do, the poor little begger 'ul die of sufferkation" (261). Adah then explains to Rachel what life is like for her and the other women: "Leah lives with 'er father an' mother and six kids—they 'ave three rooms—some clarse they are! Nine of 'em in three rooms. Esther an' 'er chap 'as one room, bit bigger nor the one I 'ave. 'Ell of a lot o' charnce any of us 'ave fur 'air-washing, barthin'—even washin' clothes. The German kid's the best orf—she lives with 'er mother. Two women can manage ter barth a bit when theer's just two on 'em. Different when you got men around the plice" (262).

In the light of Jacob's biography, one can read much of the novel as her personal wish-fulfillment fantasy. Meyer is punished for succumbing to anti-Jewish values and for beating his wife, as perhaps Jacob wished her father had been—but Rachel stands by him and he repents, as perhaps Jacob wishes had happened between her parents. The intense emotional attachment between Sholto and Rachel is probably based on Jacob's own attachment to the older Marguerite, eventually broken up by Marguerite's Jewish husband (who is presented in the memoirs as only too like Jacob's father). Unfortunately, Marguerite died soon after; in the novel,

Sholto finally wins Rachel, since her husband dies before her. This transmuted autobiographical material gives emotional power to the novel, which is the strong inducement to keep reading and so to absorb its transgressive ideological stance and accept its political message.

It seems to me typical of Naomi Jacob that, although women over the age of forty were not conscripted in World War II and she was in her mid-fifties when World War II was declared, she immediately returned to the United Kingdom and enlisted. She worked first for the Ministry of Information and then served with ENSA in North Africa and Italy, contracting malaria in the process. Her writing can be considered as of a piece with her life, which performed her resistance to narrow-mindedness, prejudice, and bullying, the thin end of the Nazi wedge. Just as she deserves respect for her outspoken courage, *Barren Metal* deserves to be retrieved from the misrepresentations of her critics and valued for its imaginative resistance to racism. Its openness made a significant contribution to the pressures working against the racial hegemony of British culture during the interwar years.

NOTES

1. The groundbreaking research in Nicola Beauman's *A Very Great Profession: The Women's Novel 1914–39* (London: Virago, 1983), was followed by the more academic discussions of Alison Light's *Forever England: Femininity, Literature and Conservatism between the Wars* (London: Routledge, 1991), Phyllis Lassner's *British Women Writers of World War II: Battlegrounds of Their Own* (London: Macmillan, 1998), and Elizabeth Maslen's *Political and Social Issues in British Women's Fiction, 1928–1968* (London: Palgrave, 2001). None of these critics pays Naomi Jacob any attention, although Lassner lists in her bibliography the article where Brothers discusses her; see note 2 below.

2. This was spelled out by Barbara Brothers's paper, "British Women Write the Story of the Nazis: A Conspiracy of Silence," in *Rediscovering Forgotten Radicals: British Women Writers 1889–1934*, ed. Angela Ingram and Daphne Patai, 244–64 (Chapel Hill: University of North Carolina Press, 1993). She discusses Samuel Hynes, *The Auden Generation: Literature and Politics in England in the 1930s* (New York: Viking, 1976), and Valentine Cunningham, *British Writers of the Thirties* (Oxford: Oxford University Press, 1988). There were two notable exceptions to the "High Art" approach to 1930s literature that both examined popular fiction: Andy Croft's *Red Letter Days: British Fiction in the 1930s* (London: Lawrence and Wishart, 1990), which mentions some women writers, but not Naomi Jacob, and Ken Worpole's *Dockers and Detec-*

tives: Popular Reading, Popular Writing (London: Verso, 1983), which discusses between-the-wars writing by Jewish men from the East End of London, but is short on women and does not mention Jacob. Similarly, *Culture and Crisis in Britain in the Thirties*, ed. Jon Clark, Margot Heinemann, David Margolis and Carol Snee (London: Lawrence and Wishart, 1979), examines mass culture including literature by working-class male authors, but not by women.

3. See for instance: Bryan Cheyette, *Constructions of "the Jew" in English Literature and Society: Racial Representations 1875–1945* (Cambridge: Cambridge University Press, 1993), and Tony Kushner, *The Holocaust and the Liberal Imagination: A Social and Cultural History* (Oxford: Blackwell, 1994). Kushner mentions Naomi Jacob as an example of the "apologist approach" displayed by Jewish writers, but cites none of her works (256).

4. The misogyny of Paul Bailey's *Three Queer Lives: An Alternative Biography of Fred Barnes, Naomi Jacob and Arthur Marshall* (London: Hamilton, 2001), becomes more evident as the biography proceeds towards retelling the cruel joke of Harold Lang inviting her to unwittingly play herself in his radio drama, *The Quest for Corbett*, that satirized her writing as "flowing from her like toothpaste" (180). The section on Jacob, pp. 67–184, is entitled "Like a Boiled Monkey," quoting from a description of her appearance at birth; that title is repeated as the heading of every page. Miranda Seymour's evaluation of Jacob's work, in "Carry on Camping" (a review of *Three Queer Lives*) in *Sunday Times*, November 11, 2001, p. 41, is repeated by other reviewers of Bailey's book, such as Geraldine Bedell: "Jacob wrote terribly trashy novels," in "When Queers Took Comfort in the Closet," *Observer Review* 30, December 2001.

5. Quoted by Bailey from Jacob's memoir, *Me: A Chronicle about Other People* (1933) in Bailey 2001, 96.

6. *Barren Metal* was first published by Hutchinson in 1936; I used a copy borrowed from Caernarvonshire County Library, reprinted in 1967 by Hurst and Blackett from Hutchinson's 1944 edition. On the back cover it said: "Naomi Jacob's continuing popularity is easy to understand, for her books have an immediate appeal to anyone who enjoys a good story well told." (There was also a 1961 edition published by Arrow Books.)

7. The story of Victor Gollancz's rejection of this novel about British anti-Semitism and Jewish self-hatred, and its eventual publication by Robert Hale in 1941, is recounted by Jane Miller in the preface to the Persephone edition: Betty Miller, *Farewell Leicester Square* (London: Persephone, 2000). Gollancz was the major publisher of Women's Novels and his response was part of the stance taken by Anglo-Jewish leaders in the 1930s of not drawing attention to the particular situation of Jews for fear of unleashing British anti-Semitism. He changed after 1942 (see Kushner 1994, 176–77).

8. For discussions of anti-Semitism in Woolf see Radford 1999 "Late Modernism and the Poetry of History," and in Bowen see Tylee 2005 "Hyphenated Identity."

9. His father was cantor at the synagogue and was left to bleed to death after having his tongue cut out; his mother died of a brutal flogging (Bailey 2001, 76).

10. Yet Bailey's quotes of descriptive passages (120) and anecdotes (115–16) from her autobiographical work, *Me: A Chronicle about Other People* (1933) and *Robert, Nana and—Me* (1952), show just how fluently and evocatively she

could write. He also begrudgingly praises her biography of Marie Lloyd, *Our Marie* (1936) for capturing "the energy and vulgarity that kept the music hall alive for so long" (184).

11. This series consisted of seven novels in total, published between 1930 and 1958. The first six were also brought out in two collected volumes as *"The Gollantz Saga"* Parts 1 and 2. The most successful was *Four Generations* (London: Hutchinson, 1934).

12. John G. Cawelti's book, *Adventure, Mystery, and Romance: Formula Stories and Popular Culture* (Chicago: University of Chicago Press, 1976), has nothing to say about family sagas nor, despite its title, does it say much about women's romantic fiction. This is discussed in, for example, Janet Batsleer et al., *Rewriting English: Cultural Politics of Gender and Class* (London: Methuen, 1985), and family sagas are dealt with by Christine Bridgwood in "Family Romances: The Contemporary Popular Family Saga" in *The Progress of Romance: The Politics of Popular Fiction,* ed. Jean Radford (London: Routledge, 1986).

13. See for instance the speech made by "Working Woman" in act 2 of *Votes for Women!,* the 1907 suffragette play by Elizabeth Robins, a committee member of the WSPU (reprinted in *The New Woman and Other Emancipated Woman Plays* (London: Oxford University Press, 1998).

14. Bailey misleadingly calls Sholto Falk "a good Christian" (1936a, 158) but there is no evidence for this. Religion is not an issue in the novel. The Baptist minister, Rev. Carter, who helps the Pardos does not do so to convert them, but because he is a socialist: "I believe in universal brotherhood" he tells them (8), sounding the keynote of the novel.

15. The response of the reviewer in the *Times Literary Supplement,* who lamented the absence of "the simple beauty of the Jewish marriage ceremony" (March 21, 1936), vindicates Jacob's strategy of "normalizing" rather than romanticizing Jewish life.

16. In one of the instances of Bailey's lazy reading or false argument, he informs us that Meyer gets "embroiled with some crooked businessmen (not Jewish, Mickey [i.e., Naomi Jacob] is at pains to tell her reader)" (Bailey 2001, 158). Bailey was criticized for his "clumsy" and "careless" writing in the review of *Three Queer Lives* by Neil Bartlett, "Queer as Folks," *Guardian,* Saturday Review, December 29, 2001. Catherine Shoard put this more succinctly, judging the book "a hack job" in "Paperbacks," *Evening Standard,* September 2, 2002.

17. In a piece of slack exegesis, Brothers implies that this speech is Rachel's, which destroys the whole political point of the novel (1993, 258).

18. Bailey at this point declares that Sarah's speech is "impossible to decipher" when she sarcastically asks Rachel, "'Ave yer got the top brick off of the chimbly?" It used to be a common saying that, for instance, a father who spoiled his daughter would get her anything she asked for, "even the top brick off the chimney"—something hard to get and useless to her that would deprive other people. The remark is a good example of elliptical cockney wit.

19. This is an in-joke: Naomi Jacob was herself known to her friends as Micky.

20. For an account of the Nuremburg Law against intermarriage, "Law for

the Protection of German Blood and German Honour," September 15, 1935, see Steve Hochstadt (2004, 44–46).

21. In the classic novels of women transgressing sexual (and racial or class) boundaries through adultery, such as *Wuthering Heights, Anna Karenina,* or *Madame Bovary,* they do not get away with it; and, of course, although Lady Chatterley did, *Lady Chatterley's Lover* was banned for decades.

22. One can place the relation between the two women along what Adrienne Rich called "the lesbian continuum" in "Compulsory Heterosexuality and Lesbian Existence" (Rich 1986, 51).

23. Tony Kushner has discussed the coverage by British papers of Nazi persecution of German Jews, especially the quality papers like the *Manchester Guardian.* He concludes that although most people in Britain were aware that Jews were being mistreated by the Nazi regime, they did not understand why. Moreover, since the experience of false atrocity propaganda in World War I, they were disinclined to credit reports of atrocities. However, after news coverage of Kristallnacht, November 1938, ordinary people took action where their government had failed to (Kushner 1994, 88).

24. The term is taken from Ervin Straub, *The Roots of Evil* (Cambridge: Cambridge University Press, 1989), 80.

25. Phyllis Bottome's novel, *The Mortal Storm* (London: Faber, 1937; Boston, Little Brown, 1938) was made into a film by MGM in 1940. This was so successful in United States as anti-Nazi propaganda that Germany banned MGM films. The novel is discussed at length by Brothers (1993, 248–52) and Lassner (1998, 219–24). Unlike Bottome, Jacob had not been to Germany.

"A Jewish womanhood attached to the soil . . . a new type of Jewish womanhood": Constructions of Israel in the Fiction of Lynne Reid Banks

Deborah Philips

A PAMPHLET WRITTEN IN 1920, FOR THE LONDON FEDERATION OF Women Zionists, frames the early pioneer dream of a socialist Jewish state with expectations of a new kind of Jewish womanhood: "There should be fostered a native type with ideals native to the soil of the country . . . In Palestine . . . there is to grow up a native Jewish woman, and of a type which will do honour to our people as a whole. . . . a Jewish womanhood attached to the soil, both as the source of livelihood as well as national possession. . . . We stand at the cradle of a new type of Jewish womanhood (Goodman 1920, 4). Such ideals may seem a long way from the postwar London of *The L-Shaped Room* (1962) but it is Lynne Reid Banks who has done more to articulate and promote the notion of a Jewish "type with ideals native to the soil of the country" than any other fiction writer in Britain or America. Reid Banks is now remembered largely for *The L-Shaped Room*, which, in its narrative of the independent, single, and pregnant woman has since been read as a protofeminist novel. But what is less remembered, and is not acknowledged in contemporary reviews of the novel that became a school set text, is that the main focus of romance in the novel is a Jewish man, and that Jane's story that begins in the L-shaped room ends, two novels later, on a kibbutz in Israel.

More than any other British writer, Reid Banks has consistently written about Jews in Britain and North America, relationships between Gentiles and Jews, and about Israel. Although not herself born Jewish, the romantic heroes of her novels consistently are; there is a recurrent trope in both the adult and children's fiction of the attractiveness to women (both Jewish and Gentile) of the exotic, sensitive, and, often, damaged Jewish man. Reid Banks did marry a Jewish sculptor, and emigrated with him to Israel, where they raised two sons on a kibbutz; the authenticity and restorative power of kibbutz life and of physical labor in the cause of Israel are persistent themes of her fiction. For Reid Banks, as a professed Zionist (and, also in her own words, a "practicing atheist"), Israel is the Jewish homeland; the Israel of her novels becomes a space that answers to her protagonists' needs for work, spiritual fulfillment, moral principle, political idealism, and romance.

Israel is for Toby Cohen, romantic hero of *The L-Shaped Room,* and for subsequent Reid Banks heroes, a projected utopia, that is fueled by his discontent and alienation from the postwar metropolis. Israel, Mother Israel, Eretz Israel, is projected in these novels as a space of conviction rather of than pretension; it is repeatedly the place where not only all Jews, but also disenchanted North Americans, north Londoners, unrecognized actors, writers, and women discontented with postwar Britain, can find a place that allows them to develop and to discover their integrity.

Reid Banks's answer to disenchantment with postwar Britain is to identify herself with the Jewish people and with the Zionist cause. Judaism (as an ethnicity rather than a religion) and Israel are presented in her fiction as beleaguered causes. Her allegiance to Israel and identification with Judaism was evident from before her marriage or residence in Israel, and is a strong element of the 1960 novel *The L-Shaped Room.* The narrator is markedly sensitive to the populist and colloquial anti-Semitism of the period; among other slights to Toby's race, Terry, the actor father of Jane's baby, is unapologetically anti-Semitic:

> "By God," he said, unable, I saw to help himself, "he *is* a Jew and no mistake—that beak! Wonder why he changed his name—and then changed it back again?"
> I thought, *He changed it because of people who feel like you, and he changed it back because*— . . . . (1962b, 269)

Despite this sensitivity to the casual racism of anti-Semitic stereotypes, the novel's declared liberalism is very uneasy. The representation of the black and gay musician John is much less attuned to racial slur than it is for the Jewish characters. While the novel does allow the narrator to question her "atavistic fear" of a black man, the narrative does not challenge Toby's assessment of John: "He's just naturally inquisitive. Like a chimp, you know, he can't help it. He could no more resist having a look at you than a monkey could resist picking up anything new and giving it the once over" (46). This unthinking assumption of racial inferiority remains unchallenged in this novel, and in the two later novels in which John appears. The representation here of what Jane refers to as "odd-coloured people" can later be seen to inform the depiction of Palestinian characters in those novels set in Israel.

The L-Shaped Room ends equivocally: both the romance and Jane's future with the baby remain unresolved. Toby continues to haunt both the reader and Jane, the narrator, and he is a pervasive presence over the course of the next two novels, which chart his emigration and the heroine's pursuit of him to Israel. By the time of the second novel in the sequence, *The Backward Shadow*, in 1970, Reid Banks had become involved with Zionism, and had herself spent time in Israel on a kibbutz; the import of Judaism is much more direct and better informed here than it is in the first novel. Jane's relationship with Toby has become tenuous; although he remains the "backward shadow" of the title, the romantic obstacle to their relationship is now that she is a Gentile. His attraction to another, younger woman is because of her Jewishness, a nobler betrayal than any other form of infidelity. As the novel progresses, Toby and his new wife are described as "getting caught up in Zionism . . . He's Jewish to his backbone these days" (1972, 250).

The final novel in the trilogy, *Two Is Lonely* (1974), explores what it means to be "Jewish to the backbone," and was written after Reid Banks had moved to Israel. Toby has now moved beyond embracing his identity as a Jew to become a committed Zionist, and a kibbutznik. The bohemian intellectual has found a pride in manual work, and an integrity that literary London fails to offer: "The manners, and values in a capitalist, urban society like London *can't* be the same as one finds in a socialist Jewish commune like this . . . I'm not important here because I have a facility for writing stories. My prestige, my place in this little world, if any, is based on my dubious abilities as a teacher of English, a picker of bananas, a layer of irrigation pipes, and a washer-up" (1976, 178). Toby here is echoing Zionist writings from the early days of the pioneers. The possibility of a utopian egalitarian community, which was hinted at in *The L-Shaped Room*, is now seen as having been achieved in a socialist kibbutz. Zionist writings from the 1920s addressed potential women settlers in very similar terms: "It is the duty of the modern Jewish woman, equipped with the resources of European civilization, to bring her gifts and talents to the service of her people in its homeland and to take her rightful place in the national regeneration of the people of Israel" (Goodman 1920, 7). By the final novel in the series, *Two Is Lonely*, Jane's rival for Toby's affection is no longer the beautiful, younger, and Jewish metropolitan princess whom he married in the second novel, but a woman of the soil, free of vanity; she is the "modern" Jewish woman of the Jewish Women's Zionist Organization, a woman with whom the Gentile Jane cannot compete: "She was about my age, not at all good-looking, with lined and shiny skin, soft skimpy hair and very pale, rather bulging blue eyes. She wore a sun-faded sleeveless cotton dress cut away at the neck, and sandals. My first general impression of her was of a comfortable, relaxed ease of manner; a rare quality to find in a plain woman" (1976, 164). The Gentile heroine, Martha, who appeared in an earlier novel *An End to Running* (1962), aspires to become this woman of the soil by immersing herself in the life of a kibbutz.

The hero of the novel, Aaron, is a wealthier and more successful version of Toby of *The L-Shaped Room*, another Jewish writer whose career and aesthetic frustrations cannot be resolved by London. Aaron Franks has many of the same defining characteristics as Toby Cohen: his semitic features are both foreign and attractive: "A strong beaky nose under sharply winged eyebrows. His face was both bony and sensual; his mouth semitically full and yet somehow austere" (1962b, 12). Aaron begins the narrative as an avant-garde writer, an opportunity for the novel to attempt a (rather unsuccessful) satire on what Martha sees as the wilful obscurity of contemporary drama: "Who really understood *Waiting for Godot*? Who understood *The Caretaker*? . . . That ludicrous dustbin thing? Nobody. Probably not even the authors. They were controversial. People felt they had to see them, or be out of the swim" (50). This rejection of modernity is in part an alliance with the professed realism of the generation of the Angry Young Man, but it also suggests that there is an "inauthenticity" and decadence in fashionable London intelligentsia. The play that Aaron writes is described as "a subtle take-off of all the new-wave playwrights he despised for writing as if half-baked ideas and demotic rhetoric counted more than craftsmanship and having something important to say" (76).

It is the fact of Israel that is the "something important" that Aaron eventually has to say; for both the Jewish Aaron and the Gentile Martha, Israel comes to represent a place of authentic values, and of personal commitment, which are not demanded by the intellectual metropolitan Jewish community (Aaron's hated sister lives in Hampstead, collects modern art, and patronizes avant-garde theater). The narrative is particularly scathing about Jewish attempts at assimilation: Aaron, until he lives in Israel, is described as "a self-hating Jew"; his sister, a practicing Jew who sees herself as a European, is the most unsympathetic character in the novel. Israel, or more particularly, the kibbutz, is counterposed in the narrative as a place where the Jew can be complete, where men are masculine laborers, and women are equal partners with no personal vanity. It is the kibbutz and the rural in particular that answer to the need for authenticity. Urban Israel is represented as hardly less strident than London; Tel Aviv is described as "brand new very brash and bright and busy, and rather dull . . . the place had no atmosphere—it was just a modern city" (181). Unlike Linda Grant's celebration of Tel Aviv's European modernism in *When I Lived in Modern Times*, Reid Banks sees the architecture of the city as vulgar and unsympathetic.

The environment where Aaron and Martha choose to settle is rural rather than metropolitan. Aaron's romanticization of Israel, as it was for Toby and the pioneers, is as a place associated with physical rather than intellectual labor; again, a sense of cultural and spiritual identity is derived from agricultural work and from the land: "The real world of hard work and clean air, of earned hunger and sleep . . . I . . . felt a sudden furious lust to stick my fingers deep into the grey earth, to lift rocks and to feel my own sweat running down my back" (1962, 166).

Israel thus becomes the site for a European Jew to prove himself as a mensch; as Martha puts it "the real battle (is) to turn yourself in to a—man" (246). Aaron imagines Israel to be "that one exceptional country where you weren't a Jew as you were a Jew everywhere else, on sufferance." (165). Anti-Semitism across the world is here directly attributed to the lack of a Jewish home-land: "What was it . . . about us? Why did we raise this blood-blister on every country we settled in? . . . Did they hate us because men must hate other men and we were a fixed target, a captive receptacle of hate, having nowhere to run to? Or had the very fact of having nowhere of our own made us provoke hate by stubborn refusal to blend, the bitterness of unbelonging making us defiant, clannish and arrogant?" (157). Israel is represented here as the missing part of Jewish identity, the space that will make a Jewish subject whole. Aaron's alienation, an anger that in effect is not so different from that of the very Gentile Jimmy Porter, is accredited to a fractured Jewish experience. It is Israel which is the remedy for Aaron, and by firm implication, all Jew-ish people. This universalizing of the alienated Jewish experi-ence outside Israel is a very particular take on the post-Holo-caust refugee Jewish experience, and one which is written about very differently by second generation Jewish writers brought up in Britain or America.[1]

Aaron in literary London is, however, a lost soul searching, a wandering Jew, who can only find a homeland in the Promised Land. Aaron and Martha find in the kibbutz an antidote to what they perceive as the pretentious dishonesty of the contemporary metropolis and find in Israel aesthetic and emotional redemp-tion. Martha becomes the ideal immigrant, respectful and well informed, who has researched the history of Jewish culture: "I waded, with fierce determination, through pages dotted with alien, half comprehended words like Histadrut, Knesset, Pal-mach, *yishuv* . . . But the story parts, the early pioneers, the ille-gal immigrants, the Siege of Jerusalem, these gripped my imagi-nation" (118). Israel thus becomes for the Gentile heroine a place of powerful narratives, of romance, of embattled and literally besieged idealists, and also the answer to her lover's alienation. Martha, sharing Aaron's perception that Jews outside Israel are a race apart, describes the kibbutzniks as comfortable in them-selves in a way that is not available to the London Jew: "They don't seem like the sort of Jews one meets in London. I never noticed it before coming here, but Jews at home are—well, dif-ferent, a race apart. There's a sort of *straining* feeling about them" (227). This honesty and sincerity is again associated with the land, and particularly kibbutz land. The kibbutz thus comes to stand as an emblem of a land properly husbanded by Jewish settlers, as if their labor naturalizes and justifies their presence. Aaron describes the kibbutz and the results of its cultivation with pride: "As we passed through the kibbutz lands, so neatly tilled and husbanded, I felt a sudden surge of confidence, even pride, that fruit-bearing trees had been coaxed out of that unyielding yellow sand. . . . The feelings of awe, consolation and stability I had had in London about my Bar Mitzvah trees returned now, only with greater validity, having their roots in real life and personal effort" (261).

Those feelings of consolation and stability are nonetheless undermined in the novel by recurrent references to an embattled nation, and a suggestion that this confidence and pride in the land will need armed support. There are indications that this is a community that is not welcome on the West Bank; the kibbutz boasts "solid-looking air-raid shelters" and the narrative also intimates that there was once an Arab community on the land which has been displaced by the kibbutz. Aaron comes to recognize that his commitment to a Jewish homeland must also involve a military pledge: "This was after all my place, and that if I had to die for it, I would" (262).

𝕶

In the L-shaped room trilogy and in *An End to Running*, Israel and Judaism are doubly alien to their heroines, associated with foreignness and with masculinity. Their English and Gentile heroines find themselves in Israel and involved in Jewish history because of a romance with a man (as did Lynne Reid Banks herself). Gerda, of the 1968 novel *Children at the Gate*, is the first of Reid Banks's heroines to herself be Jewish, and there is a more self-aware feminist edge to this novel. The heroine is another lost soul, perhaps the most damaged character in the novels.

The novel begins in Acre, where Canadian, divorced Gerda is mourning the end of her marriage and her lost child. Written in 1968, the novel is haunted by the fact of war: "Israel . . . has a smell of its own. The smell of gunpowder and bad blood, the smell of war hanging over us all the time" (62). The Arab city is associated with Gerda's own sense of degradation and grief: "dust and dirt, stale brandy, sour milk, sweat, the stench of my own misery and my own weakness" (55). Gerda has no compunction against expressing her initial antipathy towards the Arab people:

"I try to avoid even looking at them, for the Arabs seem to me an ugly race, ugly not from any physical defect but because their faces are dull with stupidity, crafty from years of subservience, first to their own kind, and now, alas, to us" (30). Arab people are thus presented, as were the sparse number of Arab figures who featured in earlier novels (and also John of *The L-Shaped Room*), as a combination of sly cunning and childlike stupidity, a race of "odd-coloured people" who represent both a threat and a burden of responsibility to the Jewish people. The children in Acre are dirty and unkempt, in stark contrast to the clean and well-cared for Jewish kibbutz children. This distinction is attributed less to poverty than it is presented as a racial difference.

The Jewish kibbutz is constructed in the novel in direct opposition to the Arab Acre: a community that is based in cleanliness and dedicated work rather than the urban degradation of Acre. The kibbutz also promises feminist values; Gerda is informed that women in the kibbutz are the equal of men and that it is the kibbutz way of life that can offer women a means of both working and of bringing up children.

Reid Banks's alliance of Zionism and feminism is also promoted in *Sarah and After, the Matriarchs*, written in 1975. This retelling of Old Testament Bible stories from the point of view of the women is designed to encourage the pride of young Jewish women in their own history and traditions. Dedicated to Reid Banks's goddaughters, this account of a Jewish female heritage is one in a long line by Jewish women writers who were concerned to transmit Jewish and Hebraic traditions from mother to daughters. Such a feminist account of Jewish history has a precedent in earlier Zionist writings by women: Dora Kobler's *Four Rachels*, published by The Education Department of the Federation of Women Zionists in 1947,[2] a year before the establishment of Israel as a state, clearly anticipates it, and lays down a marker for a female tradition of Zionism.

The Zionism and the embracing of a Jewish identity that is charted in such writings is directly related to Reid Banks's own biography and family history written to her sons from Jerusalem in 1976. In *Letters to My Israeli Sons*, Reid Banks describes her own identification with Israel and with Judaism in the same terms she has given to her heroines: Israel for her, as for her heroines, is a lover and a country:

I found a magic land more exciting, more challenging, more mysteriously fascinating and beautiful even than I had expected.

Later, much later—I came to know that it was not perfect, that
there were flaws. Terrible flaws. But by that time it was too late. My
honeymoon with Israel was over; I was married to it. (1976, 6).

The "terrible flaws" of Israel are not addressed in her adult fiction
until the 1981 novel, *Defy the Wilderness*, but Reid Banks's passionate engagement with Zionism (and Jewish men) remains
undimmed in this late novel. Its title echoes a Zionist slogan, and
a founding myth of the Israeli state, and the narrative endorses this
belief that it is the Jews who have the prowess and courage to cul-
tivate the desert, while by implication the Palestinians cannot.

The heroine, Ann, is the closest of all the heroines to Reid
Banks's own autobiography; a onetime ITV journalist, she is a
novelist, whose most "recent novel . . . had a Jewish hero" (1983,
53). Ann is researching (as was Reid Banks herself at the time of
writing of the novel) a book based on interviews about what she
terms the "First Arab-Israel war." Ann's experience of Israel
dates back fourteen years, and like Martha and Jane she has followed a Jewish lover to a kibbutz. For Ann too, Israel has all the
connotations of honesty and moral certainty: a country without
pretension. Although she purports to politically disavow the
"chauvinist mysticism" of those who cherish a mythical "Mother
Israel," nonetheless she shares a faith in the spiritual properties
of the land: "That some power emanated from it to its people and
from them back to it that made it give of its best." Musing on the
fact that she does not use cosmetics in Israel (something that
both Jane and Martha had also noted of kibbutznik women), she
concludes that Israel is a space that demands authenticity: "In
Israel it was different. How, different? She could not and never
had been able to pin it down. It was not just a practical matter of
heat . . . It had something to do with not needing disguises, or
artifice . . . It was absurd to . . . ascribe her strange sense of well
being, her subjectively rejuvenated looks to the country" (11–12).

Like Jane, Toby, Aaron, and Martha before her, Ann is disillu-
sioned with the London of the 1960s; in a retrospective sequence,
she is working as an arts journalist and despises contemporary
London as artificial and tedious. Escaping on a European trek,
she finds her experiences throughout "cheap" and stale, "exotic

dishes made of cheap ingredients." Eventually, a chance meeting with a kibbutznik takes her to Israel, where she discovers a new integrity and maturity. Israel provides Ann with a soothing balm, not only for the face, but for the troubled soul. It gives her an "inner sureness, a calm slow ascent towards maturity and fixed principles of living and philosophy— . . . I'd used all the superlatives before I got here. All the alliteratives. . . . Israel was all of them and none of them and far more than any of them to me" (20–21). Israel thus becomes for Anne a place of passionate engagement—literally—as the site of her two great love affairs; the kibbutz, especially, evokes the same language of a passionate romance that Reid Banks employed of her own relationship with Israel: "She was hooked, over-ears in love with the whole place and everyone in it, besotted with the single idea of a community of productive Jews . . . its imperfections charmed her more, endeared the place to her, as a slight limp or a crooked tooth makes a person one passionately loves all the more attractive" (24–25).

Written in 1981, *Defy the Wilderness* has to allow for Israel's imperfections, and the conflicts within a Zionist position are more apparent and acknowledged than in previous novels. The post-1977 political situation that both Ann and Reid Banks have to confront is played out against this romanticized, passionate affirmation of the power of Israel, but the Zionist cause was then a much less comfortable political alliance than it had once been; this was a period in which many liberal intellectuals in Israel termed themselves "post-Zionist." In 1977 Sadat had visited Israel, and symbolically accepted Israel as a nation, and the year also saw the election of Israel's first nonsocialist prime minister, the hardline Menachem Begin, who would remain in power until 1983. Begin's government is balefully acknowledged in the novel as part of "the chauvinist right" (48).

Defy the Wilderness attempts to represent the conflicting positions in contemporary Israeli politics, and works much as do Reid Banks's own collection of interviews in *Torn Country*, published a year later. While the novel is apparently structured as a dialogic collection of voices in the contemporary Israel of the post-Begin era of the early 1980s, and claims to present the reader with a multiplicity of positions on the current state of the nation, it is Ann who is the mediator and moral arbiter of those voices. The trajectory of the heroine's romance also suggests that there is only one, and that an extreme Zionist, political solution to the conflicts of Israel.

Ann begins the novel as the mediator for a number of dissenting and conflicting voices representing contemporary Israel. What these voices share is a nostalgia for a day when the cause of Zionism seemed certain and unassailable. There is an overwhelming tone of a sense of the betrayal of the founding principles of Israel. Ann's first lover (who betrays her) is named Menachem, a name which would, at the time of writing, have evoked Israel's then prime minister, Menachem Begin. Confronted with the complexities of a contemporary Israel, Ann reflects nostalgically on the certainties of the 1960s generation of immigrants, the generation that was so championed in her earlier novels: "The early 'sixties. Her era . . . still—idealism. Hope. Single-mindedness. . . . A period . . . after the great watershed of the '67 War, of blinkered introversion, over-confidence, and a sort of innocence—a lingering national virginity and a kind of *faux-paix*" (Banks 1983, 59).

After 1977, this nostalgic illusion of Israel as an entirely just and internationally supported cause and as a pure and proud nation can no longer be sustained. The early days of the pioneers and 1960s immigration are remembered with a warm glow of moral justice. One character remembers with regret the period that Reid Banks had written of in earlier novels, but it is a memory that erases conflict: "Those happy days when the cause was pure and the issues were clear and the Jews were all heroes. . . . When everybody knew there was only one side to be on and all the world agreed . . . How comfortable it must have been then, to be a Jew and to be sure you were right! No wonder those American Jews want to get back to it" (40). The West Bank settlements, and American financial support for them, are a recurrent source of unease in this novel. This construction of an American romantic naivete about Israel displaces Zionist zealotry away from the state of Israel itself and also serves to distance the English Ann and by implication, Reid Banks, from association with forms of Zionist extremism.

Reid Banks may recognize in this novel some of the contradictions and tensions of the contemporary politics of the Israeli state, but she nonetheless entirely accepts the Zionist position expressed in earlier novels, that the state of Israel is the only safe place for a Jew. Ann comes to accept of her Israeli lover that "he couldn't live anywhere else; if only because . . . only here could he be a complete Jew" (27). Ann's otherwise gentle and understanding English husband raises the spectre of a covert anti-Semitism—one that is less explicit than that depicted in earlier novels, but which is nonetheless perceived as a threat. There is no recognition in the novel that Ann's hardly expressed but nonetheless visceral fear of Arab people might share this unrecognized racism; in a chance encounter with an Arab she experiences him as a "man whom she felt, at a deeper level, to be an alien and an enemy, inimical to all she loved here" (43).

In *Defy the Wilderness*, the few Arab characters who appear (largely as builders and manual laborers) are described as "unreliable." Throughout the novel the Palestinians remain "they"; undignified with individuality or a national identity, they are recurrently referred to as Arabs, in a linguistic denial of their right to a state. While Ann and her Jewish friends constantly assert their own liberalism, this is nonetheless repeatedly tinged with an expressed distrust of all Arab peoples. The novel holds out no hope of concordat; Ruth, the most sympathetic figure in the novel, expresses a professed liberal Jewish position that is nonetheless full of fear and loathing: "I don't wish to insult the Arabs . . . Our being here at all is insult enough to them. But I cannot flatter them because deep down I *know* they are trying to cheat me, I know they would cut my neck if they could. I fear them" (95). The Palestinians are positioned throughout the novel as a race rather than a nation. Throughout the series of novels about Israel, Reid Banks sustains a double standard, in which the Jews are perceived as heroic in their founding of a nation-state based on racial and religious identity, while the demand for a state from the Palestinian peoples is perceived as entirely untenable. The militant Zionist Boaz goes so far as to suggest that the Palestinians are too cowardly to fight with the same conviction that the Jews have shown: "If they really wanted their freedom . . . they would fight for it! . . . That's how the Jews fought against the British. But then, the Jews *really* wanted independence. 'At the risk of their lives'—yes! That's how all fighting is done!" (98).

Boaz Schaterman, the ultimate Jewish romantic hero, haunts the novel, although he does not appear as a character until over halfway through. A powerful presence, he is described as "brave, stubborn, virile, ruthless—but crippled, . . . A man of war, with singleness of purpose and the strength of his convictions" (276).

As a contemporary reviewer pointed out, Boaz is "an heir to Mr Rochester with the added quirks that true Zionist fervour can provide,"[3] he has lost a hand to a terrorist bomb, and is, it is said, further to the right than Ariel Sharon. Boaz is also the most macho hero of any of the novels; he has "the most powerful and masculine face she had ever seen" (161). Boaz is a literally damaged Jew, but he is also a "shtarker" (a term derived from the Yiddish term *shtark*, "strong"), and he is a shtarker with "all the mensch like elements."[4] More powerful than Ann's quietly anti-Semitic husband Peter and fiercer than the intellectuals she knows, Boaz is crude, maimed and aggressive—but he represents for Ann the "real" Israel. As she breathlessly tells him: "In some almost metaphysical way, *you are Israel*" (157).

Ann, like Jane and Martha before her, rejects the coziness of postwar Britain, and allows herself to be seduced by an Israeli man and by Israel itself. There is a recognition in this novel that the pacifism and socialism of some of the kibbutz projects that were so celebrated in earlier novels are not appropriate to contemporary Israel, and that the Israeli cause is now one which has to embrace "blood-guiltiness," both metaphorically and literally, as Ann comes to embrace the aggressor Boaz. It is an aggressive masculinity that draws Ann to Boaz: the men are more exciting in Israel than in England. Israel as a nation is also presented as a stimulating and a dangerous and more exotic environment than England. Ann's husband seals his own fate when he writes her a letter full of village gossip, chat about the church and gardening, and suggests that he is "getting a wee bit bored with the Jews." Ann's militant Jewish lover (and Israel itself) seduces her by allowing her to see herself as a vibrant woman who does not belong to the dull and cozy English world: "All that—English flatness and blandness and safety—that's not for you, there's no challenge in it, it demands nothing. Israel makes demands, it hurts the flesh . . . it makes you weep . . . and drinks your tears and forces you to know you are alive" (294).

This conflation of the dangers and excitements of Israeli men with Israel as a country is bound into an eroticized fascination with military masculinity. In a description of a young English man who volunteers as a commando in the Israeli army (there is no mention at all in the novel of conscription), aggression and the military are suggested as a natural destiny for Jewish men and a source of pride for all Jewish mothers: "The deep primordial pride of womanhood in uniformed and gun-toting sons, in fierce, brave aggressive male progeny, fulfilling a destiny—of driving off marauders bred into them throughout the millennia of evolution . . . What price the tame option of a decent little semi . . . compared to the inner glory of that? . . . a woman is conditioned to hope for and expect of her men—the ultimate proofs of masculinity, the evidence that he is a young lion and not a young lamb" (243).

Reid Banks's own 1982 version of Israeli history, *Torn Country* (1982), is clearly close to the fictional book that Ann Randall researches in *Defy the Wilderness*. Like Ann's book, *Torn Country* is made up of interviews with a range of Israeli people, the great majority of whom are Jews still living in Israel. Like Ann, Reid Banks is apologetic at her inability to include other voices, and attributes this in her introduction to her position as a known supporter of Zionism. Nonetheless, her sympathies are made very clear: the book is dedicated to "Boaz"—the hero and aggressor of *Defy the Wilderness*, and the fractured star of David emblazoned on the front cover suggests an unequivocal support for the contemporary Jewish state of Israel.

Israel, though seen as flawed, remains in *Defy the Wilderness* and *Torn Country* the Promised Land, and the Jews the Chosen People. The history of the Israeli state is presented in terms of nature itself granting the Jews a right to the land. One descendant of Jewish settlers describes the establishment of Israeli settlements and articulates one of the founding myths: "The place was a wilderness! . . . When (my grandfather) came in 1905 he found the land barren, a few fields scratched out of the rock . . . No orchards, no husbandry, no thought for the future . . . It was the Jews who transformed this place" (Banks 1983, 179). It is Jews like Boaz who are now seen as necessary in defense of this place and its history. Like Ariel Sharon, Boaz's past history was as a member of Dayan's commando units in the 1950s, which had mounted aggressive raids on Jordanian territory. Boaz is described as "fascist" by several characters in the novel, and his own virulently expressed political position is indeed close to fascism. He asserts the need for perpetual war, and believes in individual heroism and in the racial superiority of the Jews: " 'Peace' he shouted. 'Peace? What is it? Who needs it? . . . Peace is for places like England . . . But it is nothing to do with real life . . . Here we live as men have to live, on an edge, and every few years we go over it when we have to fight for our survival . . . there is no doubt they are entirely different from us, and if you push me to say it, I will say it: *we are better'"* (176).

The narrative resolution of the novel ultimately supports this position, and also confirms the natural superiority of the Jews which has been an undercurrent of Ann's encounters throughout Israel. The self-defined radical Ann comes to believe that the socialist utopias of the kibbutz movements are no longer the way forward, a decision acted out in Ann's choice between her former lover Menachem, a kibbutznik pacifist (despite his name), and the right wing aggressor Boaz. Ann chooses Boaz, and an aggressive Israel, in a narrative endorsement of Boaz's undercover terrorism.

In a recent article in the *New York Review of Books*, Tony Judt has argued that "In the Middle East today each side dwells within hermetically sealed memories and national narratives in which the other side's pain is invisible and inaudible."[5] Reid Banks is a writer who has been a significant figure in the mediation of such memories and national narratives. The Israel of Lynn Reid Banks's fiction and documentary writings is a construction that is echoed in many British and American mythologies of Jewish and Israeli history. Israel becomes in Reid Banks's fictions a country that provides spiritual, political, and moral principle, combined into one neat cause. And it is Israel which is seen in these novels to provide a solution to the frustrations and elitism of a postwar secular modernity; it offers a form of spirituality that is not Christian, and it is a brave new cause, but one which stems from ancient tradition.

In the torn country of Lynne Reid Banks's fiction, desirable masculinity and a new kind of "womanhood" are knitted together with a particular form of Zionist nationalism. In the novels of Lynne Reid Banks, Israel is the place in which the Jewish schlemiel can become a mensch, and the Jewish princess a woman of the land: her heroines become the "new kind of Jewish woman" endorsed by the Federation of Jewish Women Zionists in 1920, embattled and heroic, embracing the "authentic" men and land of Israel.

NOTES

1. See for example, Anne Karpf, *The War After: Living with the Holocaust* (London: Heinemann, 1996), and Martin Goldsmith, *The Inextinguishable*

Symphony: A True Story of Music and Love in Nazi Germany (New York: J. Wiley, 2000).

2. Dora Kobler, *Four Rachels*. (London: Education Department of the Federation of Women Zionists, 1947).

3. Marigold Johnson, "Pillow Talk and Politics" *Times Literary Supplement,* October 2, 1981, 1118.

4. Linda Grant, "Defenders of the Faith," *Guardian Review,* July 6, 2002, 4–6.

5. Tony Judt, "Israel: The Road to Nowhere," *New York Review of Books* 49, no. 8 (May 9, 2002): 4.x.

Ellen Galford's "Ghost Writing": Dykes, Dybbuks, and Doppelgangers

Paulina Palmer

Introduction: Galford and Her Identifications, Old and New

ONE OF THE MOST STRIKING FEATURES ABOUT ELLEN GALFORD, A contemporary writer whose fiction inscribes a uniquely humorous interplay of realism and fantasy, is the variety of different identities—national, cultural, and sexual—of which she boasts. Though born in North America, Galford has spent much of her adult life in Edinburgh and represents herself to the reader as Scottish by adoption. In both *The Fires of Bride* (1986), a work of Gothic fantasy set on the imaginary Hebridean island of Cailleach, and *Queendom Come* (1990), which focuses on the political life of Edinburgh in the 1980s and gives a savage exposé of the destruction that the Thatcher government wrought on the social fabric of Scotland, she foregrounds her Scottish connections. The two novels explore and interrogate Scottish identity and culture, with Galford addressing the topics with a degree of ambivalence. While celebrating their endurance in the face of English imperialism, she also exposes the absurdities they display and critiques their exploitation and commercialization by financially interested parties such as the Scottish home industries and the Tourist Board. In addition, she critiques the element of machismo and misogyny apparent in Scottish constructs of masculinity, illustrating the part that the dour puritanism of John Knox and his ilk has played in its formation. Her treatment of Scottish culture and identity is poststructuralist in emphasis; it bears witness to the fact that national identity tends to be constructed rather than innate. It is a matter of culture, rather than given by nature.

Yet another identity that Galford claims, the one which, in fact, is consistently to the fore in her fiction, is lesbian/feminist. A lesbian/feminist identification helps to account for her preoccupation with themes of gender and sexual orientation, underpinning her representation of relationships between women and informing her ideological viewpoint. *Moll Cutpurse* (1984), her earliest publication in the field of fiction, explores same-sex desire and women's oppression in Jacobean England. It also examines, through the vehicle of historiographic metafiction, the topic, a controversial one in the lesbian movement of the 1970s and 1980s, of butch/femme role-play. *The Fires of Bride*, in addition to interrogating Scottish identity and culture, and critiquing their commercialization, celebrates lesbian/feminist concepts of women's community and sisterhood, while playfully exposing the flaws and contradictions that they often reveal in practice. Her subsequently published novels *Queendom Come* and *The Dyke and the Dybbuk* (1993), though differing radically in content and location, also inscribe a lesbian/feminist perspective and focus on the construction of lesbian identity and relationships.

Reference to *The Dyke and the Dybbuk* brings me, in fact, to the last identity that Galford claims—the one that, in terms of this collection, is of key importance and explains why I've chosen to discuss her work. This is her Jewishness. *The Dyke and the Dybbuk*, as well as being the novel in which her Jewish identification features most prominently, also illustrates her interest in and knowledge of Jewish history, culture, and occult lore. As is the case with her treatment of her other ethnic and cultural affiliations, Galford approaches Jewish culture with a degree of ambivalence. While celebrating its complexity and endurance, she also exposes its restrictive and oppressive aspects, especially where women and men who identify as gay are concerned.

As this introduction to Galford's fiction illustrates, what emerges from a reading of her novels is the image of her as a very unusual, not to say "eccentric" figure: an American/Scottish/Jewish/lesbian/feminist. Her work is of interest, in my view, not just for the different identities that she foregrounds and explores, most of them minority ones and some of them conflicting, but for the attitude that she adopts toward them. Not for her some wishy-washy mish-mash of global identification, à la Rosi Braidotti, of "nomadic subject" or "citizen of the world." Or if, in fact, Galford does think of herself as "a citizen of the world," it is in a very different sense from the usual meaning of the term. Instead of conflating the different identities she adopts into a general form of minority otherness and alterity, she foregrounds each one individually. She turns it round and inspects it, examining its strengths and problematic features and teasing out its contradictions. She compares and contrasts her different affiliations, playing one off against the other and juggling with them in a playfully carnivalesque fashion. Her fiction, as is generally the case with the most successful carnivalesque writing, displays a distinctly political edge. It operates as a strategy of resistance against a hegemonic conception of Britishness, heterosexist norms, and anti-semitic prejudice.

This political aspect of Galford's work agrees, it is interesting to note, with the interests and perspectives of present-day feminist and queer theorists. The French-based Julia Kristeva in her study *Strangers to Ourselves*, developing the concept of abjection that she initially explored in *Powers of Horror*, investigates the way that our ambiguous view of the stranger as a figure of fascination who, simultaneously, poses a threat to our identity and way of life, results in us attempting to abject her/him from the community, giving rise to prejudice and acts of racism. Our efforts to abject the stranger are, Kristeva argues, impossible since, in the eyes of other people, we all appear "strangers." In addition since, from a Freudian psychoanalytic point of view, we all have an unconscious, the stranger, rather than being external to us, is, in fact, within us; s/he is an aspect of ourselves. Galford, like Kristeva, devotes her intellectual energies to teasing out the complexities of the concepts of "the stranger" and "the Other." She interrogates and problematizes them, demonstrating the fact that we all exist as "strangers."

The interest that Galford displays in different forms of alterity, as I argue in my recently published study *Lesbian Gothic: Transgressive Fictions*, helps to explain her frequent literary utilization of fantasy forms, Gothic in particular. A comment voiced by the queer theorist Diana Fuss is relevant here, shedding light on the Gothic aspect of Galford's work and that of other writers of lesbian fiction. Discussing the importance that the Gothic motif of spectrality and haunting assumes in queer theory today, Fuss points out that writers frequently employ it metaphorically to represent "the return of the repressed" that lesbian/gay desire enacts in homophobic society, and to depict the tense and frequently hostile relationship that tends to exist between heterosexual and homosexual communities. Describing the two communities haunting one another in the manner of a ghostly visitation, Fuss depicts lesbian/gay literary production in present-day homophobic society as a form of "ghost-writing, a writing which is at once a recognition and a refusal of the cultural representation of 'the homosexual' as phantom Other" (1991, 4). In the case of Galford, we might add to the "homosexual" identity cited by Fuss, the identities "Scot" and "Jew" since they too are generally defined against a hegemonic norm and feature as the focus of scrutiny in Galford's work. Utilizing the strategy of humor, she devotes her fiction to exposing and critiquing the prejudiced representation of all three identities as, to borrow Fuss's aptly chosen phrase, "phantom others." And by deliberately renegotiating their relationship to the abject, she also succeeds in resignifying and valorizing them. In this respect she contributes to the agenda of queer politics as defined by Eve Sedgwick. Teasing out the resonances of the term "queer" Sedgwick remarks on the fact that "a lot of the most exciting recent work around 'queer' spins the term outward along dimensions that can't be subsumed under gender and sexuality at all." She comments on "the ways that race, ethnicity and postcolonial nationality crisscross with these and other identity-constituting, identity-fracturing discourses" (1994, 8–9). Galford's investigation of the interaction and tension that exists between a lesbian/feminist identification, on the one hand, and certain national and ethnic identifications, on the other, vividly illustrates Sedgwick's observation in fictional form.

THE DYKE AND THE DYBBUK: LONDON LESBIANS AND FRIENDLY SPOOKS

Having commented in general terms on Galford's literary and ideological interests, I'll now turn to *The Dyke and the Dybukk*, the novel in which, as mentioned above, her interest in Jewish identity and culture achieves priority. *The Dyke and the Dybbuk* is a work of fantasy creating a humorous lesbian variation on that antiquated old cliché of Gothic fiction and film, the family curse. This particular curse, as the female dybbuk Kokos who is dispatched by Mephistico Industries to execute it explains, originated in the Middle Ages in a humble European dorf when an orphan girl of mixed parentage, contemptuously known by the Jewish inhabitants as Anya the Apostate, sought to take revenge on her Jewish lover, Gittel, for betraying the vow of sisterhood the two had sworn, by agreeing to marry. Angrily watching the wedding procession wind through the narrow streets of the dorf, Anya directs the curse not only at this particular Gittel but also at all subsequent ones, until the thirty-third generation. She expresses the wish that they will disappoint their misogynistic husbands by giving birth only to daughters and, an even more scary fate, be possessed by a dybbuk, a form of Jewish demon whose mission is to posses the human subject with the aim of driving her mad. Kokos, the female demon designated to execute the curse, is initially prevented from doing so by the strategies of her archenemy the pious Hebrew scholar Shmuel ben Issachar, revered by his numerous disciples as "the saintly sage of Limnititzk" (1993, 7). In an effort to prevent her assault on Jewish womanhood, Ben Issachar utilizes his occult skills to imprison her, like Shakespeare's Ariel, in a tree. However on emerging from her sylvan incarceration in the 1980s, Kokos, by employing the services of the Mephistico Industries archives, succeeds in tracing the descendants of Gittel number one to Rainbow Rosenbloom, or "Gittel-plus-nine" (27) as she colloquially calls her. Rainbow, Kokos discovers, lives in Ilford and identifies as lesbian feminist. In order to earn a living and achieve financial independence from her Jewish family, she has taken a job as a taxi driver. "Rainbow" is not, of course, the name that her parents conferred on her. On the contrary, she has appropriated it herself after the "rainbow" gay alliance as a sign of her attempt to liberate herself from her Jewish cultural inheritance that she regards, in terms of its bigoted attitudes to homosexuality and its relegation of women to the roles of wife and mother, as deeply oppressive. Though succumbing on occasion to the pleas voiced by her numerous aunts that she return home to participate in Jewish festivals, she has made every effort to cast off her Jewish identity. Having comfortably ensconced herself in a flat comprising "three rooms above a Cypriot bakery in north London" (40), she spends her leisure time mingling with the local lesbian community, gorging herself on what Galford disrespectfully terms the "mind-candy" of "dyke-detective thrillers, biographies of self-destructing rock-stars and science-fiction tales of intergalactic sex wars" (40), and, one of her main pleasures, indulging her taste for Chinese food.

Galford's choice of London as the location for the novel and the urban focus that it permits her, as well as giving her scope to explore the interests and interaction of the London Jewish community, places her novel in the mainstream of lesbian writing. Discussing the part that an urban environment plays in the formation of lesbian identity and culture, Elizabeth Wilson describes the lesbian as "the inhabitant of the great cities," a figure defined by her sexuality and by the fact that she "stands outside the family" (1986, 169). The lesbian's relationship with the city, foregrounded by Wilson in the 1980s, has subsequently been examined by other theorists and critics in greater detail. Gill Valentine explores the lesbian "(Re)negotiating the 'heterosexual street'" (1996, 146–55), while Sally Munt, developing from a queer perspective the ideas of Walter Benjamin, discusses the concept of "the lesbian flâneur." Munt describes the woman who identifies as lesbian appropriating the male prerogative of the gaze, thus reclaiming the urban space for women (1995, 114–25). These ideas form the social and ideological context of *The Dyke and Dybbuk* that, in combining a focus on an urban environment and lifestyle with motifs of haunting and demonic possession, merits the designation "urban Gothic."

The narrative strategy that Galford employs in the novel, the intellectual game she plays, is to juxtapose and confront one form of alterity with another, deftly manipulating stereotypes in order to interrogate and problematize social and cultural norms. By emphasizing the transgressive identities of both the demon Kokos and the dyke Rainbow, the object of her haunting, she disconcerts the reader by unexpectedly highlighting the attributes the two share. She transforms Kokos, in fact, from the role of Rainbow's demonic adversary, intent on her destruction, to her friendly doppelganger who, as her sojourn in Ilford continues, finds herself involuntarily accommodating to Rainbow's interests and viewpoint. This process of doubling between dyke and dybbuk commences in the early stages of their relationship. Kokos is annoyed to discover that, like the lesbian Rainbow, she is the object of prejudice and bigotry: she is shocked to hear the attendant at the Turkish bathhouse that Rainbow frequents, on learning that the latter is the victim of haunting, assure her that the place is free from ghosts since, in her experience, "Spooks don't like soap and water . . . They're very dirty creatures" (1993, 70). Another feature that Kokos and Rainbow share is, judged by conventional standards, a strong degree of eccentricity and Otherness. Kokos's demonic mission, as she has learnt from the infernal mentor with whom she studied, is, Galford informs us, to "take control of the [human] subject, to possess her in mind, soul and body" in order "to transform her into something Other than what she was before" (39). Here, however, she encounters difficulties since, as she snidely remarks on first meeting Rainbow, "By any conventional standards, this rather eccentric individual is pretty Other to begin with" (39). Unaccustomed to lesbian fashions in appearance, she disparagingly describes Rainbow's physique as "broad, solid and topped with a grating of spikes (This she calls a haircut?)" (39). She is also surprised to find that, far from being being demure and quiet as a nice Jewish girl should be, Rainbow has "a mouth that always wants to have the last word—and often gets it" (39). Rainbow's lifestyle also strikes Kokos as decidedly outré. She refuses to dress fashionably to attract a prospective husband but, on the contrary, wears "a faded purple T-shirt bearing a clenched fist and a washed-out political slogan" (40), lives in a chaos of unwashed clothes, and forms intimate relationships with women. In addition, she has a passion for film that finds expression in the frequent visits that she pays to the local cinema and in the reviews she writes for a gay film magazine appropriately called *The Outsider.* This organ of intellectual debate, Galford informs us, has its editorial headquarters in "two rooms above an Indian takeaway in the Holloway Road" (43) where, she ironically observes, "the spiritual heirs and heiresses of Marlowe, Wilde, Sappho and Stein operate" (43).

In keeping with her heroine's cinematic interests, Galford litters the novel with intertextual references to film. These are not merely decorative but, on the contrary, serve a number of different intellectual and ideological ends. To start with, they provide a source of Gothic imagery appropriate to the theme of haunting and dybbukry that the novel treats. This is reflected in the fact that Rainbow's announcement to her friend Naomi over a meal at a Chinese restaurant that she is the victim of supernatural haunting evokes from the latter not expressions of alarm or words of sympathy but a mocking reference to the Hammer Horror film machinery of "old Gothic mansions, bats and secret chambers and Vincent Price" (74). Reference to film also furnishes Galford with a vehicle to develop the theme of lesbian urban life that provides the context for the action of the novel, and to comment on the dangers that the city holds for women. Rainbow's insecurities on this score, exacerbated by the Kokos's spectral attentions, are, in fact, reflected back to her in the examples of film noir that she watches on the silver screen. As Kokos, congratulating herself on her skills in arousing fear in the human subject, smugly remarks on accompanying Rainbow to the cinema to see a new release, "Images of cheap hotel rooms, flickering neon, midnight streets and threatening footsteps make her feel tense and lonely. Or that's what she tells herself, when she stumbles out into the watery sunlight" (53).

Another function that reference to film plays in the novel is to advertise the fictionality of Galford's narrative and foreground the lesbian recasting of classic Gothic themes in which it engages. This is exemplified by Kokos's somewhat grandiose comparison of the battle of wits in which Rainbow and she engage to the "great scene in Bergman's *The Seventh Seal* when Max Von Sydow plays chess with Death" (98). The names of film directors and film titles are further utilized by Galford as signifiers of lesbian and Jewish history and culture. References to the Jewish film moguls who dominated Hollywood in its early years and to cult lesbian films such as what Kokos fondly terms "that old lezzie boarding-school classic, *Mädchen in Uniform*" (101), feature prominently in the text. Kokos, eager as always to celebrate her own achievements and that of her infernal colleagues, even has the audacity to claim that the cinema industry itself may have originated in the inspiration of an exceptionally inventive dybbuk:

> I note, with some interest, that Hollywood, from its earliest days, has been a stamping ground of ex-yeshiva boys from Belz, Pinsk, Odessa and Etceteragrad. Next time I'm back at the office I must check the old project files—did any of those moguls, with their fruity shtetl accents and pushcart-pedlar tactics, have dybbuks of their own? It wouldn't be the first time some great, allegedly human invention was actually the work of a demon whispering into a subject's inner ear. And Movie-land certainly reminds me of home-sweet-home: tricksy phantasmagorias with lights and mirrors, plus lots of battles over the budget. (83)

Rainbow's obsession with film, particularly works focusing on lesbian relationships and female screen icons such as *Mädchen In Uniform* and *Queen Christina*, intrigues Kokos, introducing her to a fascinating new world of lesbian/feminist culture. She is astonished to find that Rainbow, far from being ashamed of her Otherness and the transgressive lifestyle she leads, positively relishes them. She happily defines herself as "a Jewish lesbian who breaks the Sabbath and most of the Commandments, eats forbidden food and hasn't put a foot into a synagogue in twenty years" (119). Nor does she see anything strange about living in jeans and a buffed faded leather jacket, with "a chequered scarf to indicate solidarity with the Palestinian struggle" (40). However, as Kokos firmly informs Rainbow, Jewish identity is a cultural construct, meaning different things to different people— and its renunciation is a good deal more difficult to achieve than she appears to assume:

> "Beloved," I say, "this may be news to you. To your Aunt Becky, you're Jewish. To old Rabbi Whatisface, you are—just possibly—Jewish. To Hitler and his henchmen, may their memory be cursed in all the languages of the worlds, you'd be Jewish. And to me, of course, you are—or I wouldn't be here. But, in the Jewishness stakes, sweetheart, the kosher ayatollas who run this neighbourhood would place you somewhere between a Tibetan lama and the fairy on the top of the Christmas tree. So break any rules, you please."

She disrespectfully concludes, parodying the controversial last line of the film of *Gone with the Wind* uttered by Clark Gable in the role of the suave Rhett Butler, "because frankly, my dear, they don't give a damn" (119).

Kokos initially finds Rainbow's lesbian identification disturbing—worrying too, as far her hopes of carrying out the contract for the Gittel family curse in the future is concerned. Rainbow's lesbian proclivities, she recognizes, do not augur well for the creation of future Gittels. How, Kokos wonders, can she make the contract of infernal possession last until the thirty-third generation "unless I can actually persuade the dear girl to succumb to a broody fit and procreate?" (41). Rainbow, unfortunately for Kokos, shows not the slightest interest in procreating. She is not, Kokos regretfully observes, "one of your self-propagating Amazonian Earth Mothers, who does it all with a test-tube and a turkey-baster" (41).

Kokos's task of possessing Rainbow demonically and transforming her into something Other is further complicated by the
fact that, as her relationship with her deepens and she gets to
know her, she discovers, against her better judgement, that she
rather likes her. Fascinated by Rainbow's alternative way of life
and speedily adapting to her passion for film and her taste for Chinese food, she decides, to her astonishment, that "I've finally met
a human I find interesting" (41). Her feelings for Rainbow inten-
sify, and she perceives, with alarm, that liking is turning into
love. Experiencing feelings of attraction toward a client, let alone
falling in love with her/him, is strictly against the rules of
Mephistico Industries. It is regarded as distinctly unprofessional,
and Kokos fears it may cost her her job.

There are other reasons too, besides experiencing feelings of
attraction for Rainbow, that make Kokos wish to prolong her visit
to London. She finds herself enjoying life in the metropolis, taking pleasure in its mix of sexual identifications and ethnicities.
As a dybbuk with a lesbian orientation, she is at an advantage
here, since she feels equally at home in both gay and Jewish circles. Her response to the latter furnishes Galford with an opportunity to interrogate and discuss Jewish history and culture.
Watching the Jewish residents of London, Kokos ponders their
history, recognizing them from her travels as "sharing common
ancestors in Krakow, Magdeburg, Avignon, Granada, Tbilisi,
Salonica, Babylon" (60). Commenting on their ability to avoid or
survive pogrom and exile, she describes them as "the descendants
of restless, wary people. Who may have sniffed blood on the wind
or have been looking for a golden city, but who, for whatever reason, took their future generations out of danger's way in time"
(60). Driving to a picnic organized by Rainbow's sociable aunts
who relish any excuse for an excursion, she admits to experiencing a sense of recognition. "I can't tell you how nostalgic this out-
ing makes me," she confides to Rainbow as they get underway.
"A bunch of Jewish women laden down with bundles. Reminds
me of at least ten different migrations, forced and voluntary. Did
I ever tell you about the time in the Persian empire when—"and
she embarks on a lively account of the various episodes of Jewish
history through which she has lived (157). Rainbow's aunts bicker
among themselves about the pros and cons of Jewish orthodoxy.
Aunt Goldie praises the young people she knows who, after experiencing a secular upbringing, have unexpectedly turned to reli-

gion in an attempt to return to their Jewish roots and affirm the value of tradition. Aunt Rebecca, however, disagrees. "So what's so great about tradition?" she snorts scornfully. "Tradition means getting massacred every time the Cossacks get restless, and catching cholera and girls married and pregnant from the time they're fifteen, and a whole bundle of medieval superstitions, and no plumbing, and women doing all the dirty work as usual. You can leave me out of it!" (164).

As for Rainbow, her reaction to Kokos, dybbuk and infernal doppelganger with whose spectral attentions she unexpectedly finds herself landed, is as mixed as is Kokos's response to her. Though initially scared out of her wits by Kokos's dramatic methods of haunting, including projecting fits of hysterical cackling on her taxi radio and transforming the film reviews inscribed on her computer into Hebrew characters, after she has heard the story of the ancestral curse and understood the reason for her visit, she quickly accommodates to her presence. Her knowledge of horror film, gained while working on *The Outsider* magazine, proves useful in this respect. Kokos's uncanny spectral appearances, as Rainbow flippantly observes, "cut little ice with someone who's seen every celluloid shocker from *Nosferatu* to middle-period Ridley Scott" (101) and who has "read, seen, heard and hummed along with every version of the Faustus legend" and "watched every piece of demonic celluloid from *The Devil with Hitler* to *Rosemary's Baby meets Damien Seven at the Senior Prom*" (96). She also finds Kokos's presence useful from a practical point of view. Tiring of Rainbow's slovenly ways, Kokos is reduced on more than one occasion to tidying the flat and doing a spot of dusting. In addition, she protects Rainbow from the nocturnal dangers of the city by employing the conventional supernatural device of rendering her invisible.

This comfortable relationship between dyke and dybbuk is, however, unexpectedly disrupted when Rainbow, unconsciously following the example of the medieval Anya the Apostate, unexpectedly falls in love with Riva, an attractive young Jewish matron colloquially named by Kokos "the Flower of Stamford Hill" (120) whom she meets when on a visit to one of her aunts. Riva, though undeniably a beauty "with eyes like blue-black plums and hair even blacker" (60), is, as Kokos points out, by no means an appropriate object of desire for the lesbian/feminist Rainbow. Not only is she married to a famous Orthodox Jewish scholar, but she has also fulfilled her wifely duties by bearing him six children. Rainbow, however, is undeterred by these obstacles and, with the husband absent in New York, makes a valiant attempt to court the beautiful Riva and win her love. With this aim in view, she gives up going to the cinema and, instead, devotes her time to boning up on Jewish history and theology. In order to see more of her beloved she even agrees to attend a family wedding and, in the hope of making a good impression, borrows some sequined feminine attire from one of her aunts, though protesting all the while under her breath that she feels she is wearing drag. This turn of events irritates Kokos who, as Galford comments, would much prefer to be "at the pictures, watching *Desert Hearts* or *Thelma and Louise*" (90) than studying Hebrew lore and attending weddings. Missing her regular diet of alternative film, she strikes a bargain with Rainbow: "You take me to as many movies as I want to see, I feed you all the right lines to attract the attention of a certain person" (99).

Rainbow's courtship of Riva, though predictably unsuccessful, gives Galford the opportunity to problematise concepts of Otherness by juxtaposing different forms of alterity and prompting the reader to compare and contrast them. She goes out of her way to disconcert us by humorously demonstrating the similarities that exist between Jewish and lesbian culture and social life, instead of dwelling on their differences. Both, she observes, are minority cultures, the members of which habitually suffer persecution and discrimination. Both display positive attributes such as a capacity for survival, a strong sense of community, and inventiveness in the arts. However, in the case of both Jews and lesbians, these positive attributes are frequently undercut by less attractive ones, including moral smugness, ideological narrowness, a masochistic obsession with the role of victim, and a tendency to take refuge in forming cliques. Both Jews and lesbians, in addition, tend to be fixated on dress codes and ritual festivities. Both, moreover, are strongly territorial and have their own closely guarded social venues. As Kokos remarks, whereas Rainbow's territory and sphere of knowledge is "every dyke bar and women-only disco between here and Brixton," her own is "the Chasidic wedding hall" (131). Even Jewish and lesbian approaches toward female separatism are proved to have something in common. As Kokos sardonically tells Rainbow, due to the fact that in Orthodox Jewish society the sexes tend to lead separate lives and "hardly talk to each other," her adored Riva is "more like a classic right-on radical separatist than you'll ever be!" (98).

Kokos's irreverent demonstration of the resemblance between the transgressive lesbian separatist and the respectable Jewish matron illustrates Galford's ability to playfully celebrate, and simultaneously deconstruct, in the manner of a carnivalesque juggler, cultural and ethnic differences. However, she uses the tactic for serious ends, employing it as a strategy to problematize and explode concepts of the Other and the alien.

Galford treats other aspects of Jewish life, such as the national diversity of the Jewish people, with similar perception and wit. The account she gives of the various migrations that have had to take place in order for the family line generated by Gittel number one in her medieval Eastern European homeland to culminate in the figure of Rainbow Rosenbloom driving her taxicab in twentieth-century London interweaves celebration with critique. It combines admiration for the tenacity and initiative of the Jewish people with a recognition of the social tensions and snobberies that threaten to divide them:

> In some chink of time between pogrom and cholera and Holocaust, Gittel-plus-five packs up husband, baby and a pair of brass Shabbos candlesticks and conveys the family genes—via wooden wagon, railway carriage and passenger steamer—to London. The Jews who have come before—Hispanic and Iberian grandees; German bankers and merchant princes who, by their manners and education, could almost pass as Christian whites—are not particularly thrilled to see her. Or the thousands like her, trooping in with their thick plaid shawls and smells of alien cooking. (26)

The narrative strategies which Galford employs in constructing the novel suit the genre to which it belongs, subtly juxtaposing episodes from different historical periods and introducing passages of authorial comment, with the effect of creating a typically complex Gothic text. She also successfully manipulates the traditional Gothic device of creating a network of interlocking stories recounted by both main and subordinate characters. Kokos's self-congratulatory account of the contribution she made to "three successful joint ventures with Islamic djinns and affrits, in medieval Spain, where Jewish and Arabic magicians explored forbidden ground together" (48), the juicy anec-

dotes of family gossip and scandal narrated by Rainbow's loqua-
cious aunts, and the intriguing Jewish folk tales that the maternal Riva tells the children in her care before they retire to bed,
are some of the most memorable of these. Describing the latter's
skills as a storyteller, Galford comments,

> We hear of the wise fools of Chelm, of clever Khashinke and silly
> Bashinke, of David and his slingshot, of the fox and the fishes. Soon
> all the junior members of the audience are fast asleep. But Riva still
> spins her tales, for Rainbow's ears alone. She brings us to a town
> where the sky is full of burning, the old synagogue about to be
> engulfed: white doves wheel round the rooftops, beat their wings,
> drive off the flames. Then deep into the countryside: midnight in a
> blacksmith's cottage, we hear the strangers' urgent knock. . . . We fly
> backwards, retracing old tribal routes—dreamed up or remembered—
> and into a city walled with honey-coloured stones, where the sage
> Hanina sends demons home to hell with their putative tails between
> their legs, and where King Solomon outwits mighty Ashmodai, Duke
> of the Underworld, and makes him do the royal bidding like any
> human flunky. Rainbow drinks it in, wants more and more. (181–82)

The passage cited above is of interest in illustrating the way
that Galford envisions Jewish culture, in a typically postmodern
manner, as comprising an interplay of different narratives, oral
and literary, in which fact and fiction, history and myth, biblical
text and occult lore interrelate and merge. It also, of course, illustrates her own impressive skills as a storyteller, demonstrating
her ability to entertain and inform the reader with her lively and
erudite narrative of Jewish and lesbian culture and lifestyles, and
the differences and interaction they display.

II
The Women's Novel

Divided Loyalties: Betty Miller's Narratives of Ambivalence

Sarah Sceats

Betty Miller's recently republished *FAREWELL LEICESTER SQUARE* is her only novel to focus on an explicitly Jewish theme—and, ironically, the only one that she had difficulty in getting published. For although it was completed in 1935 and Miller predicted that it would be "one of the best novels Victor Gollancz Ltd have ever published" (Miller 2000, x), her publisher in fact rejected it, and it was not until during World War II, in 1941, that it was published by Robert Hale. It is tempting to observe that Miller's novel is uncannily perceptive, even prescient; at the least it seems a case of nature (or in this case the British literary establishment) imitating art, for the book is concerned with rejection and what it means to be Jewish. In his book *Post-War Jewish Fiction* (2001), David Brauner suggests that prewar writers generally distanced themselves from their Jewish roots, in favor of a sort of cosmopolitanism, and this observation applies to Miller except in the single instance of this novel. Her one foray out of neutral territory and into the problematic relationship between Jewish roots and English middle-class identity exemplifies the ambivalence Brauner identifies as endemic to Jewish writers. "There is a fundamental tension between self-assertion and self-denial in British-. . . Jewish literature" (Brauner 2001, 29), he writes, a conflict between "the desire to rebel against, and perpetuate, the tradition of which [the writer] is and is not a part" (30). Though Miller shows little overt indication of placing herself in a British-Jewish tradition, her writing is marked by conflict and a similar kind of ambivalence to that anatomized by Brauner, not only in the explicitly Jewish theme of *Farewell Leicester Square* but in her other, ostensibly British and "cosmopolitan" fiction.

81

Farewell Leicester Square focuses on issues of belonging and identity. This is a slippery topic, for self-location is in many ways problematic at the best of times, and most especially so where there are conflicting or incompatible frames of reference. Experience of conflicting loyalties is the case for many British—or perhaps more specifically English—Jews, culturally positioned as both insiders and outsiders. The more English, it seems, the more problematic. Loyalty to one's country, the sense of participating in its culture, the desire for success and recognition are powerful normalizing feelings. Yet wholesale surrender to such feelings is problematic. How is it possible to feel fully part of a nation that overlooks its own anti-Semitic past, and where a casual disparagement of Jewishness was openly expressed right into the mid-twentieth century—and indeed has not fully disappeared. There is also a nagging alternative loyalty that fuels the sense of internal exile. For nonreligious and non-Zionist Jews this alternative loyalty may be somewhat amorphous (as Alec Berman points out, Palestine, as it then was, is entirely foreign to him, though he can imagine what it *might* feel like to belong there), but the feeling is no doubt intensified by mainstream culture's construction of Jews as Other.[1] Second- or third- or fourth-generation progeny of immigrant families, and even the offspring of mixed marriages, may never quite escape the sense of not wholly belonging—or indeed of not quite wanting to belong.

Such is the predicament faced by the protagonist of Miller's *Farewell Leicester Square,* a young Jewish man, Alec Berman, the son of a tobacconist, who has a burning ambition to become a film director. This aspiration sets him apart from and threatens the stability of his traditional and socially unambitious family. Indeed, his father histrionically disowns him when he leaves home to begin his apprenticeship and Alec, taking his father's words at face value, severs contact with his parents, brother, sister, and hometown. The early part of the novel provides a potent evocation of Alec's childhood home life in Brighton, emphasizing smells, atmospheres, rituals, repeated phrases, parental bluster and manipulation, sibling rivalries—things, as Alec puts it, that "one would remember always" (Miller 2000, 8). The Jewishness of the family is emphasized: the Friday-night suppers, weekly attendance at the synagogue, the manner of the engagement of Alec's sister Violet and above all, perhaps, the food: chopped herring, chollah, gefilte fish, cheese cake . . . (the nostalgia for which is one "obstinate and trivial craving" (218) Alec cannot educate himself out of). Home is a hermetic environment, within but distinct from the "English" world of Brighton outside, and the family's sense of belonging to it is ostensibly unquestioned. Within the tribal community, however, Alec nurtures a desire for separation; his intense capacity of vision—the filmmaker in him (the equivalent, perhaps, of Miller's own creativity)—perceives a world outside the family, a world of which he fiercely wants to become a part.

Alec's desire devolves upon the Rottingdean house of the filmmaker Richard Nicolls, which he goes to look at in longing homage. Before an archetypal village green, pond, and church he reveres Oldwood Lodge, catching sight of Nicolls in easy companionship with his horseriding children, a relationship apparently far removed from the Sturm and Drang of the Berman household—or at least Alec's part in it. An ideal is planted in Alec's being, as he becomes conscious of "the difference between these two, who could tread with careless assurance a land which in every sense was theirs; and himself, who was destined to live always on the fringe: to exist only in virtue of the toleration of others, with no birthright but that toleration" (33–34). Oldwood Lodge thus becomes for Alec an aspirational ideal, itself belonging to England in a way that the warm, familiar but conflicted household of his childhood cannot and perhaps will not do. It is clear from the self-excluding terms in which he conceives his aspiration, however, that its defeat is a foregone conclusion.

Alec eventually succeeds in gaining an interview with Nicolls, a shrewd but kind man who is impressed enough by Alec to offer him an apprenticeship, though he nevertheless views him with a distancing and coldly analytic eye. Nicolls's first impression is worth quoting in full:

He observed the characteristic blunt head, prominent ears; the black tough hair. It was a commonplace mask, slightly vulgar, with the energetically coiled ambitious nose. The eyes alone had distinction: dark, unusually intense, and hooded, in a fine romantic way, by heavy lids. His voice had about it a trace of racial sibilance: but that, thought Nicolls, seeing how adaptable, how anxious to conform was this young man Berman, he would soon lose. Five, ten years would see him talking, acting like the English public-school Jews whom Nicolls periodically encountered at the board meetings of his companies. Men who always gave him a slightly odd sensation as he conversed with them: who had succeeded in the extraordinary feat of ousting all trace of their origin, not only from their accent and behaviour, but actually from their physique. Despite which complex achievement (for which he was not without admiration) they struck him always as essentially unreal, hollow men. They existed in a curious limbo between the two races: their reality lost in the role they had adopted, and that role itself without reality. (38–39)

The writing here is adroit: Nicolls exhibits the utter, complacent certainty of the insider. He does not display *anti*-Semitism—indeed has no need of it, so assured is he of his position—yet his very detachment betrays racist assumptions. The use of free indirect discourse, the patrician litotes—"he was not without admiration"—the faint allusion to T. S. Eliot ("hollow men") and ostensibly descriptive but loaded phrases such as "commonplace mask," "racial sibilance," and "English public-school Jews" combine to suggest an unbridgeable gulf.

The passage also intimates the essential ambiguity of Alec's situation: he is set to lose one sense of his identity without altogether gaining another. Alec's ambition becomes tangled up with desire for Nicolls's daughter Catherine, a young woman who represents almost everything Alec desires, including the elusive possibility of belonging. Alec's subsequent marriage to Catherine has an inevitability rooted in his teenage fixation; he is in love with her before the event. She is, as he recognizes, a symbol, "the girl out of his own past," whose meaning for him is established before they ever meet. This perhaps explains why he immediately feels comfortable with her, falling into step as they walk on the beach with a sense of ease and happiness. Significantly, his proposal, or part of it, is couched in terms of belonging: "Oh, Catherine, I wish you loved me. That would make all the difference. That would make me whole. I'd belong then: like the others. I wouldn't be outside, any more, if only I had that" (145). For, although he is by now a successful filmmaker, he is acutely aware of the subtle difference between being "born a Jew" and "born an Englishman" (141). Miller has him enumerate the perpetual strains of living as an inside outsider, having to walk "on earth that doesn't belong to you, speak a language which isn't really yours (although you know no other)" (142), living in a perpetual state of "low grade fear." He speaks of casual vilifications, the fear of causing embarrassment to potential friends and a host of similar social dilemmas. Although by marrying Catherine he enters the English establishment and although to all intents and purposes he has "arrived," he does not feel he has received an inheritance. On the contrary, he is if anything even more aware of difference. The fact that his wife becomes impatient with his misgivings, dismissing his perceptions as self-wrought, only increases his sense of exclusion and isolation.

The marriage is, of course, doomed. Although for a time the couple live blissfully (Alec coming in to moments of "private joy" at "the smell of home, indefinable but positive" [156]), Catherine is too frail a vessel for the weight of his existential homelessness. Even before they are married, Catherine remonstrates that things cannot be as bad as Alec believes, for "this is England" (144). To his bitter reply that "the concentration camp is only *spiritual* here," (144) she wonders aloud whether the problem is not one of his own perception. Later, this becomes increasingly her response: Alec is creating the situation. Yet her own unthinking comments give the lie to her protestation. At their first meeting when he asks who bought Oldwood Lodge after her father's death, she replies, "Heaven knows. Oh! Yes—some awful dago, I believe." Alec is shocked: "Me, she means. Dago: Jew: Outsider. . . . She might just as easily have said 'some ghastly Jew'" (107). And the split, when it comes, follows upon their child's fight at school when he is called a Jew. *"I'm not willing to accept the same scheme of disadvantages for my son,"* she writes to Alec, "the divided loyalties . . . the fears . . . the self-consciousness"—all the things she wished Alec to ignore or deny (272).

Miller is here bringing the dilemma of societal ambivalence into the home. The child, in one sense, provides the possibility of bridging a gap, of combining "the best of both worlds" as Catherine's friend puts it. Miller loads the dice against this, however, by making him physically resemble Catherine's brother, the person most hostile to her marriage. Catherine also provides the child with a thoroughly English upper-middle-class life, complete with Nanny, silk shirt, knickers, white socks, and a friend called Timothy Hope-Sewell. Alec has little input in his upbringing, and is in any case in a state of conflict over it, wanting him to have a Jewish friend and eat Jewish food, but resisting such desires because they seem atavistic, redolent of a return to the ghetto.

The narrative concludes, predictably enough, with the failure of Alec's integrative dream: the break-up of his marriage and his return to the family home where his mother lies ill. It is a palpable homecoming: "kindred flesh; the physical warmth, mutuality of *family*, of an intimacy that is amorphous and without frontiers" (286), a repair of the longstanding breach that sets in motion his mother's recovery. But the homecoming, for Alex, is not a resolution so much as a reminder: he belongs inescapably to his (Anglo)-Jewish family. It is not an exclusive belonging, however; unlike his brother and sister he has stretched the connection. He both belongs and does not. Unable to become wholly English, he is equally unable to return to an unquestioning Jewish ethnicity. He is ambivalence personified.

I referred earlier to David Brauner's discussion of ambivalence, a discussion that self-consciously seeks to offer a more nuanced account of Jewish "self-mythologization" than that of self-hatred proposed by Sander Gilman. Now, however, I want to invoke a slightly different formulation of ambivalence, conceived largely in terms of external positioning by the "host" society, which perhaps offers a more apposite and suggestive explanation for a novel of the 1930s. In his book *Modernity and Ambivalence* Zygmunt Bauman characterizes the spirit of modernity as positioning Jews in opposition to a clean and ordered society, thus associating them with disturbance and disorder. Bauman cites Ezra Pound's metaphors of slime, swamp, miasma as creating "monsters of ambivalence." Like the horrible stereotype of the "greasy Jew" underpinning Nicolls's observations of Alec (or the "frightful Dago" that Alec's wife casually lets slip) this suggests a social abject parallel to the threat to the psyche in Kristeva's theory of abjection. Kristeva writes that what causes abjection is "what disturbs identity, system, order. What does not respect borders, positions, rules. The in-between, the ambiguous" (1982, 4). This is not so far from "monsters of ambivalence." What is formless, liminal, ambiguous is threatening precisely because it will not be categorized. But by the same token, of course—as Bauman suggests in claiming that ambiguity becomes a weapon against modernity's destructive potential—the very slippery, elusive qualities of ambivalence that make it threatening confer upon it a kind of protean power.[2]

The binary opposition of us/them, friends/enemies (such as proclaimed most crudely in recent times by George Bush in his war on terrorism) of necessity excludes neutral or ambivalent figures. Into this category falls the stranger, someone neither "with us" nor "against us," for strangers are, in Bauman's words, "spiritually remote" (1991, 60). The "otherness" of strangers is a challenge to orthodoxy for, like the abject, they remain indeterminate. As a result when they cannot be assimilated (transformed) strangers are often ousted, killed, expelled, imprisoned, marginalized—or stigmatized and labelled "exotic." Attempting to escape such positioning by means of "self-improvement" only compounds matters for, according to Bauman, this simply confirms the original difference. (Jack Zipes's splendid anatomization of the poisonous short story of attempted assimilation "The Operated Jew" [1992] illustrates the point perfectly.) Self-*improvement* implies an admission of former "inferiority," and may lead to further ambivalence and self-hatred.[3] Hence the so-called "self-hating Jew." Sander Gilman writes: "Self-hatred arises when the mirages of stereotypes are confused with realities within the world, when the desire of acceptance forces the acknowledgement of one's difference" (1982, 4). Alec is in precisely this position: his fervent desire to belong coupled with what he perceives as constant reminders of his difference produces an existential angst that may be interpreted as self-hatred. Miller certainly writes such an interpretation into the novel in Catherine's exasperated perceptions of Alec's struggles.

It is also true that the stranger may be seen in positive terms, however, as mysterious, unknown, promising, and offering an open prospect; ambivalent, perhaps, rather than embodying self-hatred, and a more open reading of *Farewell Leicester Square* sees Alec as ambivalent, as an inside outsider or familiar stranger, perhaps, rather than as self-hating. The stranger cannot be "natural" (unlike the supremely assured Nicolls) for s/he is not a native but neither is s/he necessarily a newcomer: rather, in Bauman's view, an *"eternal wanderer,"* whether spiritually or literally. It is notable that Bauman cites certain philosophers who see a parallel between this archetypally Jewish condition and that of the modern intellectual grappling with uncertainty.[4] Indeed, he goes so far as to suggest that the postmodern condition (a term he uses descriptively rather than chronologically) *is* that of the "displaced person," for while modernist society was intolerant of mess and ambiguity, postmodernity asserts that contingency is all. In other words, the postmodern individual is by definition a universal stranger. So, by some strange turn of logic Jewishness becomes interchangeable with the "universally human" (195). As Bernard Malamud put it, "Every man is a Jew though he may not know it" (cited in Brauner 2001, 38).

Without wanting to claim Miller as mouthpiece of the post-modern condition, it nevertheless seems to me that her fiction explores precisely the themes that echo from Jewish experience through modern and postmodern life. She is acutely aware of the appeal of order (a modernist yearning) yet constantly opposes it, mostly to its disadvantage, to life and mess and vigor. Alec's return home at the end of *Farewell Leicester Square* can be read in these terms, as a retreat from the sterility of an upper middle-class order to which, incidentally, he represents the negative: uncontainable, contingent existence. For Alec himself there is a resolution of sorts, for in experiencing the loss that he most fears Alec is liberated: "He was no longer afraid, because he no longer had anything to lose. He was free from his own desires: from his own apprehensions. Whatever happened now, spiritual or physical exile, he was ready for it" (Miller 2000, 306–7). In effect, he embraces the status of stranger.

Although this is her only novel with an explicitly Jewish theme, Miller's other novels nevertheless also focus on displacement, outsiders, divided loyalties, internal conflicts and acute states of ambivalence. There are allusions to foreigners from the beginning of her writing. In her first novel *The Mere Living*, the "Turkish or something" Mr. Vance is observed as alien, with "violent nostrils" and oiled hair (Miller 1933, 141) by the resentful paterfamilias Mr. Sullivan, his ostensible business partner. Sullivan is irritated by evidence of difference; Mr. Vance has the temerity to wear a strange French coat: "Why couldn't he get himself a decent English overcoat and not go about like that? Look at him now, folding it away so carefully. What a dago." (140). What irks Sullivan most, however, is Vance's evasiveness; he has a "dark expressionless face" (141) and seems to withhold. Vance is, perhaps, "spiritually remote," certainly a stranger.

Miller's second novel, *Sunday*, concerns a depressed, uptight English factory owner, Mark, who goes to stay at the country home of a French friend whom he met as a child when they were both sent away to a sanatorium. The holiday is an escape: from the mechanization in the factory and from the emotional entan-

glements of his mother and sisters. He persuades himself that he
will avoid intimacy with strangers by locating himself in the
French family but not being part of it, "released, because of his
particular position, of any necessity for participation" (Miller
1934, 46). On the first night he is acutely aware of sensations of
strangeness: the new smells, the room's odd configuration and
general unfamiliarity; even the sheets speak "an unknown language to his body" (67). Quite soon, however, he becomes
attracted to the daughter of the house, though it is foreignness
itself, and not just Janine, that attracts him: "Here was not the
silence of his own age-long culture, it did not belong to him,
sprang from another race, another direction; but all the more passionately, therefore, because of his inevitable exclusion, he loved
it, he sought to penetrate . . . (175, Miller's ellipsis). The desire to
penetrate—in all senses—is his undoing. Janine's possessive
mother resents him as "this stranger from the outside. Man. Rob-
ber. . . . Why should he come, what right had he?" (155), and when
she discovers that he has yielded to a sexual impulse with a servant girl, she manipulates his downfall. Only so long as he had
remained "the guest, the stranger amongst them" (219) was he
tolerated. He is granted no status within the family, the culture;
he must remain outside and only in himself may discover the
meaning of his stay at Laroche.

Here again the central concerns of the novel revolve around
questions of displacement, otherness, the position of outsiders,
and the ensuing conflicts, divided loyalties and states of ambivalence, recurring preoccupations in all Miller's writing. It is in her
last two novels, however, that the elements I have been discussing are most interestingly developed as variations on the
Jewish theme. On the Side of the Angels treats the theme
obliquely, playing with the idea that wartime offers a possible
resolution of ambiguity, in its raison d'etre of resisting enemy
"chaos" and with the army's inclusive order, hierarchies and reg-
ulations. An almost universal desire to be involved in the project of war unites the population and, the novel suggests, effects
a transformation in attitudes.[5] The novel examines this wartime
culture through a series of relationships. Honor is married to
Colin, a doctor in the service; her sister Claudia is engaged to
Andrew who has been invalided out; all are variously affected by
a capricious CO and a dashing newcomer, "commando" Neil

Heriot. The plot turns upon Colin's infatuation with the idea of a privileged relationship with the CO and on the intrusion of Heriot into all their lives.

Wartime engenders a polarization of friends and enemies, rendering the role of "stranger" as I have been discussing it almost untenable. Miller suggests a further scheme, opposing uniformity, order and death on one hand to abundant, disordered life on the other. It is perhaps a rather obvious polarization, but Miller complicates it somewhat. Order and neatness can be attractive, if deathly: "Claudia, walking on the crisp raked gavel [of the cemetery] looked about her with pleasure appreciating the pattern that death maintained within these precincts. How orderly, how correct (thought the young schoolmistress) and how easy to impose order once the unruly spark had gone . . ." (Miller 1945b, 33; her ellipsis).

Hierarchical structures are also appealing, as Colin's desire to be part of the CO's clique testifies, and public scenes such as the regimental sports day and dance indicate the potency of belonging to that exclusive club Miller calls "the rigid artefact of military life" (39). Both these two scenes (despite the fact that they delineate off-duty, leisure activities) and the more claustrophobic individual interactions evoke a hierarchical, determined, and bounded minisociety, in which there is both a certain security and clarity.

The "unruly spark," clearly more vital and messy, is embodied in Honor, who is characterized wholly in terms of a receptive, reproductive—and largely passive—femininity. The opposition is signaled when she meets the CO and intuitively recognizes the repugnance of the military: "Standing there before him, she became aware, in a moment of burning shame, of her own femininity: the fullness, the slipshod contours; of all that was inchoate, un-uniformed about her: of that which was capable of giving the offence, of making her innately unacceptable to the men before her" (39). Claudia comments that the CO does not like women, wives or families, for they are *rivals*. Honor may represent what it is they are supposedly fighting *for* but she is the antithesis of what they embrace.

If Honor and her babies represent one extreme and the CO the other, the four remaining characters stand in complex relation to the polarity. Honor's husband Colin ostensibly has a foot in each camp, but he does not identify with his family, so overwhelming is his desire to achieve intimacy with the powerful. The dashing Captain Heriot, excited by falling bombs, challenges the liberal position, asserting that violence is innate and accusing Claudia and her ilk of doing violence to their own nature through self-control. His argument is effectively undermined, however, for he turns out to be a fake, a bank manager and dutiful father, who has perpetrated a sustained act of impersonation so as to cash in on some of the excitement, glory, and love offered to soldiers (214).

Andrew, too, has an ambiguous relationship to the war effort. A skeptic and intellectual, his invalid status positions him outside the military world. Equally, though, his revulsion when faced with tadpoles ("jellified—nasty—primitive" [73]) suggests that he is not of the messy reproductive party either. In some ways his attitudes to war are not unlike Heriot's. He claims that there is a "force of pent-up human emotion" in everyone that needs "a regular dose of high explosive for catharsis" (77). Like Heriot he accuses Claudia of fooling herself with the notion of being civilized and rational. War, he says, "gives us a chance to discover the lie we were all living, during the so-called peace years" (31). In his case, however, these views are part of an intense effort to see the world clearly, without Colin's "colouring of enchantment" (125). In the face of a hostile audience he maintains that there needs to be a homeopathic "place for the antisocial impulse within the social framework itself" (133), and he sees war as escapism, "a flight from reason, from everyday duties and responsibilities" (141).

It is perhaps obvious where my argument is leading. Andrew's self-location is problematic. He is ambivalent, en route to qualifying as an existential stranger. Physically removed and temperamentally remote from the military, he is written off by Heriot, who tells Claudia "the day of the intellectual is over" (185). For her part Claudia is drawn to the apparent strength and decisiveness of the "rough soldier" as Heriot describes himself. She is mesmerized by the apelike hairs on the back of his hand—a palpable touch of the beast. In the end, however, she concludes that she cannot flee her convictions. She returns to Andrew, who welcomes her to ambivalent no-man's-land: "No way out for us. Caught in the trap of our own reason like a rabbit with its paw in the gin. On the side of the angels, in fact, with a vengeance. . . ." (235, Miller's ellipsis).

Miller's final novel, *The Death of the Nightingale*, again opposes order and reason to the instinctive and contingent, but this time she reverts to the literal outsider figure in Matthew O'Farrell, son of a slain Irish Republican. Matthew is in love with Léonie, who is the only daughter of Professor Newman Cain, a scholarly man who writes on reason and guilt and himself has an obsessive need for order, rationality, and control. Cain's character seems all of a piece: he prefers electric light to sunshine, aeroplanes to birds, winter to spring, and is worried by open gates and doors. He seeks to secure the "closed exclusive relationship" he has had with his daughter. Matthew, by contrast is ebullient, passionate, impulsive, and impatient to wrest Léonie away from her father for he senses that "the source of her nature was being sapped, mysteriously diverted" (Miller 1948, 26). Not surprisingly, Léonie feels torn between the two men, defending each against the other.

In a plot that is positively Hardyesque in coincidences, it transpires that all is not as it seems. Cain's housekeeper (and former mistress) is substitute mother to Léonie because she was complicit in kidnapping the child when Cain's wife left him for a lover. Matthew's martyred father turns out to have been set up by none other than Cain when they were fellow academics in Ireland during the Troubles, and Matthew's mother, Rose, reveals that she and Cain had a peculiarly intense, unconsummated, and painful relationship that both, separately, struggled to repress.

Cain himself is deeply conflicted. He is appalled by the disturbing empathy he feels with a breastfeeding baby and the "avidity" this makes him recognize in himself; as a result he embraces mechanism as an escape from strong feelings and inconsistency.[6] In a scheme in which England represents dominating intellect and Ireland rebellious emotion, Cain has no hesitation in associating himself with English "law and order" and viewing all rebellion as "anarchy." Even when Matthew taxes him about his role in Kevin O'Farrell's death, Cain maintains that the Irish cannot appreciate "justice," a dismissive as well as self-justifying judgement calculated to snub and repulse an unwanted prospective son-in-law. But Cain's repressiveness also suggests that he protests too much. To begin with, he chose a French wife in part precisely for her qualities of otherness.[7] Furthermore, Rose O'Farrell describes Cain as having been "fascinated" by her husband's vitality and the charismatic effect he had on the students, and indeed Cain is passionately attracted to Rose herself. It's only after her husband Kevin's death, when Rose feels she must refuse Cain's proposal, that he becomes "old and indifferent," or at least retreats into the world of will and mind.

Described by Rose as "the typical Britisher," Cain in Ireland was an outsider. In adopting an uptight Englishness he asserts difference; he is Us, not Them. Yet his ambivalence in relation to the O'Farrells indicates a more complicated position and his sense of being "only a visitor, a stranger" in their house (205) hints once again at a sense of displacement. Even when geographically and domestically reinstated in Hertfordshire he remains somehow inaccessible, spiritually—and emotionally— remote. His only recourse in the face of disturbing life is pained withdrawal.

On first reading this novel I took Cain to be the archetypal Englishman and Matthew O'Farrell an obvious displaced stranger, for Matthew is an exiled Irishman disparaged and held at bay by an English insider. But again the situation is more complicated: Cain is ill at ease and Matthew is an exile who seems largely at home in his new country. Nevertheless, there are several parallels between Matthew and Alec Berman. Both men's leaving home is a voluntary displacement and both are consequently rejected by a parent. Matthew's mother severs contact when he joins the RAF, for England is "the enemy." In both cases the young men fall in love with the daughter of a man who despises their ethnicity. Nevertheless, there are differences. Matthew's exile is negatively motivated, for he seeks to escape the inheritance of his father's martyrdom. In fighting for England he rejects his birthright, without becoming more than an adopted son. And yet, unlike Alec, he returns of his own volition to what he has rejected, when he visits to tell his mother of his engagement.

Inevitably, returning evokes complex emotions, and Matthew feels the force of old patterns and the power of familiarity. At one point he succumbs to the sensations of memory, which for a moment have the effect of turning his fiancée into "a foreigner, a stranger to his blood, to his own deepest experience" (193)—an episode he feels is a betrayal of her. He should have resisted "the ambivalence of the exile," he thinks, and "accepted and abided by the divorce pronounced on his own nature" (92).[8] But his purpose in returning is not to renew but to "dissolve" his relationship with the past, "finally to denude of the element of legend that surrounded them, objects and scenes intrinsically commonplace" (183). In the end this is effected by their translation to England, where his father's photograph loses its potency and his mother looks so ordinary that Matthew, to his shame, thinks she resembles "somebody's cook" (236). Like Alec, Matthew has slipped uneasily into the English middle class.

Unlike Alec's, Matthew's story ends with the beginning of his marriage, and the resolution is, in this respect at least, more optimistic than that of the other novels. In an earlier passage, when Léonie accompanies him to the station on his way to visit his mother, the idea of strangeness is given a wonderful slant. As the couple pace the platform, Léonie watches and listens to the other passengers: "It was as if the frontiers between the two countries dissolved, and there was an overlapping in which here, in the very heart of the capital she knew, she felt the tempo of an unfamiliar people invade her senses; an experience that she found oddly pleasurable, oddly disturbing" (178). There is, perhaps, some wishful cosmopolitan thinking here, as Miller projects herself into the position of welcoming insider. Even here, however, she cannot forgo admitting the existence of ambivalence. If Léonie's experience offers an optimistic intimation of consummation, it is, nevertheless, even now "oddly disturbing."

NOTES

1. See Gilman 1986, chapter 1, "What is Self-hatred," and passim.

2. Bauman 1991. See chapter 1, "The Scandal of Ambivalence."

3. As Sander Gilman paraphrases it, "the more you are like me, the more I know the true value of my power, which you wish to share, and the more I am aware that you are but a shoddy counterfeit, an outsider" (1986, 2).

4. Shestor, Mannheim, etc.

5. Indeed Miller wrote in a letter to friend and author John Verney of the "astonishing effect" of army life. People she describes as "quite ordinary civilians" and "respectable God-Fearing citizens" became, she wrote, "quite unrecognisable" as soon as they put on uniforms. Letter cited in Sarah Miller's introduction to the Virago 1985 edition of On the Side of the Angels. A penetrating analysis of the astonishing, fascinating and seductive effect of war in On the Side of the Angels is given by Jenny Hartley in "Warriors and Healers, Imposters and Mothers: Betty Miller's On the Side of the Angels in Dressing Up for War: Transformations of Gender and Genre in the Discourse and Literature of War, eds. Aránzazu Usandizaga and Andrew Monickenam (Amsterdam: Rodopi, 2001) 173–88.

6. "Avidity" is a word that recurs in Miller's writing, usually in relation to a repressed character's repelled fascination with open emotional expression, especially of yearning or passion.

7. Nothing, incidentally, is made of Léonie's dual nationality, though it secures for her a position between the two men and tangential to both Englishness and foreignness.

8. Note "ambivalence" here.

Bellow at Your Elbow, Roth Breathing down Your Neck: Gender and Ethnicity in Novels by Bernice Rubens and Linda Grant

David Brauner

Wнᴇɴ ɪ ғɪʀsᴛ sᴛᴀʀᴛᴇᴅ ʀᴇsᴇᴀʀᴄʜɪɴɢ ᴛʜɪs ᴘᴀᴘᴇʀ ɪ ᴡᴀs ᴄʟᴇᴀʀ about what I was not going to do, which was to lament the poverty of British-Jewish fiction when compared with American-Jewish fiction; the exalted reputations of Bellow, Roth, Malamud, Ozick, Paley, and others have been used for too long as a yardstick with which to beat their less illustrious British cousins over the head. No, I was determined to look at Rubens's and Grant's fiction in its own terms. However, in the week that I began writing two things happened that made me backtrack somewhat. First of all Linda Grant was interviewed on BBC Radio Four's arts review program, "Front Row," about her new novel, *Still Here.* Secondly, the story broke that the new sponsors of what was then the Booker Prize (the Man Group) were going to open up the competition to American fiction from 2004 and the *Guardian* asked a number of former winners of the prize, Bernice Rubens among them, for their thoughts on the implications of this. This is what Rubens had to say: "I don't think we can compete against the Americans. We're pygmies in comparison, which doesn't make us bad, but there's no one here to touch [Philip] Roth. . . . American literature is better than British because it is not nagged by tradition. We have the whole of the canon breathing down our necks. If you have Austen sitting at your elbow it's very hard to write, but the Americans are free of that stronghold [*sic*], and so they write with chutzpah . . . you'd never get a [British] Roth or a Bellow" (2002, 3).[1] And here is a remark made by Alix Rebick, the female narrator of *Still Here,* quoted during the Grant interview: "It *was* the Jewish century

... The century of the Holocaust but also of Einstein and Schoen-berg . . . and Saul Bellow and Philip Roth" (2002b, 244).

What struck me immediately, reading Rubens's response to the *Guardian*'s question of whether British authors can compete with their American counterparts, and listening to Grant's interview (in which she talked almost as much about Roth's fiction as about her own), and later reading *Still Here* itself, is how much both these writers have American-Jewish fiction (which is to say male American-Jewish fiction, which is to say Philip Roth and Saul Bel-low) on the brain.[2] The reverence with which Rubens and Grant regard Roth and Bellow is close to awe: they are implicitly accorded the same status as those legendary twentieth-century geniuses Einstein and Schoenberg[3] by Grant, and regarded by Rubens as so superior to any British writers that there is appar-ently no hope even of aspiring to their level of excellence.

Grant's third novel opens with a lyrical description of Liver-pool, looming like a "colossus" over the river Mersey. But then we are told that "for a hundred years my family has been trying to get to America. . . . We cannot get over the feeling that England is an interim stage. America! We still have inside us the immi-grant, greenhorn fever of our grandparents for the country where the personality expands to fill the emptiness of the continent instead of shrinking into itself, shriveling for want of air and light. . . . We want to talk big, think big, make it big, be big people without jostling for elbow room" (2002b, 2). So it's clear that, like Rubens, the Rebicks view themselves as pygmies, dwarfed by the magnitude of American life, and cramped by its style. The Rebick family are forever "looking longingly across the Atlantic Ocean to the country glimmering faintly in the western light, immense and unattainable" (151) and defining themselves nega-tively, in terms of their failure to reach America. Toward the end of the novel Alix alludes explicitly to the famous opening words of Bellow's third novel, *The Adventures of Augie March*: "I am not an American born or bred. I am not Augie March and hence also not at liberty, like him, to go at things freestyle" (343).[4]

It seems to me, then, that the intimidating, inhibiting presence breathing down the necks of Rubens and Grant is not in fact Jane Austen, but Philip Roth; the stranglehold that threatens to stifle their writing is exerted not by the venerable English canon, but by the modern canon of American-Jewish fiction. Moreover, it seems to me that Rubens and Grant deal in their fiction with the Bellow at their elbow in diametrically opposed ways, and yet neither manages to break free entirely from the anxiety of their influence.[5]

Philip Roth has often been vilified for his portrait of the suffocating, infantilizing, emasculating oedipal Jewish Mother—Sophie Portnoy in *Portnoy's Complaint* (1969)—yet Rubens was there first. Her second novel, *Madame Sousatzka* (1962), published seven years before *Portnoy's Complaint*, features not one, but two, stereotypes of the Jewish Mother. The novel deals with the battle for the allegiance and affections of a young Jewish pianist prodigy, Marcus Crominski, between his mother, Mrs. Crominski, and his teacher, Madame Sousatzka, the eponymous protagonist of the novel. It opens with a detailed account of the relationship between Mrs. Crominski and Marcus, a relationship characterised by mutual guilt and resentment. In the absence of a husband/father (Mr. Crominski having died when Marcus was a young boy), mother and son are bound together in an intensely claustrophobic, quasi-incestuous union that they can neither happily engage in, nor disengage from. They both perform (unknown to the other) a daily ritual of self-recrimination in which they berate themselves for having failed to satisfy the other's emotional needs, and vow to be more considerate of each other's feelings. They resent each other, and resent themselves for their resentment of the other. As the novel opens, however, it is clear that the balance of power in the relationship is shifting: Marcus is growing up and learning to fend for himself. When Mrs. Crominski arrives home from one of her shopping trips to find Marcus quite content, she is at once relieved (having entertained lurid fantasies of catastrophes occurring in her absence) and disconcerted, as she "always felt a slight irritation that things could go smoothly even if she were not in the house" (Rubens 1962, 8). When Madame Sousatzka, a famous piano teacher, decides to take on Marcus as a pupil Mrs. Crominski's feelings are similarly ambivalent: on the one hand proud that such an eminent figure is willing to tutor her son (free of charge); on the other hand apprehensive that this formidable Jewish matriarch might usurp her role in Marcus's life.

As it turns out, Mrs. Crominski's fears are well founded, since it is apparent from the outset that Marcus is not simply another pupil for Madame Sousatzka, but rather a surrogate son. Moreover, as with his own mother, the nature of Sousatzka's intense emotional investment in him seems at times more erotic than maternal. When an impressario and concert promoter, Felix Manders, offers to take Marcus on as a client, Sousatzka's indignation is couched in terms more suited to that of a jealous lover than a rival mentor: "Sousatzka could have killed him. He had no right to trespass on her bond with Marcus like a cheap adulterer" (88). Indeed, just as Mrs. Crominski selfishly discourages Marcus's attempts to become more self-reliant, so Sousaztska perpetually defers the date of Marcus's first public concert, deliberately arresting Marcus's emotional and musical development in order to prolong his dependence on her. The crisis in the novel occurs when Sousatzka insists (for the umpteenth time) that Marcus is not yet ready to perform in public because he is still "a little boy" and Marcus responds by finally asserting his independence: "I'm not a little boy. . . . You've always treated me like a little boy. You won't let me go" (184).

Rubens has returned to this theme of the child prodigy never allowed to grow up repeatedly in her fiction[6] most notably in her most famous novel, the Booker Prize–winning *The Elected Member*. Published in 1969, the same year as Roth's *Portnoy's Complaint*, and, like Roth's novel, clearly influenced by Franz Kafka's famous story "Metamorphosis," *The Elected Member* tells the story of a Jewish family as dysfunctional as the Portnoys. However, where Roth sees in Kafka's tale a mordant humor and transforms it into his own brand of "sit-down comedy," Rubens draws on its representation of pathology and paranoia to create her own study of mental illness. Whereas Alexander Portnoy's alienation from the (Jewish bourgeois) values of his family parodies Gregor Samsa's, the predicament of Norman Zweck (the protagonist of Rubens's novel) echoes Samsa's not simply because of the form that his drug-fuelled hallucinations take (that of silver fish crawling over his body), but also in his role as family scapegoat. In the case of all three Jewish sons, it is their relationships with their mothers that are at the root of their problems.

As Kafka's tale opens, Gregor has displaced his aged father as the family breadwinner and in his mother's affections, but after his transformation into a giant beetle she recoils from him in disgust and his father undergoes a curious metamorphosis of his own, recovering his former authority and dignity and resuming his role as head of the family. In Roth's novel Sophie Portnoy threatens Alex's manhood, repeatedly referring to his penis as "that little thing" and implicitly threatening to castrate him, while at the same time she eroticizes their relationship by addressing him as her "lover" (1969, 153, 91).

When *The Elected Member* begins, Norman Zweck's mother has already been dead for two years, but the family is still haunted by her. After her death, Rabbi Zweck, Norman's father, moves into Norman's old room and Norman begins to sleep in his parents' bed, symbolically usurping his father's place. He tries to sleep on his father's side of the bed, anxious to avoid the "cold legacy" of the mother's side, but one morning he wakes up and begins to stroke "the virgin sheet alongside him, over and over again" (Rubens 1986, 7, 9). Rubens goes on to describe how "suddenly on the skin of his palm, he felt the grazing of a curve and a line. As he lowered his hand, he uncovered, as in a brass rubbing, the head, shoulders and prone body of his mother. His hand lay paralysed where her legs would lie, and terrified, he clawed down the sheet and revealed her entire" (9). The unsettling mixture here of oedipal desire for and revulsion at the mother's body (with a hint of necrophilia thrown in for good measure) reveals the extent to which the absent Mrs. Zweck is paradoxically present in Norman's neuroses. Indeed, she is to a large extent responsible for the pathological, drug-dependent state that gives rise to this gruesome hallucination, as well as to that of the silver fish.

When, aged five, Norman arrives home one day with a Polish boy, conversing fluently with him in his native language, Mrs. Zweck, "who had long been convinced that there was something special about *her* first-born, now set about his education in earnest" (88, my italics). Before long, Norman has acquired numerous languages and, with them, the status of celebrity child prodigy. Determined that Norman should outdo his initial achievements, and conscious of the limited shelf-life of such fame, Mrs. Zweck decides, when Norman is nine years old, to lop off one year from his real age for the next three years, so that, like some vain aging Hollywood star, instead of getting older he remains mysteriously stuck at the same age. This also necessitates reducing the age of Norman's sister, Bella, since she is the second child and cannot be seen to have overtaken her brother. So it is that, on the day of Norman's belated Barmitzvah (at the age of sixteen, rather than, as Jewish custom demands, thirteen), when Bella (actually fifteen, but officially twelve) dresses herself in her finest stockings for the occasion, Mrs. Zweck demands that she take them off, remarking "Plenty time to be grown up" (90). When Bella refuses, Mrs. Zweck hits her repeatedly as she sees "her fantasy, carefully woven over the years, dismissed so flagrantly by one of her own flesh and blood" (91). This incident of physical abuse (compounding the mental abuse that she has inflicted on Bella by refusing to allow her to grow up normally) has both short-term and long-term consequences. That afternoon, while the adults indulge in the celebrations, Norman and Bella sneak off to have sexual intercourse. This incestuous coupling is clearly at one level a rebuke to their mother's attempts to postpone their maturity (by asserting themselves as sexually active beings, they defy their mother's artificial extension of their prepubescence), but on another level its perversity actually matches her own unnatural practices. Traumatized both by her mother's beating of her, and by her brother's penetration of her, Bella ironically assumes her mother's emotional (dys)function in the family after her mother's death.

Freakishly sporting the girls' white socks that her mother had insisted she wear to Norman's Barmitzvah, Bella embraces her mother's legacy with a mixture of sadism and masochism. Like her mother, she seems intent on ensuring that the men of the family (Norman and her father) cannot do without her, as a way of disguising her own helpless dependence on them: "She had always taken her father's dependence on her for granted, but now that he was going, and with such confidence, she knew that she could not manage without him, or at least without his needs, which together with Norman's, were her sole means of sustenance" (66). Condemned to a life as an old maid, Bella devotes herself to ensuring that Norman fulfils her mother's hopes for him.

If Bella is clearly damaged by her abnormal childhood, Norman seems, as a young man, to have broken away from everything that "chained [him] to his inheritance" (7), forging for himself a successful career as a barrister. Once again, however, Mrs. Zweck intervenes to prevent Norman achieving independence. Having earned some money and established himself in chambers, Norman announces his intention to leave the family home and take up his own lodgings. At first Mrs. Zweck tries to laugh this off, but when it becomes clear that Norman is intent on leaving, she becomes the most appalling caricature of the guilt-inflicting martyred Jewish Mother: " 'Go, go,' she screamed. 'Who's stopping? *I* should stop you? You had enough from your mother? Go. You want I should break my heart? You want you should break up the family?' . . . 'Then go' she shouted. 'Go' " (164). The irrationality, extremity, and perversity of Mrs. Zweck's recriminations here are revealed not simply in the hyperbole of her language but also in the fact that she addresses Norman as though he were her husband rather than her son. To accuse Norman of breaking her heart and breaking up the family home is to accord him the place not of a son but of a lover. Like Madame Sousaztska, Mrs. Zweck's possessiveness overcomes her ambition to see her prodigy succeed in his chosen career; the desire for vicarious glory gives way to the fear of losing control over the boy's destiny. Rubens's narrator's judgment of Mrs. Zweck is unambiguously damning here: "She could not for one moment believe that his life could be lived without her sanction. He was not an individual, but an appendage of herself" (165).

Faced with her hysterical, implacable resistance, Norman eventually backs down and breaks down, turning to drugs to escape from his disturbed family life into his own disturbed and disturbing world of nightmarish hallucinations. After Mrs. Zweck's death, it is left to Bella and Rabbi Zweck to deal with the consequences of her behavior, and to take the blame for Norman's spectacular collapse (he humiliates himself and his family by turning against his own client in a court case). When we are told that "Rabbi Zweck knew by instinct that his expectations and hopes for Norman had contributed in large measure to his son's breakdown" (143), it is clear that the father is simply an accessory to the mother's crime, or, to put it another way, that his greatest crime is his failure to overrule her (he is distinctly uneasy about her plan perennially to preserve Bella and Norman at ages eight and nine, respectively, but defers to his wife in spite of his reservations).

(S)mothered as he is, Norman might have turned out like Alex Portnoy (who compensates for his mother's ridicule of his "little thing" by fucking his way through as many Gentile girls as he can, though of course when confronted by the Jewish girl who resembles his mother, he is impotent); instead, he follows the path of the Freudian archetype of the mother's boy, Leonardo da Vinci (to whom Portnoy compares himself at one point), and becomes a repressed homosexual. It is no coincidence, then, that when he first begins to talk to his psychiatrist about his great love, David, Norman observes: "Throughout our childhood, it seems the only thing we gave our mothers was aggravation. And not just aggravation, but *such* aggravation. I used to think aggravation was a yiddish [*sic*] word" (148). In spite of this moment of Portnovian humor, however, the consequences of this relationship are tragic rather than comic. When David becomes romantically involved with Norman's younger sister, Esther, a jealous Norman deliberately sabotages their relationship, encouraging Esther to elope with a philosemitic Gentile librarian, John. When David learns that he has been jilted, he kills himself, and Esther is left in a loveless, guilt-ridden marriage, estranged from her family.

The novel finishes with both Norman and his family reconciled to, indeed relieved by, the prospect of his long-term incarceration in an asylum, because it spares them the horror of having to face each other on a daily basis. Norman consoles himself with the conviction that he is part of an "elite," "chosen" by God (as the Jews were chosen) to bear a special burden of responsibility.[7] In fact, his delusions are grander than this: in his own eyes he becomes a Christlike figure who takes on the sins of others and martyrs himself for their sakes: "Bella can't grow up . . . and I carry it. Esther married out, and I carry it. My father . . . failed, and I carry it. My mother wouldn't let me go and finally broke my back. Together, they sucked the life out of me with their ravenous appetite. Who am I, save their receptacle?" (223).

Unlike Christ, however, he resents his self-sacrifice. Unlike Alex Portnoy, who, though he finishes Roth's novel with a howl of existential anguish, then hears his self-dramatizing self-pity deflated by Spielvogel's punchline ("Now vee may perhaps to begin. Yes?" [Roth 1969, 250]), Norman is left trapped in his portentous, solipsistic world. Unlike Roth, Rubens cannot allow comedy in to subvert the tragedy, cannot free herself to write with Roth's chutzpah. Indeed, her fiction seems to me deliberately to insulate itself altogether from the influence of her American-Jewish contemporaries like Bellow and Roth, and yet of course such a strategy of studiously avoiding the very writers whom she admires above all others betrays a sort of negative influence.

If Bernice Rubens keeps her head down at her desk, then, writing away with eyes carefully averted from, and ears tightly shut to, the nagging presence of Roth and Bellow, Linda Grant seems all too eager to confront them and enter into dialogue with them.

She regularly reviews their fiction, and her novels are full of implicit and explicit allusions to their work. Early on in Grant's first novel, *The Cast Iron Shore,* Sybil Ross, the half-Jewish protagonist, asks her father, "What does it mean to be a Jew?" (Grant 1998a, 30). He responds with a long nonchronological survey of Jewish suffering, but Sybil is unimpressed: "I did not want to be part of the world of pain he described. . . . And what I really wanted to know was what he *did* under his prayer shawl" (31). But her father refuses to satisfy her curiosity on the grounds that "you are not a man. And the other thing" (31).

The "other thing" being the fact that, since her mother isn't Jewish (though she does convert later in the novel), Sybil herself is technically not Jewish either. As she puts it: "Almost before I was conscious that I was a girl not a boy . . . I knew that I was not a real Jew" (25). Moreover, this identity crisis is exacerbated by the discovery that her mother was in fact a Gentile German (so that Sybil becomes convinced, without foundation as it turns out, that "the enemy was in me, Nazi blood pumping my empty heart" [65]). Yet in spite of this mixed inheritance, and in spite of her youthful rejection of any ties to Jewish history,[8] Sybil is constantly affirming her Jewishness, both implicitly (in her use of the pronoun "we" whenever she refers to Jews) and explicitly (referring to herself repeatedly as a "Jew" or "Jewess"). This ambivalence toward her own (ambiguous) Jewish identity is, of course, classic Philip Roth territory and it's not difficult to imagine what Roth might have made of such rich material, but Grant deliberately avoids exploring this ambivalence in any detail—and hence avoids the comparison with Roth. Indeed, in spite, or perhaps because, of her collision with some of the most significant political and ideological movements of the twentieth century (Fascism, Communism, civil rights, etc.), Sybil Ross remains a curiously uninvolved and uninvolving figure.

The blurb on the cover of my paperback edition of *The Cast Iron Shore* is full of praise for Grant's portrait of Ross: Lisa Jardine claims that "in Sybil Ross, Grant has given us a female protagonist to match the end of the twentieth century," while Natasha Walter insists that "Sybil's story will resonate and stay with you" and goes on to throw down the gauntlet to Grant's peers by posing the rhetorical question: "Why does contemporary literature field so few smart, courageous heroines?"

Yet it seems to me that, for all the incident and action packed into her life story, there is a hollowness at the core of Grant's representation of Sybil Ross. There is something in her that goes beyond the natural desire to fit in, to belong, something about Sybil's ability to adapt herself to her environment that approaches a Zelig-like urge towards complete assimilation. In fact she refers to herself as "a reptile on a rock you wouldn't even notice if you sauntered past" (263) and as "a chameleon [. . . with the] capacity to deceive and dissemble and pretend" (356) (in Woody Allen's film, Zelig's sobriquet is "the human chameleon").

That this is a self-conscious strategy, a calculated project, is clear from other statements that Sybil makes on this theme in the course of the novel: "I observed the ways of those about me and sought to become like them" (83); "I had utterly transformed myself. Over and over again. It had become my forte." (254). For Sybil, then, this fluidity of identity is a liberation from the pressures of social conformity, an opportunity to exercise "endless choices for re-invention" and "be anyone I wished" (261). I think what Grant is aiming for here is a sort of Rothian celebration of protean selfhood (note that Sybil's father's real name is Izidor Roth before he anglicizes it to Sydney Ross), but actually Sybil's lack of a fixed self seems to me less like an agile facility for self-invention than a complete abdication of responsibility. Whereas in Roth the self is always the site of contesting ideologies, the field on which heated internal battles are fought, in Grant it seems to be an empty vessel waiting to be filled. Moreover, for all her feminist rhetoric, Sybil seems alarmingly subservient to, and dependent on, the men in her life, from her father, to her bisexual lover Stan who "had saved me from the void into which my queer ancestry had cast me" (113), to her black lover Julius, to whom Sybil concedes "I owed my moral identity . . . my very self" (272). At one point in the novel Sybil observes that "I had been in America just over a year and if you included the journey over I had had four lovers. Each time I lost myself and became whatever they wanted me to be" (161).

If the men in her life do not determine who she is, then great causes do. Sybil becomes involved with a whole series of these—Communism, civil rights, feminism, etc.—but in each case she seems to attach herself to these ideologies in the hope of defining herself rather than out of personal conviction. She admits that "I seized on the Race Question as a way of burning out of my soul that diseased part of it which I had inherited with my mother's blood" (183) and when she becomes involved in Communist politics she spends her time typing up transcripts of meetings and running errands, rather than contributing to policy. Her fellow female Trostkyites "positively glowed when they understood how blank a slate I really was" (195).

One day after hours, during a stint working in the fashion section of a department store in New York, Sybil notices one of her colleagues, an eccentric older woman, holding a silk flower to her head. As she does this, she is momentarily transformed in Sybil's eyes into a young girl waiting for her date to arrive. The spell is broken when a passing floor-walker observes that "merchandise can become very grubby if fingered," but for Sybil a kind of epiphany has occurred. Watching the woman's metamorphosis Sybil undergoes one of her own, and a "passion was born" inside her: "In time the woman became lost to view but something had been ignited which burned away my solitariness and connected me, tangentially, to the world" (176). What precisely this passion is, is never made clear (and indeed the vagueness of the word "something" and the adverbial qualification "tangentially" hint at its paradoxical tenuousness) but her allusion to this incident later in the novel—"the woman at Lord and Taylor who once was young and now was old and poor and lonely, I would be her champion" (234)—suggests a connection with feminism and with class politics. Ultimately, what characterizes Sybil, however, is not a single defining passion but rather a series of abortive attempts to define herself in terms determined by others. Like Evelyn Sert, the heroine of Grant's second novel, the Orange Prize–winning *When I Lived In Modern Times* (2000), who describes herself as "a work-in-progress, not even that; a preliminary sketch for a person" (5), Sybil has a provisonality to her that prevents her from becoming a great fictional heroine to rival Moses Herzog and Nathan Zuckerman.[9]

It is significant that the Jewish heroines of all three of Grant's novels have to leave England in order to realize themselves (Sybil Ross goes to America, Evelyn Sert emigrates to Palestine, Alix Rebick sets up home in France): in terms of her own fiction it seems that Grant has to leave the shores of England before she can write with any conviction about the lives of her Jewish female protagonists. The partial exception is Alix Rebick who, though she begins the novel as an expatriate, spends most of its duration in her native Liverpool. Rebick is, I think, the most fully realized of Grant's heroines, and yet the irony is that, to achieve this more vivid portrait, Grant has to ventriloquise a Jewish *American* male voice (the narrative responsibilities in *Still Here* are shared between Alix and Joseph Shields, a Chicagoan architect overseeing an ambitious new development in Liverpool).

Moreover, according to Joseph, Alix isn't really a woman at all, at least not in the conventional sense of the word: "You think like a man, you talk like a man, you seem to have discarded all the usual nonsense that women are interested in" (2002b, 278). Whether this is intended to be an indictment of Joseph's rather narrow—sexist, misogynist?—conception of women is not clear, but, although Alix does rebuke him, her critique is somewhat undermined by the fact that she's so willing to swoon away into his arms and ignite at his merest touch. Furthermore, any feminist credentials she might have laid claim to evaporate altogether later in the novel when she concludes that "thirty years of feminism . . . and . . . What did we wind up with? Empty cunts" (342).

When they finally consummate their relationship, Joseph describes Alix bending down to take "my Jewish cock in her Jewish mouth and it silenced her," the apparent implication being that she is going to be the subordinate, silent one in this relationship. Joseph thus has the last word, literally as well as metaphorically (it is his voice that ends the book). Is it too allegorical a reading to suggest that Joseph Shields here stands for the American-Jewish male novelist dominating the female British-Jewish novelist? Perhaps. At any rate, there is something disturbing in the evident satisfaction that Joseph takes in "silencing" Alix, and in Alix's complicity in this satisfaction (and by extension Grant's, since there is no evidence of an ironic authorial distance in the representation of Alix). It appears that whichever path of resistance the British-Jewish women writers of fiction take—Rubens's stubborn refusal to engage with the writing of Bellow, Roth, and others, or Grant's uneasy negotiation with them—American-Jewish male authors seem always to be there at their elbows, breathing down their necks, casting a long shadow over everything they write.

NOTES

1. Rubens presumably means "stranglehold" rather than "stronghold," but her argument is in any case puzzling. The Americans, after all, have their own canon and their own tradition, albeit one stretching back hundreds rather than thousands of years. If English novelists have Austen and Dickens, American novelists have Hawthorne and Melville.

2. It is perhaps rather surprising that their admiration does not extend to American-Jewish women writers of the same generation as Bellow and Roth, such as Grace Paley and Cynthia Ozick, or indeed to any of the younger generation of American-Jewish writers (male and female) who have spawned a large number of anthologies over the last twenty years or so.

3. Surely even the most ardent admirers of Roth and Bellow would not claim that they have achieved the sort of paradigm shift in the art of the novel that Einstein and Schoenberg were responsible for in the fields of physics and music, respectively.

4. The opening line of Bellow's novel is actually: "I am an American . . . and go at things as I have taught myself, free-style" (Bellow 1954, 3).

5. I am using Roth and Bellow interchangeably here, to indicate what I take to be Rubens's and Grant's conflation of the two (a conflation I would not want to endorse).

6. For example in *Spring Sonata* (1979), in which the foetus Buster, foreseeing his fate as a gifted violinist whose family would exploit and destroy his talent, refuses to be born and finally kills his Jewish mother-to-be, Sheila Rosen, rather than allow her to deliver him into the world and the clutches of her own domineering Jewish mother, his prospective grandmother, one of Rubens's most grotesque figures.

7. Being one of the elect in this religious sense of the word is of course hinted at in the title of the novel, though the clearer allusion is to the way in which Norman has been elected by his family to represent them (in the way that the elected members of Parliament represent their constituencies).

8. In this she anticipates the attitude of Alix Rebick in *Still Here* who remarks in an aside "To hell with the Jews and their never-ending sorrows" (Grant 2002b, 243), itself surely a self-conscious echo of Alex Portnoy's notorious invitation to his "people" to "Stick your suffering [Jewish] heritage up your suffering ass" (Roth 1969, 72).

9. Evelyn's blankness, like Sybil's, seems partly the legacy of her parentage (her father is an American soldier who impregnates her mother and promises to come back to England to marry her but never does). Her surname, Sert, was chosen by her mother because "it was brief and it did not seem to come from anywhere" (Grant 2000, 8) and is ironic in that there is nothing certain about Evelyn. Like Sybil, her sense of her Jewishness is precarious: "Who was I? I was a Jew. How did I know? Because of the tales they told me, of Poland and Latvia" (11) and her general sense of self no less so: "How could I know what I was anymore, when I felt just as much a composite character as I had at school where the blonde girls with blonde eyelashes felt like members of another race?" (55). When she travels to Palestine under an assumed name, Evelyn muses on her identity in terms reminiscent of Sybil: "If I have a passport in the name of this

Priscilla Jones, who's to say I'm someone else, apart from myself? I mean if I suffered from some form of amnesia and forgot completely that I was Evelyn Sert who would I be then? . . . I seemed to contain several selves and each of these seemed to me as valid as the next" (140).

Motifs of Exile, Hopelessness, and Loss: Disentangling the Matrix of Anita Brookner's Novels

Aránzazu Usandizaga

"ALL OF BROOKNER'S NOVELS MAY BE REGARDED AS CONTINUA-tions or variations of a single narrative," says John Skinner in his study of Brookner's work, and only by careful reading does "one [become] increasingly aware of a whole *matrix* of motifs" (Skinner 1992, 181). In the several interviews she gave in the 1980s, Brookner openly confessed the close connections between her own experience and those of her heroines and heroes, and it is now unquestionable that in the twenty-three novels she has written so far, she has rewritten a similar story, closely inspired by her own experience. But just as we listen to the many variations on a musical motif in a baroque composition, we keep on reading and rereading Brookner's novels because no matter how well known the scenario might be, they continue to interest, to surprise, and to deeply move us. There is nothing mechanical in her writing. Her plots introduce remarkable alternatives to similar subjects, and they question them from many perspectives.

I believe Skinner's reference to a "matrix of motifs" in Brookner's stories is a useful starting point in the understanding of her work. Yet the main motifs in her plots must be disentangled from the tightly woven web in order to come to terms with their significance. Some of her motifs have been so far hardly discussed by the author's critics. Such is the case with the use she makes in her stories of Jewish culture. Jewishness is very rarely referred to directly in her novels. It is mostly introduced in disguised and oblique ways, but like Brookner herself, most of her heroines and heroes are the children or grandchildren of central European Jewish exiles, and Jewish culture plays a central role both in her characters' destinies and in Brookner's artistic purposes.

Only a few of Brookner's novels treat Judaism directly but its more occult presence as cultural background is central in the understanding of her ambitious artistic project. Within the complex "matrix of motifs" to be found in her novels, Judaism purposefully inundates and transforms Brookner's other motifs in the elaboration of her fictional project. Brookner's novels *Latecomers* (1988), *A Family Romance* (1993), and the recently published *The Next Big Thing* (2002) are perhaps the clearest examples of novels directly concerned with Jewish subjects and with the consequences of the Holocaust. Jewish culture is also a central subject in *Family and Friends* (1985), yet all these novels tend to blur historical facts and the desire for denunciation. The same could be said about her early novel, *Providence* (1982).[1]

Very few critics seem to have focused on the subject of Brookner's representation of Jewishness in her writing. In "Paradigm and Passage: The Fiction of Anita Brookner" (1993), Robert E. Hosmer, Jr. discusses some of her early novels as "exilic" in connection to Jewish history. More recently, Louise Sylvester's "Troping the Other: Anita Brookner's Jews" (2001), offers a more comprehensive approach to the matter. After briefly discussing the three Brookner novels in which the characters' Jewishness is more obvious, *Providence, Latecomers*, and *A Family Romance*, Sylvester laments Brookner's shyness in addressing the Jewish question in her novels, to the point of bringing up the word "betrayal." Sylvester suggests that Brookner disguises Jewishness and historical reference in her novels to accommodate her writing to British reading tastes: "What one is finally left with as a reader . . . is the simultaneously offered clues for the initiated, and a smattering of exoticism and sadness for the general reader who will probably feel . . . the faint echoes of Jewishness, and the relief that its implications, and specially its recent history, are not explored in any detail. A solution perfect for the English audience Brookner has both sought and found" (2001, 56–57).

Given Brookner's obvious lack of concern in accommodating any aspect of her writing to notions of critical and political acceptability, to what could be defined as politically correct, these words might be considered to be slightly unfair. We should perhaps read them in the context of Cheryl Alexander Malcolm's brief discussion of the subject in the introduction to her book *Understanding Anita Brookner* (2002). Malcolm, who has written on several Jewish women writers, admits that "her [Brookner's] writing exhibits few of the features commonly associated with Jewish writing" and is aware of the fact that the writer is accused by critics of "a self-conscious refusal to engage with Jewish culture" (2002, 11), yet Malcolm connects Brookner's writing to Elie Wiesel's advice to writers who treat the Holocaust, that they should learn "the art of economy": "At best, they might develop the skill to condense situations and themes 'to the point at which they burst from within' thereby conveying the emotional and mental devastation that lies concealed" (11). Just as she handles other important contemporary issues with total independence of fashions and accepted positions, also in the case of Judaism Brookner may be working in a more varied, subtle, and less obvious way than other writers, but not necessarily less powerfully or less convincingly.

Some of her novels offer important clues. If Ruth Weiss, her first heroine in *A Start in Life* (1981), is the first to suffer the consequences of her Jewish grandparents' sad life of exile, *Providence*, her next novel, is more explicit on the subject. Though Kitty Maul's story, like Ruth Weiss's before her, reflects and laments her failure to attract her much-worshipped lover—a subject matter repeated with several variations in many of Brookner's early novels—in *Providence* the heroine's alienation from her English environment and from her lover is symbolized by Kitty's response to Christianity. Brookner dramatizes the incompatibility between the hero's Christian faith and the heroine's inherited beliefs and her dis-beliefs, and proves the centrality of the heroine's Jewish roots. Brookner significantly places religion at the very core and as the very reason for the unbridgeable distance between the partly Jewish heroine and the Christian hero (whose name interestingly happens to be Bishop).

Kitty's passionately felt difference, the real nature of her otherness, of her tragic alienation, a condition that will affect most of her heroines and heroes, could hence perhaps be understood as having its roots in religious faith. The matter is extensively discussed in this early novel, in a series of interesting dialogues between Kitty and Maurice Bishop, which begin when he asks Kitty: "You are absolutely without faith . . . ," to which the heroine does not hesitate to answer: "Why yes." It is at this point that the Christian hero confirms Kitty's difference from him by confirming his own beliefs: "I believe in Providence, he said" (*P*, 55). And *Providence* is of course the title of the book.

But Brookner does not leave it at that. Maurice's distance from Kitty is further spelled out for her when he lets her know he is still in love with a woman who has left him to follow a religious calling and has joined Mother Teresa in Calcutta. "When did all this happen?" Kitty wants to know. "Three years ago, he replied" (*P,* 58). What is most interesting at this point is the direction Kitty's thoughts take, without further pause or comment: "Three years ago," she thinks, "Maria Therese [her Jewish mother. The coincidence in the names is quite remarkable] had died, quickly, quietly, without the benefit of clergy, without assurance of eternal comfort" (*P,* 58). Christianity immediately and subliminally awakens Kitty to the mother she had intensely loved and to her own Jewish upbringing. These same feelings are repeated in Brookner's recent novel, *The Next Big Thing.* Now it is an older man, Herz, the son of German exiles in England, who though expecting death, cannot seek the help of Christianity. Unlike Kitty Maul, Herz defines his own relation to Jewish religion and summarizes an attitude that is common to all of Brookner's heroines and heroes: "His ancestral religion, which he did not practise, seemed to him an affair of prohibitions, of righteous exclusiveness for which he could see no justification" (*TNBT,* 16).

The centrality of the gap in religious faith between the two potential lovers in *Providence* is further emphasized when Maurice and Kitty finally meet in Paris and visit the basilica of Saint Denise because Maurice, an art historian, is studying the art and architecture of French cathedrals. As soon as she enters the church, Kitty is repelled by the atmosphere, to the point of nausea. Her perception of the basilica is as of "a dungeon surrounded by abattoirs" (*P,* 117); the church contains for her "the unreason of God" (*P,* 118), and while Maurice stands "transfixed" (*P,* 118) she craves for something "elegant and rational; an 18th century building" (*P,* 118). Next, we read, "she wonders fearfully among the tombs," and lets Maurice know, "I hate this place." "How can you? I could stay here for hours" is his reply. And again, while he forgets her in the concentration of his praying, Kitty's mind unconsciously evokes her Jewish mother.

Given the development of Kitty's character in the novel, her response to the Christian environment becomes an unexpected instance of strong self-assertion in a character otherwise consistently uncertain of itself. Her usual meekness is at this point overcome; her feelings against Christianity, strong and clear.

Though Kitty's love and longing for Maurice continue to control her to the very end of the novel, perhaps rather obsessively, given her taste for the rational, the reader knows at this stage the lovers to be incompatible, and though Kitty might try to sympathise with Maurice in every way, her religious position has been declared not to be open to change. Religious imagery is again evoked at the end of the novel when Kitty is "betrayed" by Bishop in the "last supper" he celebrates before leaving the university they both work at for Oxford.

If Kitty defines the impossibility for the daughter of Jewish immigrants to identify with Christian culture, and proves that Jewish difference lies at the root of her heroine's desolation, much could be said about the suffering and displacement of Jewish exiles in connection to *Latecomers*. Brookner's only straightforward fictionalization of Holocaust survivors, it is a novel of great knowledge and penetration. Created in the context of Freudian ideas, Hartman and Fibich, the two German friends saved by being sent to England as children at the beginning of the war, manage to become two consistent characters, though Fibich is the most interesting of the two. Fibich shows most movingly the tragedy of survival in his incapacity to forget the past, to overcome the guilt left by the last memory of his German childhood, the vision of the mother he, even at that early age, knew he was abandoning to death. His difficulties become a subtle and ultimately exemplary study of how the tragedy of the Holocaust did not end with the return to peace, because the emotional damage received at an early age can never be repaired, and the consequences of war are carried on from one generation to the next. *Latecomers* offers, I think, the kind of approach Elie Wiesel had in mind in his previously mentioned advice to Jewish writers, for the moving story of the characters' precarious personal survival conveys the personal devastation they suffered as a result of the Holocaust.

The story is rendered rich and complex by the careful analysis of the two friends, of their wives and children, and by the study of the different forms of accommodation they need to work out throughout their lives, particularly with themselves, in order to survive. And though their economic prosperity in England allows them to achieve an external peace and balance, their well-being is constantly checked by the memory of the past, and the suffering never ends. The novel ambitiously covers not only the two friends' efforts at integration in the present and assimilation of the past, but also, I think most interestingly, of their need to accept the future. Thus Fibich must learn to come to terms with his extraordinarily talented and good-looking son, the son that he, the man in constant pain, cannot possibly understand; the son for whom he finally writes his version of his past. Only after passing on his own story to his son, does Fibich achieve a degree of internal peace, a peace he has certainly not met in traveling to Germany. The suffering must be recorded and remembered.

New and different readings of Jewish exile are offered by Brookner in *A Family Romance,* though in this novel the heroine, Jane, is in many ways a well known character to Brookner readers. Yet the mood is now light; the title, openly ironic, for as the reader soon finds out, the young heroine's "romance" will not involve a hero but an old aunt of dubious morality whom the heroine will nevertheless learn to accept and love.

The setting is not unlike many of her previous and later novels: Jane, a peaceful and well-brought up young girl, is the orphaned daughter of quiet and rather low keyed parents. As expected in a Brookner novel, the heroine has looked after her beloved mother until the mother's early death, and has also inherited the family's fortune both from her mother and from her originally Austrian Jewish grandmother. But part of her maternal legacy is also the unmentioned responsibility of taking care of her French Jewish aunt Dolly. The story is a bildungsroman told by the heroine whose apprenticeship in the perception of the world from childhood to maturity is strongly influenced by her surprising aunt Dolly. But who is Dolly and what kind of Jewishness does she stand for? She is probably one of Brookner's richest characters; a woman dominated by a powerful vitality, an echo of prefeminist, traditional Jewish womanhood. In spite of her apparent moral ambivalence, Dolly's talent to survive, to adapt to changing circumstances and fortunes, her passion for life and pleasure, for sex, seduce the heroine and open up her imagination. This also allows Jane to move beyond the typically Brookner lonely, empty background. In the end, in spite of Jane's initially critical presentation of Dolly, she must recognize that "what troubled me most of all was the fact that I felt myself to be in some way inferior to Dolly" (*AFR*, 207).

Dolly's exuberance in character and experience encourages Jane to question and even oppose her American feminist friends' ideas of love: "I do not tell them that my views have perhaps been influenced by the most unreconstructed woman I have ever known." Of course "I now see that Dolly belongs to another epoch, another world," but Jane must finally recognize that she has learned vital things from her aunt, and when at her weakest, she always remembers her aunt's words: "Charm, Jane, charm!" In the process of coming to terms with Dolly's challenging differences, Jane enlarges the limits of her experience and achieves personal balance and self-knowledge. Exceptionally in this novel, though the heroine is very young, she is not interested in romance. Jane's achievements are to be seen in her professional success as a writer of children's books. She is the only Brookner character to travel to America invited by several universities. The novel was published one year after *Fraud* and *A Closed Eye*, and these three novels represent a moment in which Brookner's fictional direction seemed to be changing.

Family and Friends also proved a new approach to Brookner's more direct representation of Jewishness. In this case it is an open celebration of it. The story elaborates the life of Sofka, a Jewish widow and mother, again in English exile, and it narrates the destiny of herself and her four children. It offers a change in perspective, and manages to achieve a fair balance between Sofka's point of view and that of her four children. Though the two sisters reproduce the typical early Brookner antagonism between two kinds of women—the active and the passive, the tortoise and the hare—the young women's destinies are not the novel's main focus. The novel is committed to the painting of a broad panorama of characters and destinies determined by a Jewish culture that belongs to Brookner's own past.

As was said earlier, straightforward dramatization and discussion of Jewishness is relatively scarce in Brookner's novels. What is constant in her writing is the complex dialogue she establishes with the elements of her inherited Jewishness that concern her most and that in her novels become most relevant to late twentieth-century culture. Brookner shows the importance of the Jewish legacy she has received by proving its prophetic and universal value in representing the human need to come to terms with central aspects of life as well as with suffering and death not only in the Jewish tradition but in all cultures and circumstances. But above all, her Jewishness will help the author understand and define the functions of art.

The most intense connection with Jewish culture Brookner's many heroines and few heroes are endowed with is of a double nature. In the first place most of her characters undergo a lifelong determining experience in the complex and ambivalent relationship they have with their mothers. Not that non-Jewish children do not often experience complex connections to their mother, but it is a particularly strong feature in Jewish culture, especially in exile. In the second place, most Brookner characters also share a constant sense of displacement and a strong desire for some other place. The responsibilities to aging mothers of extremely dutiful daughters and the complex and ambivalent relations that derive from such commitments, as well as their nostalgic desire for other places become the most idiosyncratic and permanent features in all her novels, and both attitudes are centrally related to Jewish culture.

As is the case in the tradition of Jewish motherhood, in Brookner's stories mothers are simultaneously a powerful source of love and a huge burden to most daughters. The often passionate love daughters feel for their mothers can be both enriching and very destructive, and many of her novels anxiously explore the ambiguities of the mother/daughter relation in all its infinite complexity. But Brookner's exploration of mothers' influence on daughters and of daughters' feelings toward their mothers is particularly relevant to the ongoing feminist discussion on the subject, a discussion begun a few decades ago, and it becomes an important part of Brookner's contribution to the analysis of the lives of contemporary women.

In her article, "Representation, Reproduction, and Women's Place in Language," Margaret Homans summarizes and discusses Western feminist readings of current psychoanalytic interpretations of the relation of women to their mothers and to writing. English and American feminist psychoanalysts of the past three decades have radically contradicted Freudian and Lacanian theories, that is to say, traditional psychoanalysis, according to which, "the death or absence of the mother sorrowfully but fortunately makes possible the child's construction of language and culture" (Homans 1998, 650). English and American feminist psychoanalysis has radically reoriented such readings. Homans summarizes these important changes in the understanding of women's psychosocial development:

> Because the daughter doesn't share the son's powerful incentives to renounce the mother, . . . her "rejection" of her mother and her Oedipal attachment to her father . . . do not mean the termination of the girl's affective relationship to her mother . . . Because the daughter has the positive experience of never having given up entirely the pre-symbolic communication that carries over, with the bond to the mother, beyond the pre-Oedipal period . . . The daughter does not, in Chodorow's view, give up this belief in communication that takes place in presence rather than in absence, in the dyadic relation with the mother, prior to figuration. (653–54)

Though Homans and other theorists warn readers of the complexities to be found in the transition from the presymbolic to the symbolic in the case of girls, the "utopian imperative" among women writers, as defined by Susan Gubar (1983), has been very powerful in recent decades.

Yet Anita Brookner's heroines, emerging from obscure Jewish backgrounds, are among the few to have remained mostly unaffected by this new feminist optimism, and that might be the reason why criticism, feminist criticism in particular, has been rather slow in assessing her many novels, even though they are all committed to analyzing and passionately describing the difficult processes of self-development in the case of women. In order to understand Brookner's position, it might be useful to reflect on Homans's warning as to the unexplored difficulties she suggests in women's transition from the semiotic to the symbolic.

This transition has also been the central focus of recent French feminism. In her introduction to the selection of writings by the French psychoanalyst Julia Kristeva, *The Kristeva Reader*, Toril Moi explains that between 1974 and 1977 Kristeva's interests underwent an important change, from the purely linguistic that had culminated in her study, *Revolution in Poetic Language* (1974), "towards a more psychoanalytically oriented examination of the problems of femininity and motherhood. . . . as an area posing new theoretical problems to psychoanalysis" (Moi 1986, 7). Coinciding with her own motherhood, Kristeva proposed interesting though sometimes contradictory ideas on the subject of women's development, and attempted to describe some of the very complex processes women undergo in their transition. This might be helpful in understanding Brookner's writing. Kristeva's radical assumption of the problematic aspects of psychoanalysis as applied to women can be very useful in approaching Brookner's novels.

Most of Brookner's heroines suffer the consequences of a too close relation to a mother, and their lack of successful self-assertion and self-articulation seems to be intensely related to these quiet and destructive mothers; to homes that lack fathers or where their presence is blurred. Kristeva talks of the "love which had bound the little girl to her mother, and which then, like black lava, had lain in wait for her all along the path to her desperate attempts to identify with the symbolic paternal order. Once the moorings of the word, the ego, the superego, begin to slip, life itself can't hang on: death quietly moves in. Suicide without a cause, or sacrifice without fuss" (Moi 1986, 157). Kristeva's theories seem to pivot around one central notion; that of the inevitable need for the daughter to "establish the mother as abjected" (Moi 1986, 257). Her references to emptiness, to women's madness, death, or ultimate "sacrifice without fuss," sound significantly familiar to the Brookner reader. The implacable and nonnegotiable understanding of women's personal and socio/literary destiny in Kristeva's theory echoes the tragic dimensions of life for women in the past and the present, and forces us to question the limits of more consolatory interpretations.

Brookner's novels of the early nineties, *A Closed Eye* (1991), *Fraud* (1992), and *A Family Romance* (1993), seemed to offer an unexpected hope to heroines (Usandizaga 1998). But as her novels continued to appear in the following years, it was soon clear that Brookner's experiments in happiness were short-lived. Since 1993 her heroines seem to have been taken over once again by the powers of abjection; they are again dominated by an invincible nostalgia toward the mysterious drives that tear them away from the social and symbolic toward the unutterable darkness of the semiotic. In none of her novels is a mother a source of empowerment to her daughter.

If Brookner questions optimistic readings of the mother/daughter plot and determines the universal centrality of such a plot to women, she takes a further step in the direction of narrative truth by transforming another inherent condition of Jewish culture, that of permanent exile, into a general feature of human life. Certainly the most carefully hidden of Brookner's motifs in the complex web of the matrix she weaves is that of her characters' cultural displacement, their internalization of the painful experience of exile that she herself has explained in several of her interviews as being based on her own experience as the daughter of Jewish immigrants.

In the introduction to his study, *The Legend of the Wandering Jew*, George K. Anderson relates the origins of "the tedious punishment" to the three great religions of the world—Christianity, Mohammedanism, and Buddhism (1991, 3). The punishment of exile appears for the first time in Christian culture in the Book of Genesis (4:1–15) when the Lord forces it upon Cain for having killed his brother Abel, though exile can be traced back to Adam and Eve who suffered the first and most painful banishment in being expelled from Paradise. Several extrascriptural legends refer for the first time to the Wandering Jew. According to them, the condition of living in permanent exile was imposed by Christ upon a Jewish man as a consequence of his bad treatment of Christ in the last hours of his life (Anderson 1991, 12–13). What is perhaps most interesting in Anderson's study is his analysis of the fact that exile as punishment is recognized to go back to the very origins of human culture. The lack of historical specificity in Brookner's references to her characters' situation allows the author to transform the burden of displacement her heroines suffer into a reflection of a condition in human life, a condition oriented toward death. Though characters in her novels are defined by their being of foreign and Jewish origin and by not being able to properly adapt to English society, their restlessness has ultimately as much to do with their personal biography as with the common displacement inherent to life.

As a consequence of such restlessness, Brookner's daughter/heroines, dangerously close to their mothers, and also her later older characters, are always projected against foreign countries. Not that their countries of reference are remote, nor do they ever travel far. Their journeys mostly take them to Paris, to southern France, and occasionally to Switzerland, Germany, or Austria. The sadness of Jewish exile becomes in most of her novels a memory that characters internalize and that is reflected in their permanent failure to properly adapt to their London lives, in their obsessive need to seek for further horizons in other cities and cultures.

By weaving exile and difference into the very core of her fictional characters, Brookner allows it to become a metaphor essential in the construction of the contemporary bildungsroman, particularly in the case of women. Though a tragic burden to them in her early novels, in her later books Brookner's heroines seem to be greatly improved by their habits of exile; they are provided with a wider geographical and metaphorical horizon. Exile seems to establish difference in their lives, and though indeed initially painful, it eventually becomes the heroines' most valuable legacy in their processes of perceiving and understanding. Gradually and consistently exile endows characters with a perspective capable of challenging easy accommodation, ultimately allowing them to come to terms with the larger mysteries of life, and of eventually accepting death.

The artistic relevance Brookner attributes to these matters is proved in two of her latest novels, which can be read as a summary and a manifesto of her artistic project. Displacement and the complex relations between child and mother continue to be central in these latest two novels, so far her most ambitious texts; two extraordinary efforts at providing a coherent conclusion to her previous work. Interestingly, the main characters in these two novels are a woman in *The Bay of Angels* and a man in *The Next Big Thing* who repeat the pattern of Brookner's previous heroines and heroes in that they both suffer a very complex relation to their mothers and also in that they are both essentially displaced people, the daughter and the son of Jewish exiles. In *The Bay of Angels*, the mother's life and death and the character's response to it, a passionate source of love and sorrow, become the central plot in the novel. In opposition to it, Herz's relation to his own mother in *The Next Big Thing* follows a Freudian pattern of radical abjection and becomes the central symbol of the character's lifelong displacement and of his final need to search for love even at the time of death.

The Bay of Angels is Brookner's most ambitious attempt so far at reorganizing and reevaluating the matrix of motifs she has been working on for so long. Zoë, Brookner's young heroine, manages a new way of articulating the many limitations forced upon any Brookner heroine. Like her predecessors, Zoë suffers the intense attachment to a mother whom she must look after until her death. Unlike her predecessors, Zoë, who narrates her story in all its sadness in the first person, acknowledges and accepts the semiotic passion she feels for the mother she cannot abandon. Persephone in love with Demeter, she confesses, "for we had been happy, too fiercely fond of each other to tolerate outsiders" (*TBOA*, 75). Her description of her mother's death and her reflections on it are amongst the most powerful in literature, perhaps as intense as D. H. Lawrence's description of Mrs. Morel's death in *Sons and Lovers* (1913). What is most impressive is her recognition of total loneliness after her mother's death, as well as her awareness that the love she and her mother felt for each other was the only possible true love because of its total freedom. It is a secret she shares with Dr. Balbi, the man who will eventually become her lover, and who has experienced a similar feeling toward his own mother: "Yes, that love was a sort of freedom. You have it with your own mother. But, as you have discovered, it turns into something more tragic" (*TBOA*, 164). Both Zoë and her lover know that no love in life can compare to the totality, the intensity of the mother's love.

Brookner's recent heroine and even more so her last hero confirm what Heidegger defined as human beings being forced into life against their will—into a "*Dasein*" that implies the loss of the connection with one's origin, with the love and identification with the presymbolic—forced into what Heidegger calls "*Das Sein für Tod*" (Being for Death). If Zoë's passion for her mother ends in the tragedy of the mother's death, and her loneliness implies permanent displacement from her true original love, Herz's own overwhelming and lifelong sense of isolation responds to this tragic need for the love of his mother and of his past.

I wish to conclude by proposing that Brookner's use of Jewish culture is indeed the starting point in a complex and intentional fictional experiment, and that her twenty-three novels can be read as a consistent attempt in the writing of an extended *Künstlerroman*. Brookner is indeed reticent with Jewishness not because she wishes not to disturb her British readers but because her extremely coherent literary project altogether excludes political metaphors of any kind; because the most serious dialogue she establishes in her novels is not with history but with art, with literature itself, and in that sense I believe it might be legitimate to define her work as a long and tentative *Künstlerroman*.

But also this matrix seems to be intricately hidden in her texts, yet all her writer heroines fail to find true satisfaction in their work. Where modernity sees fiction as a powerful source of creativity, Brookner portrays it as a distraction from life and none of her writing heroines finds consolation in storytelling. The control they may manage over speech, over the social and the public, is there only to increase their awareness of want. Language does not lend itself to sublimation. Neither do Brookner's plots share any of the feminist or postfeminist expectations. Her early young heroines imagine redemption by becoming the objects of love, yet Brookner systematically destroys the hope of romance. Hopelessly yearning to be chosen by unapproachable lovers— *Look at Me* (1983) is the significant title of one of her early novels—they bitterly realize virtue will not save them as is usually the case with nineteenth-century heroines, particularly in Dickens's novels. Her stories are thus centrally about disappointment. Her heroines are expert at loss, disillusion, loneliness—a common condition in women, and as Brookner gradually shows, also in men. She is perhaps one of the contemporary women writers to write most systematically "beyond the ending." If psychoanalysis locates the articulation of language at the source of the tensions between the semiotic and the symbolic, Brookner's heroines, in spite of their talents, never seem to find redemption or consolation in writing. Literature, particularly romantic literature, is always seen as a dangerous temptation that prevents her heroines from comprehending themselves; it is seen as an escape from events that are too harsh and unbearable.

Significantly, Brookner initiates her career as a novelist in *A Start in Life*, with the words "Dr. Weiss, at forty, knew that her life had been ruined by literature." It takes the writing of her next twenty novels to work out the dangers of fiction to truth and to imagine the possibility of writing truthfully. Not until she writes *The Bay of Angels* (2001), her recent novel centered on one woman, does her heroine finally learn the lesson. Interestingly, it is the mother who has taught the heroine the true purpose of literature: "My mother was never at all comfortable unless living in the light of the truth. Although she had once been an avid reader she had never made the mistake of confusing fiction with fact" (*TBOA*, 208). Zoë pays homage to her mother, so far the only character in Brookner's novels capable of "living in the light of truth." The acknowledgment of fictional and artistic truth is significantly a maternal legacy, a new awareness in Brookner's fiction which rounds up the author's work. Brookner's literary theory, the final and originating core of her "matrix of motifs," is thus tightly woven to the essential motifs of motherhood and exile, the motifs she has always been particularly talented to comprehend precisely because of her Jewish background.

There is no danger of confusion at this stage and Brookner's recent heroine is finally entitled to explain the author's ideas on literature. She now importantly knows that "There would be no happy ending" to her life: "I should have to live without such consoling fictions, as most people do. The disadvantage was that the fictions exert such power that one comes to accept them as revealed truth . . . That is why one longs to believe in some kind of intervention, divine or otherwise . . . To live with unutterable truth is a very hard discipline . . . Those who manage to do so are to be congratulated" (*TBOA*, 208).

"One thinks of marriage as the end of the story. There is only one end to our story" (*TBOA*, 165), acknowledges the heroine to herself in *The Bay of Angels*. If death is the only true end to any story, Brookner's latest novel with a male protagonist, *The Next Big Thing*, offers a truthful ending, for it deals with the representation and interpretation of final exile. Like most older Brookner heroines and heroes, Herz, the main character in this allegory of the human heart, has suffered a destiny similar to that of many other Brookner heroines and heroes, but unlike earlier characters, he manages to define his tragic condition: "the sadness which had nothing to do with hardships and disappointments but was rather an inheritance he did not fully understand" (*TNBT*, 26). Herz's reference is both to his condition as a Jew in exile and of course, much more broadly, as a man who knows himself to be very near death.

These two recent novels represent a powerful effort on the author's part to summarize and reelaborate the meanings of her complex fictional "matrix of motifs." They are the last words she has said so far[2] on a series of motifs, all of them connected to Jewishness, which have affected her own life and which she has managed to transmit and share through her books. They also happen to be motifs that shed light on Brookner's long efforts at trying to redefine some of the most relevant questions concerning our understanding of ourselves as human beings in our contemporary world and become of great relevance to all of us. But most ambitiously, these stories offer Brookner's brave and original reflections on the ultimate responsibility of literature and art in the eternal search for artistic truth.

NOTES

1. Page references to Brookner's novels will cite them in parentheses as follows: *A Family Romance* (*AFR*), *Family and Friends* (*FF*), *Latecomers* (*L*), *Providence* (*P*), *The Bay of Angels* (*TBOA*), *The Next Big Thing* (*TNBT*).

2. Since this paper was prepared, Brookner has published two further novels, *The Rules of Engagement* (2003) and *Leaving Home* (2004), which make no radical departures from her central themes.

III
Multicultural Literature

"Goy Israels" and the "nomadic embrace": Mina Loy Writing Race

Alex Goody

QUESTIONS ABOUT THE MODERNIST POET MINA LOY'S RELATION-
ship to and representation of race, and particularly her own jewish heritage, have not been prominent in explications of her
work. Loy's marginalization has featured in critical discussions,
but most often the focus is on her feminist sensibilities and her
ambivalent presence in different circles of modernism. The
recent collection of essays, *Mina Loy: Woman and Poet* (Shrieber
and Tuma, 1998) has one index entry for "Judaism" but this is a
mention of Christianity and Judaism as organized religions and
perpetrates the common, but problematic, conflation of the
"Judaeo-Christian." In contrast to the mainstream of Loy criticism, therefore, this chapter considers the relationship of her
racial identity to her modernist writing and to the avant-garde of
the early twentieth century. In doing so it attempts to highlight
how Loy's aesthetics and politics of identity are articulated, in
part, through a response to the construction and reception of jewishness in turn-of-the-century British culture.[1]

Loy certainly writes about race in her critiques of the structures through which various subcultures and underclasses are co-
opted into the service of hegemonic culture and consumption. In
a draft manuscript of "Mass-Production on 14th Street" (1942, in
Loy 1997, 111–13) for example, Loy's critique of the "mobile sim-
ulacra's" of the fashion industry points particularly to the racial
exploitation (and commodification) that underpins this most
modern of industries:

> Production — reproduction —
>   Astronomically countless flowers
> Of kind incontinence — —
>   O Negro, so subdued, who being

> Loosely knit excite the tempo
> Of our relaxation
> O jew, so much despoiled —
> To glorify the garment worker
> In flowerage of her hands —[2]

Loy's work is particularly conscious of the way that modern Western civilization projects and manipulates conceptions of racial otherness in both its high and popular cultural forms. Constructions of jewishness appear as part of that aesthetisization and cultural manipulation of race: the banal and/or genocidal results of this are presented in poems such as "Hilarious Israel" and "Photo after Pogrom." These works from the 1940s when Loy had settled in the United States are, however, clearly engaging with *American* culture in which race and racial identity hold a very particular position. So, rather than simply point to Loy's general awareness of race and jewishness as evidenced in her work, the concern here is to examine the relationship between her exploration and (re)writing of her own Anglo-Jewish heritage. The focus of this chapter is thus Loy's autobiographically based work of the 1920s and 1930s where, similar to her critique of the (commercial) exploitation of racial others, Loy explores the possibilities of identity and identification outside the predetermined stereotypes of an imperialist, capitalist economy.

The details of Loy's parentage are not a simple or easy way to "ground" a discussion of her jewishness because they are reworked over and over again in the autobiographical and "automythological"[3] work that she wrote. The only published version of these "self-writings" is *Anglo-Mongrels and the Rose*. There, Loy's mother Julia Bryan, daughter of a Bromley artisan, becomes "Ada" the "English Rose" epitome of English "arrested impulses"; Loy's father Sigmund Felix Lowy, a Hungarian Jewish tailor who had emigrated to England in the 1870s, becomes "Exodus," the "jovian hebrew" or "wondering jew" [*sic*]. The "facts" of Loy's family circumstances seem to be that Sigmund Lowy retained his jewish faith, but his daughters were brought up in their mother's (Protestant) religion and as Sigmund rose to become a bespoke gentleman's tailor the Lowy family achieved the bourgeois respectability of the merchant and professional class and moved to a "decent" North London suburb. It might be possible to read in this family narrative an example of the incorporation (along

an Arnoldian model) of the "hebrew" into the successful (impe-
rialistic) "hellenic" nation. However Lowy's acculturation was
as much the result of the class/economic aspirations of his wife
as of the cultural identifications of the aspirant immigrant. His
narrative (as rewritten/mythologized by Loy) is not that of the
acculturated "Jew" as symbol of the promise of modernity; it is
a narrative of the forces of capitalism, mass consumption, and
the commodification of desire seducing and perverting the racial
other.

Loy then was not part of an Anglo-Jewish community,[4] and
seems to have had little contact with the Judaic religion itself.
She also changed her name in about 1900: "Lowy" (a name her
mother apparently never pronounced correctly—parodied in *Goy
Israels* by Mrs. Israels's pronunciation "Eyes-Raells") becoming
"Loy," an excision of the "foreign" phoneme, if one wishes to
read her "renaming" in that way. But, despite her elided heritage,
the memoirs and accounts of the heady days of modernism and
avant-garde experimentation do identify Loy racially, fixing her
as a dark, beautiful jewess. Indeed, until the "recovery" of her
poetry and other writing, Loy's reputation persisted mostly in the
margins of modernism as a version of the femme fatale with
"Beauty ever-young which has survived four babies, and charm
which will survive a century if she lives that long, are sustained
by a gayety that seems the worldly-wise conquest of many
despairs — all expressed in a voice which . . . is rich with all the
sorrows of the world" (Monroe 1923, 96).

That Loy may have figured similarly to the "belle juive" of
decadent art and writing for her modernist peers cannot have
escaped her notice. In her 1914 "Three Moments in Paris"
sequence, for example, she clearly satirizes a decadent/symbol-
ist construction of woman as dangerous, morbid physicality:

> Little tapers leaning   lighted diagonally
> Stuck in coffin tables of the Café du Néant
> Leaning to the breath of baited bodies
> Like young poplars fringing the Loire
>
> . . . .
>
> Nostalgic youth
> Holding your mistress's pricked finger
> In the indifferent flame of the taper
> Synthetic symbol of   LIFE

In this factitious chamber of   DEATH
The woman
As usual
Is smiling as bravely
As it is given her to be   brave

While the brandy cherries
In winking glasses
Are decomposing
Harmoniously
With the flesh of spectators
And at a given spot
There is one
Who
Having the concentric lighting focussed precisely upon her
Prophetically blooms in perfect putrefaction
Yet there are cabs outside the door.

(Loy 1997, 16–17)

Any exploration of Loy's specific negotiation of her racial heritage and its impact upon her writing and (self) presentation needs to be placed within the broader contexts of how "the indeterminate Jew" was rewritten and reconstructed in modernism (Cheyette 1993, 207). Similar to Tamar Garb's argument that the Jew "marks the point of rupture" in the narrative of Western civilization (Nochlin and Garb, 1995, 20), Bryan Cheyette explores how "with the advent of explicitly modernist texts the very incoherence of 'the Jew' was to be a potent expression of the impossibility of fully 'knowing' anything" (1993, 9). This was to have different resonances for different writers: T. S. Eliot was desperate to disavow his own repressed semitic identifications through the anti-semitic overdeterminations of his work, and Ezra Pound projected the jew as feminine messiness, confusion, the negative principle. In *Ulysses* however, James Joyce actively exploits the "instability of 'the Jew' as a racial and cultural signifier . . . to undermine any dominant discourse" (206). As Cheyette demonstrates, Joyce's text offers an ambivalent construction of racial difference, particularly in the "disruptive capacity of Leopold Bloom's unstable 'greekjewish' identity" (267) and attempts to "break down the binary oppositions between 'Jew and gentile' or 'Hebrew and Hellene'" (267). A crucial feature of "the Jew" as a point of textual and cultural uncertainty was the fact that he/she was not an identifiable, external Other, but a presence within the imperial urban center. As Cheyette says: "What distinguishes semitic discourse from colonial and racial discourse in general is the extent to which 'the Jew' could directly encroach upon the consciousness of the metropolitan white bourgeoisie" (271).

Like Joyce, Loy deploys the uncertainty of "the Jew" (as identity, as racial marker, as cultural sign — particularly of modernity) to challenge the monolithic narratives of Western progress. In her work racial ambivalence — identity that exceeds or undermines fixity — often results from and also metonymically represents the uncertain zone of the modern city:

> The city
> Wedged between
> Impulse and Unfolding
> Bridged
> By diurnal splintering
> Of egos
> Round
> The aerial news-kiosk
> Where you
> Statically
> Hob-nob
> With a nigger
> And a deaf-mute
> Of introspection
> Plopping finger
> In Stephen's ink
> Made you hybrid-negro
> A couple of manuscriptural erasures
> And here we have your deaf-mute
> Beseech him
> He will never with-hold so
> Completely
> As the tattle of tongue-play
> Or your incognito.
>
> (Loy 1916)

Although this 1915 poem, "To You," is not specifically concerned with jewishness,[5] its voice does identify (with) the racial others of the city. Loy's text, like Joyce's, attempts to inhabit/ enunciate a space of indeterminacy. "To You" identifies and deploys the urban space as radically and racially indeterminate:

it allows for a subversive uncertainty of identity and subjectivity that is mirrored in the complex address of the poem where the speaking I/eye is doubled as the addressed "You."

Loy's own reading of Joyce's *Ulysses* (in the 1922 poem "Joyce's *Ulysses*") celebrates the novel's challenges to the norms and commonplaces of literature and culture. She highlights the living language ("The loquent consciousness / of living things," the "torrential languages" [1997, 88]), the critique of imperial and economic exploitation, and the corporeality of Joyce's text. While suggesting that *Ulysses* enacts a profound disturbance of those primary Manichean oppositions "Spirit and Flesh," at the same time her poem manifests an equivocal attitude to the semitic representation, sexual politics, and overall ontology of *Ulysses*. The poem points to a narcissistic intellectualism in the text, which feeds upon itself but is also predicated upon the realm of the maternal body (and the control of the mother's voice). That Loy reads *Ulysses* as offering a sexualization of its racial politics and representation of the "indeterminate jew" (who both is and is not Joyce-as-writer) can be seen in the following:

> Master
> of meteoric idiom
> present
>
>   The word made flesh
>   and feeding upon itself
>   with erudite fangs
>   The sanguine
>   introspection of the womb
>
>   Don Juan
>   of Judea
>   upon a pilgrimage
>   to the Libido.
>
>   (Loy 1997, 89)

The alliterative impact of these lines is both (with the "J") to connect Joyce with (a jewish) Bloom's libidinous perambulations ("Don Juan of Judea") and (with the "m") to emphasize the semi-articulate, manipulated maternal flesh on which the text is founded ("Master," "meteoric idiom," "womb," "pilgrimage,"

Molly/mother). Implicit in Loy's poem is a critique of Joyce's deployment of the racialized body/voice of Molly Bloom. As Cheyette points out: Molly, in the final "Penelope" section of *Ulysses* "is constructed so as to deliberately reproduce and redouble the ambivalent Semitism of the previous chapters" (1993, 231); "she gives full expression to the racial and sexual other-world which supplements the dominant Christian discourse" (232). This may be radical in terms of Molly's potential to disrupt the closure of fixed subjectivity. However, Joyce's strategy, of instating the female *body* as the site on which a cultural and textual "utopia" can be founded, serves to reinforce the reductive association of the (jewish) women with carnality and the body. Loy, acutely conscious of the construction and exploitation of Woman and women,[6] as well as of her own feminine position, reveals the problematics of Joyce's gendered, raced vision.

Loy's poem "Joyce's *Ulysses*" was written at the time that she was exploring and rewriting her own past, including her own ambivalent identification with jewishness as represented for her by her father (who had died in 1917). Loy's jewishness, particularly when she took her own childhood and background as her subject matter, came to acquire a metonymical function in her explorations of identity and artistic expression. In works such as *Anglo-Mongrels and the Rose,* in the unpublished novels *Goy Israels, Islands in the Air,* and *The Child and the Parent,*[7] and elsewhere, Loy examines the semitic discourses of British culture and makes her own use of the dominant (mis)conceptions of jewish character and identity. While participating in racial generalizations, Loy does offer a sharp critique of the relationship between imperial British, capitalist, consumer society and the immigrant jew, and identifies her (fictive) self with her father's jewish sensibilities and estrangement.[8]

The long poem *Anglo-Mongrels and the Rose* appeared in parts in the *Little Review* (1923–24) and in the 1925 *Contact Collection of Contemporary Writers.*[9] In its attack on contemporary cultural degeneration and critique of imperial England the sequence inhabits similar terrain to the contemporaneous work of Ezra Pound. Loy's use of language ("logopieia"), assonance, and her snatches of quantitive verse also connects *Anglo-Mongrels* to Pound's poetry.[10] However, unlike *Hugh Selwyn Mauberley* or *Homage to Sextus Propertius,* Loy's critique is not predicated upon a privileged individual consciousness asserting itself within society; her epic opens with the epitome of the dispossessed and displaced individual, the inside-outsider of Western culture—Exodus, a Hungarian Jew:

> Exodus lay under an oak-tree
>   Bordering on Buda Pest   he had lain
>   Him down   to over-night   under the lofty rain
>   of starlight
>   having leapt from the womb
> eighteen years ago   and grown
> neglected   along the shores of the Danube
> on the Danube in the Danube
> —or breaking his legs behind runaway horses—
>   with a Carnival quirk
>   every Shrove Tuesday.

(Loy 1923, 10)

The equivocal opening of *Anglo-Mongrels* establishes Exodus as both a heroic individual and a figure of ridicule; Loy reproduces the assumptions of Western culture in which the jew is the antithesis of heroism but also, through the very irony of her identification of/with Exodus, she undermines the complacency of the structure of cultural consolidation and individual identity. Offering to replace the heroic individual with a poetry of the alienated and dispossessed, *Anglo-Mongrels* explores the possibility of an outsider aesthetic founded upon the uncertain space of textual and racial ambivalence. The central character Ova—the artist as a young *girl* whose portrait this is; the offspring of "the alien Exodus"—is a "mongrel-girl" of "Noman's land" (Loy 1925, 150). Through the sequence that, like *Tristram Shandy*, starts before the protagonist's conception, Ova begins to formulate an "Opposed Aesthetics" (the title of the sixth poem), one in which Beauty is not the sole domain of a genteel, imperial tradition. And Ova's vision of "moon—flowers out of muck" (Loy 1925, 150) inextricably emerges from the mis/dis-placement effected by her interpellation in British culture through her mixed jewish heritage.

It is in the first poem of the sequence that Loy depicts most fully the "construction of the jew" through the figure of Exodus. As suggested above, Exodus is represented as both heroic and ridiculous, and the fusion of these two extremes, at the opening of *Anglo-Mongrels* for example, highlights his inherent/inherited ambivalence. Exodus is heir to a legacy of language and science, a realm of secrecy and power which connects him to his distinguished paternal origins.[11] He is also, however, disinherited by his father's death and his mother's remarriage, consigned to a spiritual and material poverty and oppression:

> Sinister foster-parents
> who lashed the boy
> to that paralysis of
> the spiritual apparatus
> common to
> the poor
> The arid gravid
> intellect   of jewish ancestors
>   the senile juvenile
>   calculating prodigies of Jehovah
>   —Crushed by the Occident ox
>   they scraped
>   the gold gold golden
>   muck from off its hoofs—
>
> (Loy 1923, 11)

Loy depicts Exodus's spiritual paralysis and his foster parents' own ignorance as the necessary results of social and economic oppression by the "Occident ox"; they are the products of capitalism. The "prodigies of Jehovah" are *allowed* (required) to deal in money and finance, the necessary underside of Western culture. As a result, the jewish population appears culpable of their own ostracism and jews effect their own repression of racial instinct and heritage; they deny their intellectual legacy (as this might mark their difference) and accept their only possible role as (ostracized) businessmen. The duality of this internalization of the contradictions of semitic stereotypes is reflected in the oxymoronic rhyming phrases "arid gravid" and "senile juvenile."

Exodus's subdued intellectual heritage and spiritual instinct emerge in a distorted form, in the alien environment of England, as a mastery of "business-English" (Loy 1923, 13), an interest in painting, and an obsession with financial calculations and with his own physical body. The link between these facets of Exodus's character and his place as dispossessed immigrant is made clear. His mastery of "business-English" and finance is directly linked

with a desire to "read" the adopted culture and so gain control
(presented as a masculine interpretation of arcane symbols) of his
cultural context (gendered feminine):

> speaking fluently   "business-English"
> to the sartorial world
> jibbering   stock exchange quotations
> and conundrums of finance
> to which   unlettered immigrants are instantly
> initiate
>   Those foreigners
> before whom   the soul
> of the new Motherland
> stands nakedly incognito
> in so many ciphers.
>
> (Loy 1923, 13–14)

As becomes clear later in the sequence, Exodus's position in society, although one of extreme alienation and horrific abasement
to his English Rose (and through her to imperial England),
remains that of man and father. He thus retains control over two
crucial (symbolic) areas of life. Exodus embodies the power of linguistic signification in "The Surprise" where he plays a trick on
Ova and then designates her a "Liar" (Loy 1925, 177). He also
demonstrates and asserts his dominion over material wealth in
"The Gift" where the "sovereign" he gives/is to Ova proves only
to be a "new farthing" (Loy 1925, 182).

In contradiction, the other aspects of Exodus's character—"He
paints / He feels his pulse" (Loy 1923, 17)—are much more tenuous and instinctual, and are connected to a vital and ineffable
force, a potential source of disruption of imperial, material hegemony. Exodus perceives his pulse as "a beating mystery" (12),
and works "at leisure / painting knowing not why / sunflowers
turned sunwards" (14). These interests are aesthetic and spiritual
in nature, and are not connected with the desire to control that
underlies Exodus's business acumen; they are aspects of Exodus's
intellectual potential (his creativity) that are inherently linked to
his position as interloper, and encapsulated in the phrase "wondering jew" (15). Loy emphasizes this racial/social-spiritual/
physical heritage as the point at which Exodus and Ova, the
would-be artist, are connected—"Behold my gift / The Jewish

brain!" states the "least godmother" "Survival," at Ova's birth (Loy 1923/24, 50).

However, Exodus's impulse towards art and his own physical consciousness fall victim to the cultural climate of England and become incorporated into the overwhelming desire for control and mastery. His aesthetic instinct becomes acclimatized into an acceptance of symbolic worship of the Ideal Feminine, embodied in the "English Rose." At the same time Exodus attempts to overcome the fact of his "alien" status, his inability to make "contact" with his adopted culture, by focusing on his body:

> —becomes   more tangible to himself   the exile
> mechanism   he learns   is built
> to the same osseous structure   shares
> identical phenomena   with those
> populating the Island.
>
> (Loy 1923, 17)

Thus, Exodus's artistic potential is subsumed into an *adopted* culture of neurosis and obsession that serves to regulate the spontaneous individual and implicate him in a dualistic system. As Sander Gilman points out, the assumption that Jews were racially prone to neurosis (often linked to their urban "nature") had gained scientific status so that "[b]y the 1880s the linkage of the Jew with psychopathology was a given in anthropological circles" (Gilman 1986, 288). But Exodus's "psychopathology" is not natural; it is the product of his cultural situation wherein he can only exist as "body":

> The only
> personal reality
> he brought from Hungary   he takes
> to Harley street   where medicine
> sits   the only   social science   applied to the outsider.
>
> (Loy 1923, 17)

It is the "English Rose"—ideal femininity/idealized nation— that imperial England offers as the object and solution of self-introspection, the means of transcending the contingencies of circumstance. But the complete possession and control of the "English Rose" is as unrealizable, for Exodus, as complete self-possession. Loy highlights how such idolatry (of the female, of the English "motherland") controls and contains the aspirations of the displaced individual, offering as a surrogate for an unobtainable ideal the assuaging illusion of (masculinist) possession and control. Ultimately, alienated from his jewish lineage and context, Exodus's only hope of mastery in an alien country, and hence existence as an independent *man*, is to possess knowledge of the material fact of England, or to possess the incarnation of England—his choices are money or sex:

> Exodus knows
> no longer father
> or brother
> or the God of the Jews,
> it is his to choose
> finance or
> romance of the rose.
>
> (Loy 1923, 18)

Clearly, as *Anglo-Mongrels* demonstrates, this reduction of humanity to a system of exploitation (whether of the body or the "surplus value" of goods) is as damaging to (English) women as it is to the jewish immigrant. The ambivalence of Exodus's eventual compromise is clearly demonstrated in his reduced power; his is initially a "lying-in-state of a virility" (Loy 1923, 13), but he ends up "despised" and "ostracized" (Loy 1925, 194). Exodus's (paternal) control over language and commerce is small compensation for a fundamental dispossession and denial. Despite his attempts to elide his alien status he is, as jewish-outsider, almost inevitably identified with the body, the feminine, the other, and rejected:

> The gently born
> they turn away
>
> from the tailor
> Who knows?
> "Man that is born of woman"
> Perhaps he chose
> an occupation all too feminine
> ___ ___ ___ ___ ___ ___ ___
>
> (Loy 1925, 194)

The ambiguity of Exodus's character, with his tentative won-
dering/wandering finally subsumed by his internalization of and
capitulation to patriarchal authority, is indicated in the biblical
resonances of his name which encapsulates the doubleness of
this father figure. The book of *Exodus* is about exile, displacement, wandering, and the hope of freedom and spiritual renewal,
and also depicts the establishment of Mosaic Law, the epitome
of patriarchal social organization. Similarly, the arcane mystery
and virility of Exodus (as jewish immigrant and as Hebraic text)
is amalgamated into a restrictive and divisive culture—jewish
ambivalence is compromised and contained in a dogmatic, hierarchical system of ownership and obedience.

In its depiction of Exodus, *Anglo-Mongrels* also demonstrates
how the ambivalence of "the Jew," which imperial English culture fixes within contradictory stereotypes, returns to destabilize
the certainties of the narrative of Englishness and identity. As
tailor, Exodus represents and reveals the constructedness of all
culture and identity.[12] He is the disavowed other that constructs
the Christian self/Christianity. The modern "gentleman" is his
fabrication, rather than Ruskin's "pure gens." He is the manu-
facturer of modernity:

> And there arose another
> greater than Jehovah
> The Tailor — —
> — — the stitches of whose seams
> he is unworthy to unloose
>
> Out of the hands of Exodus
> the Oxonian
> seeming
> a sunbeam that has chanced to stray
> into a cut—away
> (Gentlemen
> wear
> clothes
> with an easy air
> of debonair
> inevitability)
>
> Clothed and shod
> the tailor's concept of the man made God

(Sartorial peril of the yellow race
looking so out of place)
peoples the sod — —[13]

(Loy 1925, 193)

There is a clear equivocality to *Anglo-Mongrels'* depiction of jewishness; it is the source of Ova's displacement which thus creates a space of alterity for her immanent aesthetic. But also, in Exodus, *Anglo-Mongrels* reveals the complicity of "the Jew" in an oppressive and exploitative patriarchal capitalist economy. That Exodus gains the illusion of "control" by being co-opted in this way does not detract from the text's clear critique of the father's collusion in the commodification of identity and desire.

Anglo-Mongrels and the unpublished texts such as *Goy Israels* do deploy stereotypes of "the Jew" and do deal, to a greater or lesser extent, in a racialism which has its origins in nineteenth-century pseudoscience. But throughout her explorations of her past and jewish heritage Loy exposes jewishness as the contradictory construct of the Occident—the product of an attempt to fix and contain radical and ambivalent racial and cultural forces which persist in exceeding and undermining such attempts at control.

The impossibility for Loy of ever fully identifying with/through the jewish father as Outsider and interloper in Western culture is a matter of gender relations, rather than an "internalized anti-Semitism" (as Loy's biographer Carolyn Burke claims, [1996, 375]). That is made clear by a key moment in the (unpublished) *Islands in the Air.*[14] In this epiphanic moment the protagonist encounters her paternal great-grandmother and achieves a revelation of identification in the nomadic embrace of a female, jewish ancestry:

> In the pantomime a beneficent apparition declares "I am your . . . fairy God-mother," — — — "Urgrossmutter," gasps the most crude perhaps of all realities, an aged woman, appearing as if from nowhere to totter towards me on superannuated tiny sinewy feet. She also has the starkness of images and is covered with black brocade and bugles, all fringed and lacy; a bonnet encloses her head in a crescent and is tied under her chin with almost that violaceous shrill proper to Episcopal silk.
>
> She is so thin, so straight. The copious wave of her jet black hair might be that of a doll who is kept in a drawer. Before her noble nar-

rowness her tremulous hands spired as if in prayer as she peers at me unpoint and part to patter upon my face, and raising the vessels of these tears that fall on me, in praise to Iahweh, she chokes, "Mein schönes Kind."

At once a bestowal and a reception the unctuous schön in the unvanquished croon of an ancestry over its foredoomed offspring soothes me and swathes me for once in the nomadic embrace. A fallen fledgling I am picked up and the aching quills are redressed. (*Islands in the Air*, chapter 6, "Disappearances")

This moment is not simply one of racial recognition: the oxymoronic phrase "nomadic embrace" suggests the momentary revelation of a "raced" becoming that has not been fixed into this or that stereotype. In the same way that *Anglo-Mongrels* appropriates the Wandering Jew, outcast prototype for British culture from Maturin's *Melmoth the Wanderer* to Joyce's *Ulysses*, and transforms him into the unsettling "wondering" jew, the "nomadism" evoked here appears as a rewriting of the dispossession and homelessness of the jew. Neither migrant nor exile, the "nomad does not stand for homelessness, or compulsive displacement; it is rather a figuration for the kind of subject who has relinquished all idea, desire, or nostalgia for fixity" (Braidotti 1994, 22). Rather than deficiency or loss, then, this nomadic embrace, can be read as a "re(ad)dress," a homecoming without a home that simultaneously discovers and multiplies identity.

If the supposed "lack" of jewish nomadism is transformed into an excess of identification, this excess also extends into the "gift" that the jewish great-grandmother bestows, very different from "The Gift" given in poem seventeen of *Anglo-Mongrels:*

The eyes we instantly recognize are those in which we find ourselves instated. These of the ancestress, swallows disorientated in migration dipped to captivity under the arch of her brow have flown onto my face looking up into hers as she bestows upon me an even greater dower than compassion: the right to choose; for pointing to the window of the little sweet shop she asks me a question I have never heard, "What would you like?"

So, as I watch her sere beauty in return to a puzzling exile fade, retrogressive as age, into the fog, my hands are holding a bag of iced biscuits molded with rose and citron sugar stars. (*Islands in the Air*, chapter 6, "Disappearances")

This gift, which incurs anger on the protagonist (for buying and eating sweets on a Sunday), is clearly an unconditional act of giving, one which the narrative of *Islands in the Air* links to the death (in a fire) of the great-grandmother a short time later. There is a corollary in "Jews and Ragamuffins of Kilburn" (the thirteenth poem of *Anglo-Mongrels*) a poem which details Ova's first encounter with anti-semitism. Told by her Nurse that "the Jews killed Jesus / and are bound for Hades / with r—o—u—n—d noses" (Loy 1925, 170), Ova nevertheless identifies with the "common children" of Kilburn, struggling to free a girl who has her leg trapped between iron railings. The poem ends, in characteristic wordplay, with Ova's recognition that outside bourgeois, Protestant respectability lies the possibility of nonrational consumption:

> The common children
> Have the best of her
> —though dressed in
> rags—They feed on muffin.
>
> (Loy 1925, 174)

In a similar way the great-grandmother's gift of forbidden food suggests a transgression of the capitalist demand for the utilitarian deployment of resources. This demand, projecting and maintaining identities within the rigidity of economic predeterminism, is described by Bataille as a *"restrictive* economy" in opposition to which he poses a *"general* economy" of "unproductive glory" and the squandering of excess (Bataille 1991, 25, 23). For Bataille "in a world of material abundance . . . the rational—according to the principle of balancing payments—use of material and spiritual goods [does] not leave room for a radically different form of consumption—namely wasteful expenditure in which the consuming subject expresses himself" [*sic*] (Habermas 1985, 222–23). To step outside the rational, restrictive system into useless, transgressive consumption (wasteful excess which mirrors that of ritual sacrifice) is to free subjectivity from the bondage of objecthood.

The question "what would you *like*" and the bag of iced biscuits can therefore be read as acts that take the female protagonist of *Islands in the Air* and her jewish great-grandmother beyond the domination of rational economic necessity that would make them objects (the economic rationality that co-opts and objectifies "Exodus"). Their shared nomadic consciousness is a form of "resisting assimilation or homologation into dominant ways of representing the self" (Braidotti 1994, 25): the excess of the "gift" allows for the expression of a kind of sacred intimacy that is engendered from the blatant disregard for rational necessity. Both of these possibilities can be read as a substantiation of the multiplicity of "the jew" who, in Loy's textual explorations, escapes attempts to fix and exploit her difference.

NOTES

1. A focus on Loy's racial heritage, moreover, suggests interesting parallels to another British, "jewish" woman poet who, like Loy, settled (both physically and aesthetically) in America: Denise Levertov. Levertov's own interest in Loy's work is exemplified by her piece "Notes of Discovery" in Loy's collection *Lunar Baedeker & Time-Tables* (Loy 1958, 14–16). The other contributors to the prefatory section are William Carlos Williams and Kenneth Rexroth.

2. Manuscript held in the Mina Loy Papers, Yale Collection of American Literature, Beinecke Rare Book and Manuscript Library; hereafter cited as YCAL.

3. See "Autobiography/Auto-mythology: Mina Loy's *Anglo-Mongrels and the Rose*" for an explication of this term (Goody 2000).

4. Although some contact with Anglo-Jewry in suggested in Loy's unpublished autobiographical work: fragments of the autobiographical *Goy Israels* make mention of childhood socializing in Jewish circles (*Goy Israels* c. 1930s, Mina Loy Papers, YCAL), and the eight-year-old protagonist of *Islands in the Air* is enlightened about sex and racial identity by a jewish holiday friend who explains how "Jews get babies the same way as Christians" (*Islands in the Air*, chapter 7 "Ethics & Hygiene of Nightmare," Mina Loy Papers, YCAL).

5. It is possible, however, that the reference to "Stephen" parallels Joyce's own use of this name as an allusion to St. Stephen, the prototype of the Christianized Jew. What is clear is that the term "hybrid" plays an important role in Loy's later *Anglo-Mongrels and the Rose* whose protagonist is an Anglo-Jewish hybrid or "mongrel" (see below). "To You" is discussed in greater detail in Goody 2001.

6. As expressed in a range of work from the 1914 "Feminist Manifesto" onward; see Burke 1985, Arnold 1989, and Augustine 1989 for a discussion of Loy's "feminist" awareness.

7. These three autobiographically based novels, which probably date from the late 1920s to late 1930s, are all at different stages of completion and are held in the Mina Loy Papers, YCAL. *Goy Israels* is a fragmentary, mostly handwritten account of the youth and adolescence of "Goy" and her family the "Israels"; *The Child and the Parent*, in two different typed manuscripts, describes the earliest experiences of an infant protagonist and the "pre-history" of her Vic-

torian parents; *Islands in the Air*, two versions in typescript, describes key moments in the life of the protagonist from her first memory to her year in Munich studying art. In each manuscript the protagonist is the daughter of a jewish father and an anti-semitic, repressive mother.

8. Jaskoski explores some of the racial resonances of *Anglo-Mongrels*, making an interesting case for Loy's use of the legend of Ahasuerus and for parallels with Joyce (Jaskoski 1994). Her reading complements that undertaken here.

9. The text given in *The Lost Lunar Baedeker*, ed. Roger Conover (Manchester: Carcanet, 1982) draws on the first published version of the text and the text given in Loy 1958. For full details of the variations between different published version of *Anglo-Mongrels and the Rose* and a critical edition of the sequence, see "Appendix: *Anglo-Mongrels and the Rose*" in Alexandra Goody, Mina Loy's Modernist Aesthetic, (PhD dissertation, University of Leeds, 1997).

10. Pound's championing of Loy's verse has been well documented, see for example Burke 1987. Loy also "celebrates" Pound's achievment in her 1925 article "Modern Poetry," reprinted in Loy 1997, 157–61.

11. While this suggests that Exodus may have privileged access to a kabbalistic tradition, his status as Eastern-European immigrant clearly designates him as Ashkenazi; Molly's lineage in *Ulysses* is apparently Sephardic.

12. See Schaum 1986, 274–75, for an overview of the "many and intriguing "echoes of Thomas Carlyle's *Sartor Resartus*" in Loy's sequence.

13. Keith Tuma reads *Anglo-Mongrels* somewhat differently, seeing this last poem as a "discursive statement of the theological issues at stake in the entire poem" (Tuma 1998, 199). In his interpretation, "[T]he tailor—whom we might read as a figure for secularized Christianity, for Freudianism, or just simply as modernity—has remade humanity, but he also denies us, or at least that part of us which is spiritual" (201).

14. Mina Loy Papers, YCAL.

"The link of common aspirations": Wales in the Work of Lily Tobias

Jasmine Donahaye

LILY TOBIAS WAS BORN IN YSTALYFERA IN THE SWANSEA VALLEY IN 1887. Her father had emigrated from Poland to England in about 1876 and, following his brother to Wales, established a shop in the tin-plating and coal-mining town of Ystalyfera. Although he was an educated man in the Jewish tradition, his wife was religious, traditional, and suspicious of non-Jewish culture. The reading of secular literature was not encouraged in her home and, to evade her mother's strictures, Tobias and her sister Kate, the future mother of Leo and Dannie Abse, had to resort to reading in the toilet (Abse 2000). In the period, mandatory schooling ended at age fourteen and as a consequence the education that Tobias received was minimal. The language of the community around her was predominantly Welsh, but that of the school system in Wales was English, while at home Tobias's family spoke Yiddish. Although she and her siblings were all Welsh speakers, she had no formal education in the language.

Tobias grew up in a time and a place of accelerated social and political change. The industrial exploitation of Wales resulted in intense economic and social distress and Ystalyfera was a fulcrum of political activity at the western edge of the coal field. The Welsh language pacifist poet Gwenallt and the socialist painter Vincent Evans both attended school in Ystalyfera, and the influential left-wing and predominantly Welsh-language paper *Llais Llafur/Labour Voice* was published in the town between 1898 and 1915. It was in this environment that Tobias was politicized. Her writing was supported by her husband, Philip Vallentine Tobias, whom she married in Swansea in 1911, and it was encouraged by the radical editor of *Llais Llafur*. It was reputedly in this paper that she published her first story (Abse

147

2000).[1] In the 1920s she and her husband lived in the tenants' cooperative of Rhiwbina, which was a small but vibrant enclave of radical politics in Cardiff (Peate 1976, 84–99; Abse 2000).

Although Tobias was a founding member and president of the Cardiff women's Zionist organization and a lifelong Zionist, Wales and Welsh concerns were central to her political awareness. Three of her five books are set in Wales, and her last two novels, which were written after she had left, include significant Welsh components. Her earliest story, "The Nationalists," explores "the link of common aspirations" between the Jewish and Welsh protagonists Leah and Idris, and the majority of stories in the collection *The Nationalists and Other Goluth Studies*, in which it appears, take place in Wales and draw parallels between Welsh and Jewish culture (1921, 15). So, too, does her first novel, *My Mother's House*, which was published in 1931. Her second novel *Eunice Fleet*, published in 1933, is based on her experiences as a pacifist assisting conscientious objectors in Swansea and Cardiff during the First World War, and is located in a carefully coded Wales with Anglicized place-names. One of the subplots of her third novel, *Tube*, explores the class tensions experienced by a Welsh cabinet minister, while her last book, *The Samaritan*, which was published in 1939, takes up some of the cultural comparisons made in *My Mother's House*, to which it is a sequel.

This collection of work shows elements of both Anglo-Jewish literature and of Welsh literature in English, but the political concerns that arise from her dual cultural background distinguish her work from any other. In the period, for example, Welsh women's writing in English consists largely of central characters who, according to Jane Aaron "frequently identify with and feel most at home with natural rather than human phenomena," and most of whom "one way or another . . . are alienated from the human communities in which they dwell" (Aaron 2000, ix). While many of the characters in Tobias's work are alienated from the communities in which they live, it is an alienation that Tobias uses to make arguments against attempted assimilation, and where the natural world appears in her work, it is as a background to an examination of complex social relationships. Unlike the "view across the valley" of the women identified by Aaron, the view of many characters in Tobias's fiction is limited by their position *in* the valley. Indeed in her first novel *My*

Mother's House, the protagonist Simon strains to see the town of Swansea in the distance. Swansea, later Cardiff, and finally London become the focus of his longing for urban life and the greater opportunities for Anglicization and social elevation that he believes it offers.

Tobias's fiction is written in a style typical of the period: it is polemical and often didactic, which can be something of a barrier to a modern reader. This didactic style of writing and her limited formal education perhaps bring her closer in kind to the working-class socialist writers of industrial south Wales who, during the 1920s and 1930s, according to Aaron, "characteristically wrote of and for the human communities from which they sprung, expressing and identifying with the struggles of the working class" (2000, x).

However, while Tobias wrote somewhat parenthetically of these communities, it is not clear that she wrote for them. Her work was published by London presses, which is part of the reason why she has until recently been overlooked in Wales. In the absence of supporting evidence, identifying an intended audience is speculative, but the fact that the Yiddish in her writing is translated might suggest that her intended audience—or the audience intended by her publishers—was not solely a Jewish one, despite the predominance of Jewish concerns in four of her five books. On the other hand, an intended audience of Welsh speakers certainly cannot be deduced from the fact that the Welsh dialogue is *not* translated. Whether intended or not, this lack of translation has the effect of highlighting and reinforcing for an English and an Anglo-Jewish readership the distinctiveness of the Welsh context of her writing.[2]

Regardless of this intended audience, the central concerns of Zionism, Welsh nationalism, and pacifism distinguish her work from that of other working-class members of the Anglo-Welsh generation of writers, although it shares something of their didacticism and internationalist socialism.[3] Unlike the coal miner heroes of *Cwmardy* and *We Live* by Lewis Jones, for example, the hero of her second novel, *Eunice Fleet*, is a teacher. Nevertheless, he uses some of the same idealistic socialist rhetoric as the characters of Lewis Jones, indicating the rhetorical environment in which Tobias grew up and, presumably, some of her literary influences.

While the stories and all four novels are structured around thwarted romantic relationships, these relationships are thwarted by the political differences of the lovers. Unlike the conservative agenda of middlebrow writers in the '20s and '30s who sought to restabilize society between the wars (Bracco 1993), her work attempts to politicize her readership and argues for radical social change. It is in the service of these arguments that her romantic relationships are deployed: thwarted love can only be resolved through the political enlightenment of the beloved (whether a man or a woman), and romantic love can only flourish with the growth of political engagement that results from such enlightenment.[4]

Her writing could therefore be categorized as political or propagandist, using the positive connotation that the word "propaganda" had when she was first publishing her stories. In the pages of polemical journals such as the *Zionist Review*, the organ of the British Zionist Federation, where many of her early stories were published, or in the *Labour Leader*, which was the organ of the Independent Labour Party, "propaganda" included lectures, pamphlets, membership and subscription numbers, as well as literature. The success of "propagating" the political message of the journals was listed in each issue. Between 1917 and 1923 *The Nationalists and Other Goluth Studies* was the only book promoted by an insert and order form in the *Zionist Review*, which places it firmly in this "propaganda" category, and suggests its significance in Zionist circles.[5] Indeed in the introduction that Leon Simon wrote for the book he presents the work as propaganda in this positive sense:

These sketches come as something new in kind. Zionist literature is rich enough both in reasoned argument and in emotional appeal. But here is neither argument nor pleading, but just a presentation of the way in which the Zionist spirit gets hold of Jews of various kinds, lifts them in some degree out of themselves, gives them a new sense of pride and dignity and responsibility, and makes them feel that to be a Jew is worth the cost. And this imaginative and sympathetic presentment of the Zionist idea at work among people such as we meet every day, can do as much for the Zionist idea as the reasoning of the philosopher or the eloquence of the platform orator.

Simon qualifies his assessment of the work by observing that he is of course being "unfair to Mrs Tobias in writing of her sketches as though they were merely so much Zionist propaganda. Yet not so unfair as might appear. For the best propaganda literature is that which stands on its merits as literature. . . . It is because these sketches are well done as sketches, . . . that they can help the growth of the Zionist idea" (Simon 1921, 9).

The interest of this collection is not solely a Zionist one, however. The cover depicts a Welsh dragon intertwined in a Star of David, and in a review of the book Paul Goodman recognizes the significance of this joint political concern: "Mrs Tobias has introduced us to a new *milieu,* for Welsh Nationalism, unknown to most of us, has had its effect on her, blending harmoniously with the Jewish Nationalism with which Mrs Tobias is so deeply imbued. Those of us who only England know are struck by the self-assertion of Welsh Nationalism in its own home" (Goodman 1922, 161).

It is unfortunate that the only republication of work by Tobias before 2004 appears in an anthology whose editor dismisses its literary value in an introduction that is marred by inaccuracies (Davies 2002, 216–18).[6] These political sketches are important examples of the comparison of Welsh and Jewish concerns in Tobias's work (Donahaye 2001), but the most fully developed use to which she puts Wales occurs in her first novel *My Mother's House.* Vera Coleman describes *My Mother's House* as presenting "as well as the spiritual pilgrimage of the protagonist, a panorama of contemporary Anglo-Jewry, portraying with penetrating psychological insight its various political, religious and cultural milieux" (Coleman 1989, 759–60), but she overlooks the significance of its Welsh location and concerns.

The narrative follows the political evolution of the protagonist, a Welsh Jew named Simon Black who, to adapt queer terminology, is politically "brought out" by the idealised Zionist heroine Edith. The relationship between these two has its parallel in several stories and two other novels: one member of the romantic couple is politically informed and engaged, and "brings out" the apolitical other, raising him or her to political awareness and awakening political passion.

Edith, the Zionist, is beautiful and elegant, and is sensuously and almost erotically described. Clearly an ideal, she propounds on social, Jewish, and Welsh cultural and political matters in occasional set pieces that reflect positions taken by Tobias in articles such as "Jewish Women and Palestine," which was pub-

lished in 1919. In contrast to her somewhat flattened characterization, Simon is depicted as a complex and engaging if unsympathetic character, in whom Tobias has perhaps invested some of
her own unconscious or sublimated conflicts.

The novel opens in the early years of the twentieth century in
a fictional Welsh village, Blaemawe, which is a thinly disguised
Ystalyfera, where Tobias grew up. A ten-year-old Simon sees for
the first time a blonde English gentry woman who has stopped at
his father's picture-framing shop. More importantly, for the first
time Simon hears gentry English. From the beginning of the book
Tobias mocks his attitude to language. Until this moment he has
only heard Welsh, Anglo-Welsh, and the Yiddishized Welsh and
English of his parents, and this exposure to *English* English
causes a kind of linguistic epiphany: "Wings had sprouted in
Simon's ears, and were bearing him up—up to the ceiling on a
rushing air of delight . . . the accent—the accent was sheer revelation. For the first time in his life Simon heard English perfectly
spoken by an Englishwoman" (7).

This experience, which sensitizes him to his own linguistic
environment, results in an intense Anglophilia and a contempt
for Jewish culture and for the Welsh milieu in which he lives:
"That Welsh women should speak English badly was, to him, a
matter of indifference: that his mother should speak it badly,
and in the presence of an English lady, was anguish and morti-
fication in the extreme" (8). The impact on his attitude to Yiddish is unequivocal: "The other horrid tongue, already impa-
tiently endured, only now suggested itself to him as a factor in
the mutilation of the true speech," and it is only his father's
"soft, pleasant voice" that can minimize that "most disturbing
of jargons" (9).

This childhood experience initiates the pursuit of an entirely
assimilated *English* identity, in which Simon rejects Judaism, his
parents, and the Welsh culture in which he has grown up. Here
Tobias expands on the class and cultural conflicts of second generation Jews in Wales that she had first sketched in the story
"Glasshouses" (1921). In 'Glasshouses' she uses a metaphor of
greasiness and contamination to convey the insecurity of these
children of immigrants, struggling with the pressure of dual
assimilation to Welsh society and to English society. With Simon
she portrays a full range of subtle social tensions both within the
Jewish community in Wales and between Jews and their host

community. She also compares the social aspirations of Simon and his Swansea cousins with those of the Anglicized urban Welsh who similarly dismiss their cultural heritage in pursuit of an English identity.

Having succeeded in casting off both Jewishness and Welshness, and having acquired middle-class English friends and a civil service job in London, Simon finds that he is still uneasy, for "the dislike and distrust of the Jew that he had taken for granted, where provoked by distinctive habits, were as deep, he found, when these obvious agents were lacking" (349). Despite his ability to pass as a Gentile, he finds he cannot put his Jewishness behind him for he had "not realised how keenly his consciousness of his race would persist when he abandoned all connection with it" (349).

Although the unredeemed self-absorption and boorish insensitivity of Simon and his parochial social aspirations are foregrounded for didactic reasons, his need for insider acceptance becomes something pitiable and tragic rather than contemptible. When he meets Edith, with whom he falls in love, the consequences of his attempted assimilation are brought home to him for, as he discovers, she is not the idealized Englishwoman he thought her to be. To his great discomfiture he finds that she is not only Jewish but also an ardent Zionist. Worse, she places a high value on the Jewish religious tradition from which he has so categorically removed himself (although it is not for religious but national cultural reasons that she values the tradition).

Edith suffers a fall from grace when Simon discovers her Jewishness: "Something of glory had vanished from his world. The halo round Edith Miller's head was gone. It was no longer possible to worship in her a perfect English goddess" (194). Nevertheless, this fall from grace is nothing compared to that which Simon suffers when he reveals to her his contempt of Judaism: "I despise you. I think you're a coward," Edith informs him. Summing up the didactic message of the book, she continues: " It seems to me a despicable thing for a Jew to turn his back on his own people. . . . his first duty is to keep faith with his race. I can't endure the Jew who's ashamed of it, who pretends he belongs entirely to another" (240–41).

Her outright rejection of Simon precipitates a crisis in which, during a return to the Swansea valley, he becomes involved with his childhood friend Jani. As the daughter of a Seventh Day

Adventist Jani, like Simon, had been excused at school from religious study. Their friendship had been reinforced by a shared outsider status, for Jani was an immigrant from the Welsh settlement in Patagonia and was mocked at school for the old-fashioned Welsh she spoke.[7]

Simon brings Jani to London where he eventually marries her, but her irredeemable Welshness soon becomes a burden to him, and the indicators of her nationality and class a social liability that he tries repeatedly to correct and change. Both he and Jani are socially alienated, fractured, and ill at ease: London intimidated Jani's "essentially rustic soul" and "was a desert without the personal human tie" (316). Having cut himself off from family and Jewish acquaintances, Simon's slow acquisition of English friends is fraught with an acute awareness of his Jewishness, while Jani is patronized in society for her "quaint" Welshness.

It is Jani who regains a kind of integration by connecting with the London Welsh community and, through it, reconnecting with her own traditions, religion, and language. Finally she leaves with their mutual childhood friend Ieuan, and at this juncture Simon meets Edith once again. The experiences Simon has undergone have by now moderated his attitudes to Zionism, if not to religious Judaism—he has read Disraeli with sympathy and understanding, and is now more receptive material for Edith's evangelising Zionism. However it is not until the beginning of the First World War, when he enlists in the Jewish brigade and goes to Palestine as a more integrated Jew, that Edith accepts him. They marry, and the book ends with him being shot by a sniper shortly after.

The disharmonious complexity of Simon makes him rather than Edith the most fully realized of Tobias's characters, and her most interesting one. That it is he who is drawn with psychological depths, rather than the political mouthpiece Edith, suggests that the dilemmas experienced by Simon perhaps reflect a sublimated longing for assimilation and Anglicization on the part of Tobias which, through his example, she can reject.

A similar complexity is evident in the layered writing of an early scene in the book when, as children, Simon and Jani are to go berry gathering.

> Simon seized a jug from the dresser, heedless of Mrs Black's cry from the scullery,—"wait—wait—not that one! I'll wash the milk jug."

"Bother!" said Simon, impatient to be off. "I'll take care of this one, mother —

He knew she prized the piece of rainbow ware, brought home with other trophies from his father's last "sale." Simon thought its crude glitter ugly, and despised its conservation as ornament. Of course, his mother's regard for it was half fear of pollution,—might not the jug have held impure fats—lard, or soap, or trifa gravy?" (36)

When Simon and Jani are set upon by a group of hostile children from the next village, the jug is broken. This breaking of an unkosher vessel perhaps foreshadows his marriage out to Jani, but more interesting is the irritable response of Simon to his mother's fear of unkosher contamination. The small detail of the jug is a resonant one, not only by virtue of its symbolic narrative value, but also by virtue of the cultural anxiety with which it is invested: the jug captures both the uncertainty of the immigrant in a non-Jewish environment, and the tension between first and second generation immigrants over such anxiety. In addition, the realism of the scene is also of cultural historical interest, suggesting as it does that Jews in Wales imitated Welsh custom in decorative dressers, which tradition itself has complex social and class meanings (Vincentelli 1994). The fact that this image is evidently indigenous to Tobias informs its effectiveness.

In this scene and indeed throughout the book Jani is depicted as a fiery, passionate, and impulsive character, repeatedly referred to as "kittenish" and as a red-haired "sprite." However, if this depiction of Welshness as a force of nature suggests the influence on Tobias of Matthew Arnold, Ernest Renan, and the Celtic Twilight,[8] her portrait of Ieuan, the childhood friend of Jani and Simon, is more politically sensitive (even if her efforts to render his Welsh English are awkward). When Simon finds him playing truant from school, and protests the importance of education and of getting on—a social pressure on Welsh and Jewish children alike—Ieuan responds: " 'not me,' . . . spitting, like his collier parent did. 'I ann't going to any of those dam' things. I'll pass the labour exam. all right next time, and then I'm going down the pit.' " Simon argues with Ieuan about learning "proper" English, but Ieuan sees no need: "whaffor? . . . My dad don't care tuppence about English—I can talk proper Welsh. I'm a Welshman." Simon replies: "Well, I'm not," to which Ieuan drawls "no-o. U arr a Jew," but continues "but never mind about that, mun. You're as good as me, ann't you?" (18).

Tobias is careful to distinguish between overt antisemitism and this observation of difference that Ieuan makes. In *My Mother's House* and throughout her work she attributes antisemitism almost exclusively to Anglicized Welsh people who dismiss the Welsh language and mimic English ways. By doing so she implicitly compares their less than admirable social aspirations with the aspirations of Anglicized Jews such as Simon and his cousins, who similarly distance themselves from their traditions. In *My Mother's House,* for example, while attending the County School in Dawport (a fictionalized Swansea), Simon is attracted to a popular blonde girl from Devon.[9] Reluctantly, she reveals that she is in fact from Pembroke. However, according to her, "Pembroke's not real Welsh, you know—thank goodness! I hate everything Welsh. It's so frightfully common! . . . a mean, snivelling lot, aren't they?" (60). When Simon doesn't treat her to the level of luxury she expects, she dismisses him as "a mean, stingy beastly Jew!" (64).

In contrast to the antisemitism expressed by the Anglicized Welsh, among the Welsh-speaking Welsh the Jews are welcomed: "Merch annwyl,"[10] exclaims Christmas Jones in the story "Glasshouses," "and proud I am to meet you, for sure. Why, I do love the Jews, indeed I do. You are the people of the book and the Lord will show His wonders through you yet" (1921, 46). As the Jewish protagonist of the story struggles to come to terms with her tenuous social status, it is Christmas Jones who brings her to Zionist awareness: "You have got a big job in front of you my gell," he tells her: "the return to Zion" (46). Indeed her conclusion, at the close of the story, is that "if there was a Jewish country, one wouldn't have to worry" (49).

The appreciation of the Jews as the "people of the book" expressed by Christmas Jones is repeated several times in the stories and in *My Mother's House,* where Jani's father proclaims the Jews "the best people in the world" (35). It is also echoed by Tudor Watkins, a Welsh official in Haifa who appears in *The Samaritan* (38–40).

These positive attitudes to Jews that Tobias attributes to the Welsh-speaking Welsh, although clearly "philosemitic," need qualification. While Rubinstein and Rubinstein define philosemitism as "support and/or admiration for the Jewish people by non-Jews" and regard it as "the other side of the coin of anti-Semitism" (1998, 5), this does not adequately account for some of the contradictions within philosemitism that are illustrated in the work of Tobias. For example, the case of Christmas Jones indicates that the philosemitic sentiments attributed to the Welsh can be millenarial, although they are by no means exclusively so. As millenarianism anticipates the conversion of the Jews, this does not sit easily within the Rubinsteins' definition. Bryan Cheyette provides a more nuanced discussion of "semitic discourses" (1993, 8) while David Cesarani claims:

> The term antisemitism is as problematic as the subject itself. It is preferable to speak of a discourse about the Jews which operates through stereotypes that can be either positive or negative depending upon the intention of the agent employing them, something which can be deduced by careful attention to the context in which they are used . . . Discourse about Jews is of ancient provenance, deeply rooted in western Christian culture and pervasive. So-called philosemitism is part of this stereotypical system. (1998, 255)

This discussion perhaps accounts best for the range of Welsh attitudes to Jews presented by Tobias. Her construction of the antisemitic attitudes of the Anglicized Welsh, in their juxtaposition with similarly anti-Welsh and anti-Jewish attitudes among Anglicized Jews, warns on the one hand of the dangers of deracination. On the other hand, in her construction of the philosemitic Welsh—and, indeed of "philo-Cymric" Jews, such as Edith —Tobias argues that international sympathy and understanding arise not from delocalized internationalism but from an engagement with cultural particularity. As Idris argues in "The Nationalists": "Only a national life can restore self-respect to a people . . . and bring out the best that is in them. The noblest idea is to serve one's people." His Jewish opponent Israel retorts: "The noblest ideal is to serve humanity. . . . Nationality is narrow. Art is universal." But Tobias gives Idris the last word: "I have read somewhere," he responds, "that fire burns brighter when you narrow the draught. The genius of your race would shine brighter in concentration, and so serve humanity too" (1921, 20).

The "Goluth" in the title of the collection in which this story appears refers as much to the social disruption, migration, and dispersion of the Welsh, and the belief Tobias has in the consequent need for Welsh political autonomy, as it does to the Jewish Diaspora and the need for a Jewish state. This construction of Welsh culture, combined with what Tobias suggests is the

futility of either Welsh or Jewish aspiration to an English identity, implicitly serves as a critique of Britishness, despite the fact
that her vision of a Jewish homeland relies on a British imperial
model: "The idea was to create a home, a motherland, which
would be to the Jew what the mother-country was to the colonial Britisher. A centre from which every member of the race
would draw dignity and self-respect" (1931, 492).

There is an important historical context to the construction of
the philosemitic Welsh in Tobias's work. She is responding in
part to a long-standing tradition in Welsh culture of identification with biblical Jews, which can be traced back as far as Gildas
in the sixth century (Llywelyn 1999; Llwyd Morgan 1994). The
more recent expressions of that tradition involved a widespread
positive predisposition towards contemporary Jews and, in the
twentieth century, resulted in supportive attitudes to Zionism
(Donahaye 2002; Davies 2003). In addition, under the influence
of the *Cymru Fydd* ("Young Wales") movement for Welsh political autonomy, and the near attainment of Home Rule before the
First World War, one could speculate that there did not exist in
Wales the same accusation of divided loyalties against Jews as
existed in England (Henriques 1993). There was certainly not the
same pressure on Jews to demonstrate their "British," which is
to say their *English*, patriotism. The fact that the uptake of Zionism was greater in Wales than in England was perhaps a product
of these circumstances (Henriques 1993, 37). Certainly the first
two books written by Tobias suggest the cultural context for this
discrepancy.

The cultural and political nationalism of late Victorian and
Edwardian Wales, as well as the growing internationalist socialism of south Wales were clearly influential in forming the Zionist beliefs espoused by Tobias. Her Zionism was also influenced
by George Eliot, upon whom Edith, with her similarly part Welsh
background, might be modeled.[11] Indeed Tobias co-wrote a
dramatized version of *Daniel Deronda*, which was produced in
1927 at the Q Theatre and starred Sybil Thorndyke.[12] Though
Tobias read Israel Zangwill and was evidently influenced by
Ahad Ha'am, her attitudes to language—and her equal espousal
of Yiddish and Hebrew—are distinct from theirs. This can, I
believe, be attributed to the particular linguistic environment in
which she came to political consciousness.[13]

In many places her vision of Zion constitutes one of world peace rather than a vision of a national home for the Jews. In 1920, for example, in an article entitled "Zionism and Militarism: Some Other Considerations" she writes: "The authentic voice of Israel pleads for 'Peace—Peace—Peace.' It is not for us to hush a single note of that compelling cry. For, unless we fulfil its message on the soil of Palestine, we shall be false alike to the most vital teaching of our past, and to the greatest present need of racked mankind. We shall have neither gained the world nor kept our souls" (90).

This pacifism was informed by the First World War, and by the conscription of her brothers and their conscientious objector status in 1916. Her second novel, a socialist pacifist polemic entitled *Eunice Fleet* draws on her wartime experiences in the Swansea Valley and Cardiff, when she assisted conscientious objectors.[14] In *Eunice Fleet* her observations about the war and about the moral and political positions of those imprisoned, tortured, and sometimes killed for their beliefs, remain highly topical. The novel also provides a personally informed depiction of the activities of the Independent Labour Party in Wales and England, and narrows the gap in knowledge about Welsh women pacifists during the war years (Beddoe 2002). However the novel is not only a polemic. Like the psychological development of Simon Black in *My Mother's House*, that of the title character, Eunice, makes compelling reading. Through her experience of romantic and political betrayals she develops from a self-involved and apolitical social reactionary into an unequivocal pacifist.

The relationship between the socially conventional Eunice and the martyred conscientious objector hero, Vincent, has its parallel with the political "bringing out" of Simon by Edith. In *Eunice Fleet*, Vincent tries and fails to convert the self-involved Eunice either to socialism or pacifism. When he is imprisoned for refusing to serve in the army, Eunice rejects his political commitment to conscientious objection, aborts their baby, and refuses all contact with him, despite reports of his illness and mistreatment. It is not until after his martyrdom that she comes belatedly to share his pacifist vision.

Eunice Fleet is internationalist in its polemic and although large sections of the novel are set in Wales, its cultural specificity is minimized. The location is heavily Anglicized and coded, and specifically Welsh and Jewish responses to the war, by which Tobias herself was politicized, are parenthetical to the narrative. As a consequence the novel loses some of the literary power that the complexity of her own world might have offered her. Possibly Tobias delocalized the setting and reduced overtly Welsh and Jewish markers in order to make her pacifist message more palatable to an English audience. It is also likely that this Anglicization arose out of a desire not to provide anti-Jewish or anti-Welsh ammunition to British patriotic opinion (Donahaye 2004). Nevertheless, the location of historical events and characters in the novel, as well as her own experience in south Wales during the war, give a particular cultural slant to this response to the war.

With her third novel, Tobias returned to an overtly Jewish theme. This is once again juxtaposed with a Welsh concern. *Tube*, published in 1935, is an experimental and not entirely successful novel. Set in about 1933 or 1934, the narrative follows the experiences and fantasies of Angela, a country girl hungry for city life who has just arrived in London. She observes people traveling on the London Underground, three of whose stories, imagined by her, constitute the subplots to her own. Elements of her own life—books she has read and conversations with colleagues—are woven into these stories, and the characters appear in one another's stories as well.

One of these narrative subplots concerns a Welsh cabinet minister who comes to the realization that by marrying into the gentry he is betraying his political and working class roots in industrial south Wales. The second subplot concerns a young German woman who has been tortured by the Nazis; she has been rescued by Quakers and her Jewish fiancé has been imprisoned or killed. The third subplot, which is the dominant and most successful section, concerns an assimilated Anglo-Jewish woman named Gracie and her encounter with the Portuguese Jew Pedro. Pedro, who is interested in the history of Portuguese Jews and the Inquisition, brings Gracie to an awareness of her ethnic history, and their relationship is similar to the protagonists in Tobias's other novels.

Gracie, the name of the protagonist, points to the debt the book owes to *The Vale of Cedars* by the nineteenth-century Anglo-Jewish author Grace Aguilar. Indeed Tobias indicates that Angela has been reading both this book and the *History of the Inquisi-*

tion in Spain by H. C. Lea (1901). Gracie is brought to Pedro's ancestral home, where she undergoes a dream vision or psychic experience in which her forebear Gracia is betrayed to the Inquisition by her servants. There is the suggestion of eroticism in the extended attention given to the torture Gracia undergoes, which is powerfully written. Unfortunately much of this is not the work of Tobias, but has been lifted almost verbatim from the transcript of torture experienced by Elvira del Campo, a historical victim of the Inquisition, which would have been available to Tobias in Lea's *History*.[15] In a letter to Leo Abse in 1945 Tobias claims that Cecil Roth, whom she knew, had read and appreciated *Tube*, but it is likely he would have recognized this material.[16]

The martyrdom of Gracia echoes that of other protagonists, such as Vincent in *Eunice Fleet*, Simon in *My Mother's House*, Idris in "The Nationalists" and Eva/Una in two unpublished play versions of *Eunice Fleet*.[17] However the most overt use of martyrdom occurs in *The Samaritan: An Anglo-Palestinian Novel*, which was the last book that Tobias wrote. In the mid-1930s she and her husband had moved to Haifa in Palestine and the book was almost finished when her husband was killed in a riot in 1938. The novel was published a year later and its dedication reads "in memory of Philip Vallentine Tobias Who fell in Palestine . . . A Sacrifice to the ideals that inspired this book."

The novel is a sequel to *My Mother's House*, and opens in Palestine in about 1926. Musa, the mysterious Samaritan of the title, is a distinctly Christ–like figure, and offers what seems to Tobias to be an authentic, original Judaism. In "Zionism and Militarism" she had observed that in Palestine "we Jews have to unlearn the perversions of the un-Jewish world in which we are steeped" (1920, 90) and she appears to find in Samaritan culture just such a Judaism uncontaminated by the Diaspora. Musa describes his people as "the remnant of Israel, that has never left the land—that has guarded the ancient ways of Jew and Arab with faith and fidelity—in the mountains of Samaria" (313–314). His solution to conflict in Palestine would be for Arab and Jewish peoples to fuse. He dies a martyr to that cause, and his death at the end of the novel echoes other narrative deaths and ambiguous closures by Tobias: "Jews and Arabs were standing together, brothers with heads bowed in a strange truce, the sons of Israel and the sons of Ishmael. The corpse of a murdered policeman lay in the dust at their feet. And between them, hostage or deliverer, was borne the body of the Samaritan" (320).

Like her other books, *The Samaritan* contains a significant section set in Wales, in which it is Musa who notes the difference between Welsh and English cultures, and in which once again Tobias compares Welsh and Jewish concerns: "The change of speech struck his keen ear. He had learned already that another race inhabited the British principality that was once a separate kingdom. . . . he burst into a spate of questions. Had the Welsh merged into the English? Did their common tongue supersede the Celtic vernacular? Were their institutions, their system of religion and education, identical? Was there complete political equity?" (178). While he is astonished to see that "the little dark people are just like Jews" (178) and disappointed that the Welsh language does not resemble Hebrew, Edith (whom the reader first encountered in *My Mother's House*) is shocked by what she finds in Wales, and is "overwhelmed by the confirmation of all she had heard of its economic stress. . . . Everywhere was evidence of a stagnant and derelict life. Docks were idle, pitheads deserted, factories and workshops closed, furnaces extinguished. Men stood about in queues at labour exchanges, and at gates where any job was offered. Others sauntered hopelessly about the streets, or leaned in apathetic silence against walls. Melancholy towns and still more melancholy villages were full of anxious and disheartened faces" (179). With this description of the desperate conditions that existed in Wales in the '30s, Tobias indicates that after she left she retained her connection with Wales and with the particularity of Welsh experience. It is the particularity of this culture that, throughout her work, provides her with a comparative context in which to place her primary concern with Jewish experience. Her work, which until recently has been virtually unknown, reveals much about Welsh-Jewish experience that has been overlooked, in particular the class tensions that existed within the Jewish community in Wales. It also highlights the significance of the relationship between Jews and other minority cultures, and the role that this relationship can play in the formation of Jewish humanitarianism. It is almost always in the context of similar struggle in Welsh culture that she examines the Jewish struggle for recognition and autonomy, and it is both her Welsh and Jewish cultural backgrounds that inform her vision of and hope for international peace.

Notes

1. As *Llais LLafur* does not identify authors, this story is hard to locate with confidence. W. H. Stevenson, the editor of *Llais Llafur*, asked Tobias to join his staff at the second paper he edited, the *Daily Voice*, and this event is fictionally reproduced in her 1935 novel, *Tube* (Samuel 1958).

2. C. W. Daniels, who published her collection of stories, published radical and pacifist works, and hence the potential audience for this book would have been a political one. I am grateful to Claire Tylee for this observation.

3. For the distinction between "Anglo-Welsh literature" and "Welsh literature in English" see Meic Stephens, ed. (1998).

4. This makes her work not entirely dissimilar to that of Ethel Mannin, although Mannin's style and use of the popular romance form differs from hers. See Andy Croft (1993).

5. It appears in the December 1921 issue, vol. 5, no. 8

6. The piece in question is "The Outcasts," published first in the *Socialist Review* and subsequently in her collection *The Nationalists and Other Goluth Studies.*

7. The Welsh community in Patagonia was established in the mid-nineteenth century as a form of Welsh Zion under the leadership of Michael D. Jones.

8. See Mathew Arnold (1861), *Lectures on Celtic Literature*; Ernest Renan (1854), *Essai sur la Poésie des Races Celtiques.* See also Meic Stephens, ed. (1998) for a discussion of the Celtic Twilight with respect to Welshness.

9. The Welsh are traditionally seen as being dark—e.g., see *The Samaritan*, 178. Similarly in the character of Edith, blondeness and Englishness are equated.

10. "Dear girl."

11. However, it is also possible she is modelled on Kathleen Manning, later Lady John Simon, to whom the first book is dedicated.

12. The co-writer was Linda Lewisohn. Excerpts were published in the *Jewish Quarterly* in 1975. Edith can be compared to Daniel Deronda himself for, raised in a gentry home, like him she must reclaim the Jewish identity and Jewish side of her family that has been denied to her. In a more metaphorical way, like Deronda she saves a Jewish soul, and her idealized fusion of English socialization and Jewish background is, in many ways, similar to his, as is her commitment to the Zionist cause.

13. See J. Donahaye (2001) for discussion.

14. Republished by Honno Press 2004. Originally published in 1933 by Hutchinson & Co.

15. It is quoted in Sachar's *Farewell España* (1994, 171–72).

16. October 11, 1945. Leo Abse archive, National Library of Wales G/a/168.

17. These plays are in the possession of the author and the family of Lily Tobias.

Denise Levertov and the Poetry
of Multiculturalism

David Fulton

Denise Levertov (1923–1998) has been variously called an English poet, an American poet, a Jewish poet, and a woman poet, thereby reflecting the fluidity of a cultural identity that resisted neat categorization. She was certainly a woman, who wrote poetry, yet she, like Elizabeth Bishop, rejected any gendered description of herself as a writer because women's concerns, either traditional or feminist, were not, she felt, at the center of her work. In any case, she argued, poetry resisted all categories that were extraliterary: "a poet is a poet, a poem is a poem" (*PbW*, 99).[1] She can be said to be English to the extent that she was born in suburban Ilford and went through most of her formative experiences in Essex and London before immigrating to America as a GI bride in 1948, but neither of her parents was English, her father coming from Russia and her mother from a Welsh-speaking part of Wales. ("British" would be more satisfactory in its inclusiveness were not the label itself problematic.) Her first collection, *The Double Image,* was published in London in 1946 and Kenneth Rexroth subsequently welcomed the young writer to America by selecting her for his 1949 anthology, *New British Poets,* a welcome that involved a firm reminder of origins; yet little more than twenty years later he was claiming Levertov as an American poet who had helped change the course of postwar American verse. She did indeed become an American citizen in 1955 and wrote much poetry about her adopted country in the native objectivist style, yet not only did her free verse retain the greater intonational flexibility of British English in a way analogous to Thom Gunn's, but the source of her poetic imagination also remained stubbornly British. This commitment to origins is reflected in her pronunciation: recordings of poetry readings show that she retained an English way of speaking throughout

her life, the only concession to America being—as with Auden—
the introduction of a flat æ/ae/ sound for the longer Southern
English /a:/; but whereas Auden, despite his early communist
sympathies, always spoke in the received tones of the ruling
class, Levertov preserved in her speech a slight hint of the prole-
tarian East End.

With a name like Levertov one might expect a Jewish connection, an expectation sharpened by the way the poet plays with its
"Hebrew" connotations in "To Kevin O'Leary, Wherever He
Is"—"entrance, exit, / way through" (F, 26)—and indeed her
father, Paul Levertoff, was a Jew, though he converted to Christianity in his early twenties, eventually becoming an Anglican
priest. In any Orthodox assessment Denise Levertov would be
considered non-Jewish not merely because of her father's final
religious affiliation, but, more crucially, because her mother,
Beatrice Spooner-Jones, was a Gentile. Yet the subtle ways both
Judaism and the secular tradition of Jew as political radical
inform her work allow us to insist on her status as Jewish poet.
Levertov herself expressed the belief passionately, if somewhat
prosaically, that not just her father, but she and her mother too
were in some sense Jewish:

> As a devout Christian, my father
> took delight and pride in being
> (like Christ and the Apostles)
> a Jew. . . .
>
> My Gentile mother, Welsh through and through,
> and like my father sustained
> by deep faith, cherished
> all her long life the words
> of Israel Zangwill, who told her,
> "You have a Jewish soul."
>
> I their daughter ("flesh of their flesh,
>   Bone of their bone"). . . .
>
> (OP, 33; T, 142)

Jeni Couzyn chose Levertov for *The Bloodaxe Book of Contemporary Women Poets* (1985).[2] She tried to show how apt her
choice was by selecting pieces that, according to Couzyn, made
Levertov seem prefeminist, pieces like "The Mutes" on catcalls,

or "The Ache of Marriage" on the way women choose a wedded state, "however joyless," as "the only alternative to being swallowed by the deep" (Couzyn 1985a, 19). Yet even in these seemingly committed examples a quietly contrary perspective can also be heard: the woman of "The Mutes" is "disgusted" by the catcalling, but at the same time recognizes it as, in some sense, a "tribute" to her attractiveness (SD, 46–47); an institutional weight in "The Ache of Marriage" does lie heavily on the woman, but that repressive force seems inextricably bound up with a sacramental sensuality, which holds within it the potential of spiritual transcendence:

> The ache of it:
>
> thigh and tongue, beloved,
> are heavy with it,
> it throbs in the teeth
>
> We look for communion. . . .
>
> (OTS, 5)

Selections like these, even when their polyphonic nature is conceded, fail to do justice to the complexity of Levertov's position. Men can feature as dumb harassers and—primarily in the shape of her husband, Mitchell Goodman—difficult beings with whom to negotiate personal relationships, but they can also be thrilling in their otherness and can, in fact, be accorded a support sometimes denied to fellow women. "A Psalm Praising the Hair of Man's Body," for instance, celebrates Mitch's black "fleece of silk" and her son's dusting of dark hair; while "Hypocrite Women" stigmatizes wombs as "dark and wrinkled and hairy, / caves of the Moon" that are "not for the eye" and accuses women of dishonestly suppressing the suspicion that their genitals are ugly (OTS, 82, 70). Similarly, in her memoir of wartime work for the Essex Civil Nursing Reserve she writes: "I found more to admire in men as patients than in women. Men usually are neighbourly to each other, and help the overworked nurse as much as they can" (LUC, 254). She even reduces the classical myth of three female Fates, spinning the thread of each individual existence, to masculine monotheism by substituting a Christian God, weaving "the great garment" of Life (OP, 72).

Against this absence of female solidarity, however, can be set "A Blessing," in which two women writers empower each other through mutual support, or "The Showings," where Dame Julian of Norwich's mysticism is vigorously defended against implicitly male suggestions of "neurosis" (*BW*, 13, 70–75). In representing her family, Levertov manages to produce individual poems of intense engagement with her father, husband, and son, yet she displays a much more sustained interest in the female side. There is, for instance, no verse about its male members to equal the powerful sequence of extended lyrics on the decline and death of her mother in *Life in the Forest* (1978) or the three substantial elegies on her elder sister, Olga, in *The Sorrow Dance* (1967). Indeed Olga dominates the whole of that volume from its opening page, which dedicates the collection to her "memory," through "A Lamentation," the first of the elegies, which lends its central metaphor to the title of both section and book, until the final two pages, which contain an elegy on her father written by Olga herself. Nevertheless, as if to prevent any persistent pattern of sisterly support from establishing itself, Levertov published "A Young Man Travelling," in which, by allowing her narrator access to the man's mind only, the poet is able to coax us into seeing the group of three women as frank and spontaneous, yet ultimately insensitive, exclusive, and merciless: when they add the man to their number, they refuse to make the slightest adjustment for his gender (*LF*, 18–19).

Marital union can be burdensome and restrictive for women, yet it does not have to be, as "About Marriage" makes clear: while "wedlock" does, as its name suggests, contain the danger of "lock[ing]" the woman "in," it can also free her through a mutually respectful, unrestricted meeting with the man "in a green // airy space" (*OTS*, 68–69). Indeed marriage does not prevent a relationship from becoming so close that a couple, like Levertov and Goodman, can be figured as "Siamese twins," unsure whether they can "survive" separation (*FD*, 66). Even after divorce, the poet can continue to portray marriage as a dignified institution: though discarded in a basket, her wedding ring cannot be given away or sold because it retains its talismanic power as an emblem of "solemn betrothal" (*LF*, 99).

Levertov likes to subvert the "chauvinism" that says women, being nonpoetic themselves, can only participate in poetry as "Muses or servants" (*PbW*, 98–100). She tends to overturn this stereotype by making her own muse male: he is the romantic "hero" on horseback, who, while inspiring the woman writer with his colorful visit, only functions, after his departure, as a creative trigger: when "she begins to write," it is "not of him" (*CB*, 67); or he is an angel who will wrestle her, like Jacob, into prophetic utterance (*DH/ET*, 58). Another strategy is to set the ungendered muse within a domestic environment: thus the muse in "To the Muse" becomes an ever-present, though not always acknowledged, guest in a writer's house (*OTS*, 25–27). In contrast to this protofeminist maneuvering, however, Levertov can present her verse in traditional female terms—one sequence, for example, which was issued as a pamphlet (1969), is called "Four Embroideries"—and she can assign men and women within her poetry hackneyed gender relations: "Abel's Bride" shows man going "out alone on his labors," while "woman" stays behind worrying about him, though it is the worry of the socially assured for the naive (*SD*, 13); and the woman in "Song for a Dark Voice" regards her lover as "taller . . . than the ten / towers of Jerusalem" with strong "arms," which "hold me from falling" just as God's " 'everlasting arms' " in "Suspended" seem to uphold her "leaden weight / from falling," although the speaker, fixed "in the void," cannot feel them (*JL*, 23; *DH/ET*, 210). Yet these stereotypes are in their turn contradicted by "Stepping Westward," in which the poet refuses to conform to the clichéd characterizations of women as either "inconstant" or "true," and "Relearning the Alphabet" where she relishes the imagination's ability to reverse established gender roles: "In childhood dream-play I was always / the knight or squire, not / the lady: / quester, petitioner . . . not / she who was sought" (*SD*, 15; *RA*, 110–20).

Levertov's American, objectivist poetry might suggest a traditional femininity with its domesticated marital saga, its parade of chores in rooms, gardens, or shops, and habitual perspective on the outside world from an apartment window; but these gendered specifics are subsumed beneath the act of perception: what remains crucial is that she is making scrupulously exact notations of metropolitan New York just as William Carlos Williams is of Paterson, and not that her sensory apparatus is female and his is male. Similarly, when during the sixties she begins to write political poetry about American policies in Vietnam or during the eighties commits herself to Christianity, it is as engaged cit-

izen or individual soul rather than as woman that she does so.
She is aware the institutions of politics and religion could be
called patriarchal, but makes an issue of the perception in less
than a handful of poems scattered through more than twenty volumes. Thus "Watching TV" blames "our wretched history" on
"men," "not the worst of them, / the brutally corrupt," but "others" whose "likeable eyes" are contradicted by "weak, cruel,
twisted" mouths; while "Salvator Mundi: Via Crucis" inserts
into a meditation, which seems to find no difficulty in the male-
ness of the Godhead's earthly incarnation, the slyly subversive
interpretation of an unmarked pronoun as female: Jesus with his
unbearable "burden of humanness" is "like any mortal hero out
of his depth," but also "like anyone who has taken a step too far
/ and wants herself back" (*DH/ET,* 172, 206). Generally, however,
sexual politics are avoided in favor of a wish to be categorized in
terms other than those of gender, a wish evident as much in the
criticism as the verse:

> I do not subscribe to the idea that "women's poetry" is a special *lit-*
> *erary* category. . . . It is a *social* category; and . . . only *that* as long as
> the present social condition continues. . . . The case is somewhat dif-
> ferent for the new Black poets, because most of them are . . . far more
> concerned with Black culture and struggle as *subject* than are most
> women poets with the oppression or . . . nature of women *as subject.*
> There are of course many poems being written about what it feels
> like to be a woman, but though these are . . . of interest to the social
> historian and . . . psychologist, many of them are of little or no aes-
> thetic interest, and are often written by people who are not poets at
> all but . . . are "using" . . . verse, to "express themselves" or propa-
> gandize. (*PbW,* 99)

Feminist critics, when commenting on Levertov, cannot help
betraying a sense of disappointment, a sense that she let the side
down not only in her choice of viewpoint and subject, but in her
stylistic allegiances as well. Suzanne Juhasz and Linda Kinnahan,
for example, place Levertov within a modernist tradition, running from imagism through objectivism to the Black Mountain
School, a tradition which they characterize as forbiddingly masculine. It is a line of writing, Juhasz declares, which "many
women have found alien, or, in the present tense of feminist
poetry, destructive, oppressive" (Juhasz 1976, 62). Poems of this
tradition generally start promisingly in the female zone of per-

sonal "particulars," but then in a typically male manner open out into an "objectifying, abstracting, and generalizing" of "subjective experience" (62). The result is a cold masculine poetry of "distance," which fails to satisfy the female need for sympathetic "involvement . . . in self and others" (82). Juhasz's argument begs a number of questions. If H. D., Amy Lowell, Marianne Moore, Muriel Rukeyser, Lorine Niedecker, and Denise Levertov were all imprisoned within a style that repressed their gender, why does their writing exhibit so little discomfort? Is Juhasz not, as she herself surmises, falling back on the oppositional stereotype of emotional women, drawn to "the immediate, sensual evocation of . . . personal, private experience" (74) and intellectual men, who prefer abstract universals? (Admittedly, Kinnahan rejects Juhasz's simplistic characterisation for the more flexible notion of Levertov's writing exhibiting a constant and complex shift between various "subject-positions"—"poet, wife, mother, immigrant . . . Jew" and so on [Kinnahan 1994, 129].) If we adopt Juhasz's terms of reference, are we not forced to view imagism and objectivism as in some sense feminine in that they are, when true to their original ideals, content to stay with an individual's sense reactions, refusing to generalize from these into abstract thought and feeling?

Young poets have always learnt their craft from older ones, sometimes directly by means of an informal apprenticeship, but mostly indirectly through study and imitation of the older writers' works. What feminist critics seem to find particularly galling is that Levertov made the demeaning choice of a man for her teacher. When she could have contacted Moore or Rukeyser to be instructed in the strategies of American poetic modernism, she turned instead to William Carlos Williams and wrote to him so frequently that their collected correspondence has been published in a separate volume (MacGowan 1998). Although she ultimately rejects the idea, Juhasz is not surprised other critics have stigmatized Levertov as that androgynous thing, "a 'female Williams'" (Juhasz 1976, 61). Kinnahan, on the other hand, presents Williams as father to Levertov's "literary daughter," having "poetic authority" over her in the same oppressive way a traditional father has over his daughter (1994, 125, 127). She sees Levertov's poetic journey as one from this authority's implicit "masculine assumptions," of which the most significant was an isolating "individualism," to a female authority, which foregrounded the sense of "community" (128, 147–49). This is a strange argument to apply to a poet who ended up accepting, however reluctantly, the masculine assumptions of Protestant theology. It could also be objected, more generally, that American poetic modernism's repudiation of collectivist for individualist solutions was more an expression of economic base and class than gender.

Although Rachel Blau Duplessis characterizes Levertov as a liberator, who breaks through the old genteel barriers of women's poetry by using—and thereby reclaiming—obscene, sexist language and by confronting shocking subject matter, most female commentators on Levertov find her insufficiently feminist (DuPlessis 1985, 123–24). To Juhasz, the poetry exists in an unrealized, "transitional" state, containing "both the dominant masculine and the emerging feminine traditions" (1976, 61). The quotation's penultimate adjective is particularly damning: in its refusal to concentrate on "feminine . . . themes and forms," Levertov's verse is not even fully "feminine"—let alone " 'feminist' " (57). Later in her analysis Juhasz reveals the full extent of the problem: "Poems that describe experiences that are specifically feminine do not form the majority of Levertov's work: I have made a list of thirty poems from the seven volumes, containing hundreds of poems, that I am discussing" (68). This paucity of material has driven some critics to desperate measures, the most amusing of which is probably Kinnahan's attempt to read Levertov's sequence of children's poems, "Pig Dreams: Scenes from the Life of Sylvia," as an allegory of her experiences as a woman poet "in a male tradition" (173). Thus Sylvia's "fraternal" relationship with her brother pigs reflects Levertov's with the Black Mountain poets, John the "Catpig," for instance, being the homosexual Duncan. The choosing of Sylvia as a pet by the "[hu]man world" represents the way Levertov the "p[o]et" found acceptance in an implicitly patronizing, masculine poetic world (176). Sylvia's porcine id, however, finally rebels against this male repression of female experience: in "Her Nightmare" she dreams a Freudian dream of blood, which stands for "the blood of menstruation and birth" (177). These strained interpretations, based more on wishful thinking than solid textual evidence, merely reflect how difficult it is to sustain a feminist reading of the poet's work.

Levertov's status as Jewish poet seems as difficult to assess as that of woman poet. Her verse reflects how much Judaism meant to her as a system of beliefs that has produced distinctive cultural forms, yet when it deals with specific religious practice it is generally the Anglican ritual of her childhood the poet summons up.[3] It therefore comes as no surprise that it was to Protestantism that Levertov returned in old age after a life of secular struggle. "The Opportunity" celebrates a dreamed reconciliation with her dead father that is both personal and doctrinal:

> Much has happened, over the years,
> many travels.
> In the world,
> in myself.
> Along the way,
> I have come to believe
> the truth of what you believe.
>
> (DH/ET, 160)

Nevertheless, that belief, though primarily Protestant, should not be interpreted too narrowly for Paul Levertoff was, in his daughter's words, not simply a "fervent Christian," but also a "learned Jew" (PW, 77), trained in an Orthodox seminary, holder of a chair in Rabbinics at the University of Leipzig, and "part translator" of the Cabalistic books of "The Zohar" (SP/BN, 440). He was, in particular, vitally connected with that mid-eighteenth-century, East European variety of the Jewish faith, Hasidism, as a descendent of the "the noted Hasid, Schneour Zalman," who is anonymously commemorated in "Illustrious Ancestors" as "Rav / of Northern White Russia" (SP/BN, 440; CEP, 77–8). Levertov has said of the Jewish tenor of her early years: "My father's Hasidic ancestry, his being steeped in Jewish and Christian scholarship and mysticism, his fervor and eloquence as a preacher, were factors built into my cells even though I rarely paid conscious heed to what, as a child, I mostly felt were parts of an embarrassing adult world, and which during my adolescence I rejected as restrictive" (DLW, 75). However, in America during the fifties she began to feel "a renewed interest . . . in the Hasidic ideas with which I was dimly acquainted as a child" (SP/BN, 441). Hasidism expresses at once a "joyful affirmation of life" and "a sense of mystical ecstasy in the communion of God and man" (Newman 1987, lvii). This tension between acceptance and transcendence of physical limitation is perhaps best embodied in the

Hasidic notion of dance, which can signify legitimate pleasure in the body, as in the wedding dance, but also pleasure at leaving the body in death. While a storm was threatening to sink his ship, Rabbi Moshe Leib of Sasslov "engaged in a joyful dance." When asked why by Rabbi Schmelke, he replied, "I am overjoyed at the thought . . . I shall soon arrive at the mansion of my Father." (Newman 1987, 67–68). "In Obedience" pictures Levertov in her New England garden performing her own dance of "joy" that is also one of grief, for her father, "dying" in London:

> ... into whose eyes
> I looked seldom enough, all the years,
> seldom with candid love. Let my dance
> be mourning then,
> now that I love you too late.
>
> (*CEP*, 67–68)

The joy she refers to comes not so much from the classical dancing, which she studied for four years in prewar London (*LUC*, 244–53) and which takes the student through the sweat and pain of exercises to—in the words of "Dance Memories"— "the joy of leaping," which, "while it lasts," is "the deepest, the only joy" (*RA*, 60), but more from a dance firmly rooted in Jewish tradition. "It was only later," Levertov has written, "I learned . . . my father rose from his bed shortly before his death to dance the Hasidic dance of praise" (*PW*, 70). Olga Levertoff, the elder sister who tricked the poet into taking ballet lessons (*LUC*, 244), is commemorated in "A Lamentation" for performing a lifelong dance of "*Sorrow*," a dance which recognizes the Jewish "autumn birthright" of suffering and "grief," a dance the poet herself wilfully ignored while she concentrated on her own dance of "Summer" (*SD*, 52). However, the primacy of Olga's performance is signaled by the title of the volume in which the poem appears, *The Sorrow Dance* (1967), and by its final selection, a poem by Olga herself called "The Ballad of My Father," in which she extends the meaning of Paul Levertoff's dance into a joyful rebuttal of the tragedy of not just individual extinction, but also the Jewish history of diaspora, persecution, and exile:

> *My father danced a Hassidic dance the day before he died.*
> *His daughters they were far away, his wife was by his side.*

"Yes, from concentration camps, and, yes, from gas chambers:
    from thousand years' ghettos, from graves old and new—
Our unremembered bones come to caper in your drawingroom,
    And join in the death-dance of one holy Jew!"

(*SD*, 93–94)

Olga's mention of concentration camps reminds us that her younger sister defines her Jewishness less in terms of the Holocaust than of Hasidic mysticism. Indeed the poetry only contains one extended treatment of the Final Solution, "During the Eichmann Trial: When We Look Up," and this work is remarkable not merely for its magnanimity—far from being demonized, the accused becomes a focus for empathy ("pitiful man whom none // pity, whom all / must pity if they look // into their own face")—and for its startling detachment: Eichmann's massive failings are reduced almost to an objectivist problem of visual perception; when he saw a crowd of Jews, he did not scrutinize them carefully enough to sense the marvelous idiosyncrasy of each face: "**Here is a mystery, // a person, an / other, an I**"; he lacked, in other words, Keats's negative capability (*JL*, 61–66). The reason for Levertov's signal avoidance of a topic, which, as George Steiner has often remarked, almost destroyed the possibility of poetry for our age, can be found in her poetic credo (1960): "I do not believe that a violent imitation of the horrors of our times is the concern of poetry. Disorder is ordinary . . . hides grow thicker. I long for poems of an inner harmony in utter contrast to the chaos in which they exist" (1959; ed. Allen 1960, 411–12).

She clearly has in mind here confessional poetry's messy extremism—Lowell's *Life Studies* and Snodgrass's *Heart's Needle* were both published in 1959—but she is probably also thinking of the strenuous breast-beating in many Jewish poets, writing on the Holocaust, by which they try to assuage the guilt of surviving. On the single occasion she tackles the problem of guilt directly, "Thinking About Paul Celan," it is significant that although her subject is a German-Jewish poet, whose parents were killed in a concentration camp, she chooses to make the theme both general and contemporary, contrasting her own culpable contentment as citizen, not as Jew, to go on living in a millennial "world / where children kill children" with Celan's exemplary refusal:

Saint Celan,
stretched on the cross
of survival,

pray for us. You
at last could endure
no more.

(*GU*, 58)

In any case, a Wordsworthian assertion of joy rather than self-accusation is her favored mode—"so I do smile," she declares in "Not Yet," "what else to do? / Melancholy is boring" (*RA*, 52)—and when dark thoughts of pain and death impinge, she "force[s] to mind" a more optimistic "vision" (*JL*, 46–47) or, more rarely, like the old man in "Shalom" going down "dark stairs" into the "corridors" of death, expresses the wry, optimistic stoicism of Yiddish tradition (*OTS*, 37). However, after her sister's manic existence ended in 1964, its major issues unresolved, she began to wonder whether her determination to think positively at all times was not a kind of evasion:

Grief, have I denied thee?
Grief, I have denied thee.

(*SD*, 52)

An example of denial can be found in her treatment of the neo-Romantic motif of life as adventurous quest or pilgrimage, which she herself has singled out as the "dominant" one in her poetry (*PW*, 62–86). Only rarely does she allow the reader to glimpse this theme's obverse—life as constant rootless journeying, life as a wandering Jew:

. . . the Old World, the New World, my soul is scattered
across the continents
in the named places and the named and unnamed
shadowy faces. . . .

Levertov presents herself here in "Wind Song" as a "fiery ember, dispersed / in innumerable fragments" (*RA*, 62) and this notion of the unredeemed soul as fragmentary seems to hold an important place in Hasidic thinking. The poet chose as epigraph to *The Jacob's Ladder* a quotation from Martin Buber's *Tales of the Hasidim: Later Masters* (1948): "Rabbi Moshe (of Kobryn) taught: It is written: 'And he dreamed, and behold a ladder set up on earth.' That 'he' is every man. Every man must know: I am . . . one of countless shards of clay, but 'the top of it reached to heaven'—my soul reaches to heaven" (*JL*, [v]). It is easy to extrapolate from this the notion that a modern Jew's existence has been rendered fragmentary by history. This is perhaps why Levertov sees her life in "For Paul and Sally Goodman" as "an egg of colored stones, / half-made, yet the dome of it implied / by the built-up . . . curve of the mosaic" (*RA*, 20) and why she calls the fragmentary, decentered autobiography, in which she has "no pretensions to forming an entire mosaic," *Tesserae* (*T*, [v]).[4]

Though this motif does assert an authentically Jewish dimension to her identity, it simultaneously functions as a means of reminding the reader of the modernist nature of the poet's literary enterprise. In this sense *Tesserae* can, for example, be viewed as deliberately providing an initially confusing, yet ultimately illuminating reading-experience in the manner of Pound's *Cantos*, about which Levertov has written, "the chaotic aspects of the mosaic method began to be comprehensible when I realised that I had all along been standing too close . . . so that all I could see were the chips of stone . . . not the larger design" (*PW*, 252–53).

Israel is never promoted as the place where the fragmented mosaic of Jewish lives can finally find completion. Indeed the sole poetic reference to Israelis suggests that by allowing "so-called Christians" at Shatila to "wreak pogrom" on the Palestinians, "a tribe / anciently kin to their own, and now / concentrated in Camps," they have acted little better than Nazis or Slavic anti-Semites (*OP*, 33).

Levertov's poetry is given an added Jewish texture by the titles of volumes and individual poems (*The Jacob's Ladder, Candles in Babylon*, "Abel's Wife") and by its use of Jewish poetic genres ("Psalm Concerning the Castle," "City Psalm," "Psalm: People Power at the Die-In," "A Lamentation"), although this strategy could equally have been adopted by a Christian poet steeped in the Old Testament. Her developing experience is often interpreted in terms of Jewish religion and history: carols sung in "Christmas 1944" bear "a burden of exile, a song of slaves" (*DI*, 24); her deceptively various existence becomes "all my multitudes, / the tribes of my years passing" (*LF*, 48); to divorce her husband is "to send a lifetime into exile" (*FD*, 54); the painful memory of the dying Lily Bloom, to whom she could bring no comfort as a wartime reserve nurse, is described as a "covenant" by which she is "Living for Two" (*LUC*, 260; *FD*, 55–56); and the apocalyptic sense of how near "the obscene silence" of nuclear annihilation is prompts her to remember (in a style that recalls Shakespeare's Shylock as much as Judaic rituals):

> It was the custom of my tribe
> to speak and sing;
> not only to share the present, breath and sight,
> but to the unborn.
> Still, even now, we reach out
> towards survivors. It is a covenant
> of desire.
>
> (*F*, 34)

Hasidism's religious zeal (its masters are called Zaddikim or "Righteous Ones," its disciples Hasidim or "Pious Ones") and its absolute certainty of the distinction between right and wrong easily led the agnostic daughter of a Hasidic-Christian scholar into political idealism, and the numerous poems Levertov has written about her adopted country's imperial misadventures in Vietnam, El Salvador, and the Gulf certainly have the moral righteousness one would expect of somebody from her background.[5] These political subjects, together with her careful delineations of American urban and rural landscapes, make her verse seem very American, an impression reinforced by their American mode. Shortly after arriving in the States, she was introduced, via Black Mountaineers Creeley, Olson, and Duncan, to the objectivists—not so much to the Jewish adherents (Zukofsky, Reznikoff, Rakosi), though she did later forge a strong friendship with Muriel Rukeyser, but to William Carlos Williams.

Objectivism represented an American reaction to the decadence of a once-dynamic imagist movement: loose free-verse structures were to be replaced by tight "formally . . . extant" ones, constructed from expressive cadences (Williams 1967, 264); fin-de-siècle preciousness had to give way to notations of metropolitan sense impressions, seemingly pragmatic, yet informed by a radiant attentiveness that transfigures the ordinary; the poem was to become once again an image, a series of concrete particulars, unsoftened by abstractly expressed thought or emotion—if poets have to think or feel, they should embody the experience in a presented object: "no ideas but in things," as Williams declared (1967, 264).[6] By adopting the surface stylistic tricks that went with these criteria, Levertov made her verse seem very American—only Tomlinson, Gunn, and perhaps Fisher among the English have seriously engaged with objectivism—but appearances can be deceptive. Levertov tried hard to seem orthodox—she dutifully recorded simple urban particulars; she gave her volumes unimpeachably sensuous titles: *With Eyes at the Back of Our Heads* (1960), *O Taste and See* (1964); she even wrote poems explaining Williams's aesthetic and mourning the gradual silencing through death or debility of "the old great ones" of the imagist-objectivist tradition, H. D., Pound, Williams (*CB*, 59–60; *OTS*, 9–11); but, ultimately, she failed to apply its axioms with sufficient rigor and the reason for that failure can be traced to her joint British and Jewish inheritances.

The problem can viewed in "The Garden Wall" where she cannot be content with the purely presentational—the "bricks of the wall" and the striking color pattern sprayed water makes on them—she must do the readers' job for them and draw the conclusion: "archetype / of the world always a step / beyond the world" (*OTS*, 60). This tendency toward abstraction, which vitiates her political poetry, affects her verse down to the smallest detail: she loves, for instance, images that yoke together concrete and abstract like "skirts of sorrow" or "wall of refusal" (*F*, 35–36) in a manner recalling the Old Testament or a poet like Blake, steeped in biblical rhetoric, but flouting Pound's injunction: "The natural object is always the *adequate* symbol" (Eliot [1918] 1954, 5).[7] In self-conscious repudiation of Pound's ideal of the imagist poet as the sculptor who achieves Gautier's marmoreal hardness, Levertov dismisses the purely presentational approach in her verse for producing works that are mere inert " 'statue[s],' " unable, like the phoenix, to bring themselves back to life (*BW*, 11). Such pieces, according to her, end up as an "inventory" that fails to catch objects' "Gestalt" (*CB*, 59–60; *BW*, 11; *DH/ET*, 136). Elsewhere she enlists Hopkins's inscape to her cause.

This parade of charismatic terms, however, does little to obscure the fact that Levertov did not so much want to reveal the taut inner structure of things as surmount them altogether through poetic vision. Thus her programmatic poem "The Common Ground" starts with two eminently objectivist presentations, signaling poetry's true subject matter: the ordinary (the grass and stones of "the common ground") and the urban (a city square of blossoming trees and office workers gossiping during the "lunch hour"); but the third section repudiates the "'common speech,'" which Williams advocates and she herself manages to smuggle into a number of early poems, in favor of:

> the uncommon speech of paradise,
> tongue in which oracles
> speak to beggars and pilgrims . . .
>
> speech akin to the light
> with which at day's end and day's
> renewal, mountains
> sing to each other across the cold valleys.
>
> (JL, 1–3)

Levertov's one and only English volume, *The Double Image,* was published in 1946 at the end of the New Apocalypse movement and is, like this passage, very much a neo-Romantic product. Levertov's conception here of poetry as prophetic utterance seems to allude to Shelley, just as her collocation of oracles and beggars tries to lead us back to Wordsworth's oracular blind beggar; and the whole passage is typically instinct with Romantic transcendentalism, the urge to leave behind the city's dirt and all-too-human bustle for nature's elevated and ultimately sacred revelations.

This quest for epiphanies, however, originates as much from her mother's Celtic reverence for nature as from British Romantic poetry. Beatrice Levertoff, we are told in "The 90th Year," "taught" Denise "to look; / to name the flowers when I was still close to the ground / . . . or to watch the sublime metamorphoses / unfold and unfold / over the back gardens of our street" (LF, 24–25). This ability to transform natural phenomena like clouds into ecstatic visions through the power of the imagination is seen again in "The Instant" where her mother takes the young Levertov early one morning up a mist-shrouded mountainside to pick mushrooms:

Then ah! suddenly
the lifting of it, the mist rolls
quickly away, and far, far—

"Look!" she grips me, "It is
Eryri!"

(*CEP,* 65–66)

So overcome is the woman that, though nurtured in "sombre nonconformism," she passionately throws off her repressions and intones "the charged, legendary name" for Snowdon, thereby summoning a wealth of mythical associations: "home / of eagles, resting place of / Merlin, core of Wales" (*PW,* 69–70; *CEP,* 66). The poem is at once a celebration of her mother as guide to nature's transcendental powers and an attempt to set its author firmly within the British Romantic tradition by replacing Wordsworth's heroic imagination, which tames Snowdon and the surrounding "sea of mist" (*The Prelude,* Book Thirteenth), with a more modest, democratic version, which shares with family and reader its distant glimpse of sublimity.

After the revelation at Snowdon, Beatrice's younger daughter duly instituted her own acts of imaginative transformation back in Ilford: she encountered the Muse, looking like Helen Keller's teacher from the Hollywood film, in Valentines Park, the water from whose tributary became a kind of Pierian spring, transmuting a tongue-tied Keller-like girl into an eloquent poet (*JL,* 38–39, 40); she imagined under the extensive root of one of the park's trees "long steps to another country" where she and Olga "would live without father or mother / and without longing for the upper world" (*SD,* 57–58); she felt in the proper Wordsworthian manner the river Roding holding "my head above water when I thought it was / drowning me" (*JL,* 19–20; *RA,* 7–8); she mentally transported the kitchen's "greenish thickwoven cotton tablecover" to a Moorish Casbah in Cordova, from where her father's family were "expelled . . . at the end of the fifteenth century" (*BW,* 16; *T,* 18); she metamorphosed "Old Day the gardener" into "Death himself, or Time, scythe in hand" and the weekly washerwoman into a "primordial" presence (*OTS,* 29–30; *T,* 47–51; *DH/ET,* 156); she had "visions in Ilford High Road," in which the "passing faces" were "oblivious" to their transformation, at an Essex country crossroad where a tramp became a "Christian

saint gathering deeds of charity in his pack to take to the recording angel" and at an ordinary Essex shed, made so extraordinary
by a rainbow that she exclaimed to herself, "*Erde, du liebe*" (*F*,
21; *PW*, 77; *DH/ET*, 21). Only in her penultimate collection,
Sands of the Well (1996), did she feel called on to examine this
propensity for escaping into romantic hyperbole:

> Sometimes I'd make of Valentines, long ago,
> A wilder place than it was—
> the sluice where a man-made lake spilled into Cranbrook
> perceived as a cascade huge in mesmeric power. . . .

Her justification is that by seeing "more than there is" she was
able to bring out existence's latent potential (*SW*, 63).

Levertov has declared: "All that has taken place in my life
since [childhood]—all, that is, that has any bearing on my life as
a poet—was in some way foreshadowed then" (*DLW*, 78). Thus
she reveres the Essex and, to a lesser extent, Hampstead of her
youth as formative sites, "place[s] of origin" (*JL*, 38, 40). So talismanic do settings like these become in her imagination that her
American poems tend to interpret each new event in terms of
childhood experiences, thereby initiating an irreversible process
of Anglicization. Her involvement in anti–Vietnam War activism
is contrasted with the peace of Beachy Head where her mother
took her to convalesce after measles (*RA*, 23); her excitement at
living alone after a long marriage is placed as "childhood's song
. . . / sung in Valentines Park" (*FD*, 59); her ecological concerns
are traced to a youthful nightmare in which farmyard animals
suffer a sudden holocaust (*DH/ET*, 174; *LUC*, 29–30); and her
approaching death is seen to be like the "great wave" that swept
her out of sight and sound of family one English summer holiday
(*CB*, 106–7).

Though Britain remained an unfailing imaginative resource
throughout her life, she never forgot it was simply one of the
multiplicity of cultural influences playing upon her:

> . . . though my fathers
> and mothers came from Cordova and Vitepsk and Caernarvon
> and though I am a citizen of the United States and less a
> stranger here than anywhere else, perhaps,
> I am Essex-born. . . .

> (*JL*, 19–20)

Such a diversity of identities could have resulted in the bewilderment and grief of alienation: "among Jews a Goy, among Gentiles . . . a Jew or at least $1/2$ Jew . . . , among Anglo-Saxons a Celt, in Wales a Londoner . . . : all of these anomalies predicated my later experience: I so often feel English, or perhaps European in the United States, while in England I sometimes feel American." However, Levertov has confidently asserted that "these feelings of non-belonging were positive, for me" (*DLW*, 76). Her identity's complicated mixture and her fate of being an outsider in whatever place she found herself—"I in America, white, an / indistinguishable mixture / of Kelt and Semite, grown under glass / in a British greenhouse"—helped her to understand not only "the far-away daughters and sons of / Vietnamese struggle," but also "what it is to awaken / each day Black in White America" (*LF*, 53). Beyond this, her intimate experience of a variety of cultures, each with its own language or dialect, must have fueled her productive passion for translation, which found outlets in versions of Bengali poetry (1967) and the French writings of Guillevic (1969), Joubert (1984, 1989) and Beckett (1988).

Paul Levertoff combined in himself the Jewish and Christian traditions, "his lifelong hope" being "towards the unification" of the two faiths (*SP/BN*, 440). She herself was descended from "Schneour Zalman, the founder of Habad Hasidism," on her father's side and "Angel Jones of Mold, a Welsh tailor whose apprentices came to learn Biblical interpretations from him while cutting and stitching," on her mother's. These confluences made Levertov and her sister Olga wonder whether they themselves might not have the "definite and peculiar destiny" of bringing greater reconciliation between related, but often competing systems (*PW*, 70; *CEP*, 77–78). Certainly, the younger sister can be said to have achieved just such a syncretism in her poetry. "A Letter to William Kinter of Muhlenberg," to take one example, successfully conflates the Christianity of the Stations of the Cross with the wandering rabbis of *The Zohar* and the "prophets and / hidden angels" they meet on the road (*JL*, 44–45).

However, is Levertov being slightly disingenuous in asserting only the positive aspects of her mixed identity? Surely it produced sorrow and unease as well as empathetic knowledge and linguistic skill. After all, Bülend Şenay's dissertation, "The Making of Jewish Christianity in Britain: Hybridity, Identity and Tradition," which has a section on Paul Levertoff, portrays Jewish Christians as an "'in-between'" group, existing uneasily between a Jewish faith which repudiates them and a Christianity which does not fully accept them (Şenay 2000, 232). Şenay also shows how Levertoff's attempt to synthesize Judaism and Christianity by creating at Holy Trinity, Shoreditch, a church that would have Jewish forms of worship and obey as much of Judaic law as was consonant with Christianity, but be affiliated to the Church of England, died with his death (167). Denise Levertov, of course, was not in London to live through the ultimate defeat of all her father's efforts, but she must have sensed from across the Atlantic that his religious mission had ended in failure. She and Olga believed, like their father, that " 'Christianity is Judaism with its hopes fulfilled' " (167) and that progressive politics is a natural expression of religious faith, yet did the two sisters at the end of their lives really feel they had achieved their destined roles as unifiers of all these—often antipathetic—ideologies? Olga certainly did not, but perhaps Denise did at both a personal and a literary level. The absence of bitter feelings of alienation in Denise Levertov could be due to the fact that her hybrid identity seems never to have been tested severely: she was educated at home in multicultural Ilford and, as an adult in Essex, London, and New York, moved among liberal Jewish and libertarian socialist circles, in which the notion of a Jewish Christianity presented no problems. Her otherness was therefore always supported by a variety of emotional and intellectual buttresses.

Nevertheless, Denise Levertov—English, Welsh, Jewish, American poet—retains her importance as a writer who continually reminds us that cultural hybridity need not be experienced as grief. The Gants Hill district of Ilford where she grew up has lost its overwhelmingly Jewish character as Indian and Pakistani Britons, and, more recently, refugees from Eastern Europe, the Near East, and Africa have moved in, but, in general, a high degree of racial harmony has been preserved. Out of this even more diverse ethnic mixture a new Denise Levertov may perhaps emerge to reassert the advantages of multiculturalism.

NOTES

1. Quotations from Denise Levertov's works are cited in the text with the abbreviations listed below:

BW   *Breathing the Water* (Newcastle upon Tyne: Bloodaxe, 1988; New York: New Directions, 1987).

CB   *Candles in Babylon* (New York: New Directions, 1982).

CEP   *Collected Earlier Poems 1940–60* (New York: New Directions, 1979).

DH/ET   *The Door in the Hive; Evening Train* (Newcastle upon Tyne: Bloodaxe, 1993; New York: New Directions, 1989, 1992).

DI   *The Double Image* (London: Cresset, 1946).

DLW   "Denise Levertov Writes," in *The Bloodaxe Book of Contemporary Women Poets: Eleven British Writers,* ed. Jeni Couzy, 75–79 (Newcastle upon Tyne: Bloodaxe, 1985).

F   *Footprints* (New York: New Directions, 1972).

FD   *The Freeing of the Dust* (New York: New Directions, 1975).

GU   *The Great Unknowing* (Tarset: Bloodaxe, 2001; New York: New Directions, 1999).

JL   *The Jacob's Ladder* (London: Cape, 1965; New York: New Directions, 1961).

LF   *Life in the Forest* (New York: New Directions, 1978).

LUC   *Light Up the Cave* (New York: New Directions, 1981).

OP   *Oblique Prayers: New Poems with 14 Translations from Jean Joubert* (Newcastle upon Tyne: Bloodaxe, 1986; New York: New Directions, 1984).

OTS   *O Taste and See* (New York: New Directions, 1964).

PW   *The Poet in the World* (New York: New Directions,1973).

PbW   "Poems by Women," in *Denise Levertov: In Her Own Province,* ed. Linda Wagner, 98–100 (New York: New Directions, 1979).

RA   *Relearning the Alphabet* (London: Cape, 1970; New York: New Directions, 1970).

SD   *The Sorrow Dance* (New York: New Directions, 1967; London: Cape, 1968).

SP/BN   "Statement on Poetics," "Biographical Note," in *The New American Poetry* ed. Donald M. Allen, 411–12, 440–41 (New York: Grove, 1960).

SW   *Sands of the Well* (New York: New Directions, 1996).

T   *Tesserae* (Newcastle upon Tyne: Bloodaxe, 1997; New York: New Directions, 1995).

2. Couzyn significantly classifies Levertov as a British, as well as a woman, poet.

3. The important exception to this is "Wings in the Pedlar's Pack," in which her father's Judaic idealism as a young man is given the layout of "Talmudic tractates" with a Mishnah of oral traditions commented on by a Gemara of marginal glosses (*DH/ET*, 90; *LF*, 6).

4. In the same spirit the East End artist Rachel Lichtenstein finds in *Rodinsky's Room* (1999) the artistic correlative for a photograph of twelve family members in prewar Poland, of whom only four survived the Holocaust, in a mosaic recreation of the original image, made out of shards of ancient pottery from Herod's city of Caesarea, and Daniel Libeskind designs the Jewish Museum in Berlin and the Imperial War Museum North as monuments to fragmentation.

5. Ironically, as Professor Jacob Lassner pointed out at the conference "Jewish Women Writers and Twentieth-Century British Culture" (Brunel Univer-

sity, July 2002), the American heirs to the Hasidic tradition, far from espousing radical causes, have in general supported right-wing presidents. However, Levertov's father saw no contradiction between Hasidic-Christian belief and progressive politics: he mounted the soapbox during the thirties to denounce "Mussolini's invasion of Abyssinia . . . [and] Britain's lack of support for Spain" (*DLW*, 78). This, no doubt, set a precedent for Levertov, though she did claim she got the main part of her radical activism from Olga (*SD*, 88–89).

6. Levertov wilfully tweaked the meaning of Williams's dictum to accord with her own abstract, transcendental tendencies:

> "No ideas but in things" does not mean "No ideas." Nor does it specify:
> "No ideas but in everyday things
>   modern things
>   urban things."

(*PW*, 57)

This stubborn refusal to understand or pay due respect to the mode of poetry that is the foundation of her own reaches its apotheosis when she attempts to defend Williams against the charge that he is, in her words, "a sort of witless imagist miniaturist" (*PW*, 261).

7. Pound's advice, which precedes this declaration, is highly pertinent: "Don't use such an expression as 'dim lands of *peace.*' It dulls the image. It mixes an abstraction with the concrete."

IV

Post-Holocaust Writing

Writing the Self: Memoirs by German Exiles, British-Jewish Women

Sue Vice

IN THIS ESSAY, I WILL CONSIDER THE RELATIONSHIP BETWEEN BRITISH-ness, Jewishness, and the condition of exile in three autobiographical works by women writers, all of whom arrived in Britain just before or just after the Second World War: Silvia Rodgers's *Red Saint, Pink Daughter: A Communist Childhood in Berlin and London* (1996), Anita Lasker-Wallfisch's *Inherit the Truth, 1939–1945: The Documented Experiences of a Survivor of Auschwitz and Belsen* (1996), and Karen Gershon's *A Lesser Child: An Autobiography* (1992). I have chosen these particular memoirs because the first-generation immigrant experience, of which all three memoirists write, shows up starkly the process of adopting a British identity for these Jewish women.

The very fact that such an act of "becoming British" is possible—Rodgers married a future member of the House of Lords, Lasker-Wallfisch founded a British chamber orchestra, Gershon became a British poet—suggests both that there is little essential about Britishness, but also that while Jewishness can form an element of a British identity, it risks losing its own distinctiveness in the process.[1] It is not for nothing that the first volume of a recent history of British Jewry is called *Radical Assimilation* (Endelman 1990). While recent British-Jewish history has not been characterized by the violence and sanctions undergone by Jews in mainland Europe, it has featured an understated, relentless pressure to conform—to white, Protestant, preferably middle-class Britishness. Anne Karpf, the child of survivors, writes with sharp humor of her mother's habit of asking whether or not people were "English," which was "her euphemism for non-Jewish," as if the two were mutually exclusive (Karpf 1996, 51).[2] On the other hand, Lore Segal, who arrived in Britain in 1939 and left for the United States in 1948, claims—with what might be the good humor of distance—that two of her British guardians were "trying to bring a new soul into the Church of England, and, instead, turned out a temporary snob and an Anglophile forever." Segal reports a conversation with a French friend in which the young Lore claims that she is fifty per cent English: " 'Fifty per cent? Ah!' Monique said. 'You're one hundred and fifty per cent English. It's just that hundred per cent that will always elude you and me" (Segal 1974, 168, 172).

The memoirs that I discuss below are therefore part of a dual heritage. On the one hand, they are part of the growing international area of women's Holocaust writing.[3] On the other hand, they are also a part of the British-Jewish literary canon. Although writings by death-camp survivors who came to Britain after the war are uncommon,[4] Kindertransport narratives[5] and twentieth-century memoirs by British-Jewish women are less so.[6]

Each of the works I focus on is by a woman born in Germany just before the Second World War: Silvia Rodgers was born in Berlin in 1928, Anita Lasker-Wallfisch in Breslau also in 1928, and Karen Gershon in Bielefeld in 1923. Rodgers and Gershon arrived in Britain in 1939 and 1938 respectively, Gershon on a Kindertransport train, while Lasker-Wallfisch arrived in 1946 after imprisonment in Auschwitz and Bergen-Belsen. Although only Rodgers's parents managed to leave Europe—Lasker's and Gershon's were killed—all the texts are written under the influence of parental, particularly maternal, authority.[7] It is partly the survival of Rodgers' parents that enables her to bring her story up to date; it ends with the death of her mother in 1998. Lasker-Wallfisch and Gershon, however, end their accounts just before their arrival in Britain, as the death of their parents created a stark break between childhood in Europe and adulthood in Britain. Although only Rodgers gives an overt account of life as an "outsider" in Britain, Britishness is implicit in Lasker-Wallfisch's and Gershon's texts as the context of writing and of their readership. In all three memoirs there is a clear division between European child and British adult, signaled partly by a change of name: the children were respectively Silvia Szulman, Anita Lasker and Käthe Loewenthal. Gershon is so conscious of the divide between her childhood and adult selves that she is "unable" to write her memoir in the first person (1992, ix) or in English, choosing instead the more novelistic third person, in German. By contrast,

Lasker-Wallfisch describes her efforts to learn English and shed German while still in Belsen at the war's end; and on a visit to Germany in the 1980s, Rodgers attracts the scorn of shopkeepers for not knowing contemporary German vocabulary.

Each of these works is generically hybrid. Despite this, I argue that each is a *memoir of exile*—itself a diverse category—where "exile" is both geographical and subjective. I will follow the definition of "memoir" given by Mary Jean Corbett, which conveys its combination of personal and historical perspectives. She notes that, formally, memoir tends to avoid autobiography's "interplay of I-past and I-present," focusing solely "on the I-past";[8] and adds that, in terms of content, the term "memoir" does not denote "an autobiographical text that tells a story about a centered self, but one in which the writing subject recounts stories of others and events or movements in which she and/or other subjects have taken part" (Corbett 1998, 262 n. 5). Each of these three texts does just this; indeed, in each case the prompt for writing at all is the "events" of the Second World War, the Holocaust, and the death of family members. Calling the three works "memoirs" offers a way out of the difficulty of categorizing them. Silvia Rodgers's autobiography has been variously described as an example of "exile writing" (Hammel 2001), and—in the book's blurb—as an "account." Although the title of *Red Saint, Pink Daughter* suggests that it is, like Art Spiegelman's *Maus*, an autobiography that is also a biography of a parent—indeed, the photograph on the jacket is a close-up of Rodgers's mother, who, like Vladek Spiegelman, tape-recorded her reminscences not long before her death—its perspective is entirely that of the "pink daughter," and not the "red" mother. Lasker-Wallfisch's *Inherit the Truth* is subtitled *The Documented Experiences of a Survivor of Auschwitz and Belsen,* and it too is not so much an autobiography as an account with a very clear agenda: to inform succeeding generations about prejudice, evil, and the Holocaust. Again, because it is presented in a documentary manner but is narrated by an individual, *Inherit the Truth* is best categorized as "memoir" (the blurb uses the terms "story" and "book," signaling an inability to classify the text). Gershon's self-styled "autobiography" uses novelistic techniques, and is again a memoir, due to its focus on the "I-past" and positioning of the narrator amid historical "events and movements."

"MY OTHERNESS WON'T LIE DOWN":
SILVIA RODGERS, *RED SAINT, PINK DAUGHTER*

In her memoir, Silvia Rodgers describes her childhood in Berlin, where she was born in 1928 to recent arrivals from Poland, Frida and Hersz Szulman. The Szulmans managed to leave Germany in 1939; Silvia describes their lives as refugees in Britain, and her eventual marriage to the Labour MP Bill Rodgers, who went on to found the Social Democratic Party. Silvia, as I will call the narrator of *Red Saint, Pink Daughter*, insists throughout on her marginal status: "I was always 'off-centre' . . . on the periphery" (1996, 1), "an outsider" (2); "Being born a Jew and a woman and a foreigner, I was marginal from the start" (12).[9]

The marginality of the Szulmans' status in prewar Germany— as Polish emigrants who were Communist Jews—is replicated in Britain, ironically, this time by Silvia's identity as a German immigrant. This became clearest when, as a nonbeliever, she attended Jewish schools: paradoxically, Jewishness could be either the cause or the effect of marginal status. Silvia points out that Germanness in Britain carried with it the stigma of wartime enmity; during her school days, she would instead describe herself as Polish, which conjured up a different stereotype: "To be German was to be an enemy alien, to be Polish was not only to be a friendly alien, but a brave exile and a dashing freedom fighter" (194). Polishness also refuted the Jewishness that Germanness did not, as Silvia points out: she learnt to "advertise my Polishness rather than my Jewishness" (230). This is an odd formulation, as if—like Anne Karpf's mother's view of Englishness—the two were mutually exclusive. It reveals Silvia's perception of an unstable relation between nationality and ethnicity; while Germanness might suggest Jewishness as well as enmity, neither Polishness—nor Englishness—do.

The title of Silvia's memoir hints at an ironic genealogy: her mother's Communist fervor has been commuted into social democracy in the daughter. Silvia's parents subscribed to Karl Leibknecht and Rosa Luxemburg's Communist paper *Die Röte Fahne*, which took frequent issue with the milder German Social Democratic Party (10): this is a fact Silvia notes with some relish, laying the trail for her involvement in the founding of Britain's Social Democratic Party. In 1989 Silvia reads contemporary German accounts of May Day 1929, when Communist rallies were brutally put down by the police in Berlin: "'the Social Democrat agents of the bourgeoisie have declared war on the workers of Berlin'" (42). This is quoted with at least a glance at Silvia's mother, who was firmly on the side of the "workers" and had been expelled from Poland for revolutionary activity.

Throughout *Red Saint, Pink Daughter*, Silvia describes Communism in terms of Christian conversion and observance. This is not an unusual analogy, but here it implies that Frida Szulman's political activism—she appeared as a "red saint," like her heroine Luxemburg, to her adoring "pink daughter"—prevented her from being either a mother[10] or a Jew. Frida "converted" her husband and siblings "to the new and godless creed" (11, 19), despite the fact that her husband Hersz was only susceptible to Marxism's "prophet," his wife, rather than being "hit" by the ideology itself "on any road to Damascus" (35). Frida's idea of heaven, according to her daughter, was a mass rally in Berlin of the German KPD, her guardian angel in this heaven a Weimar policeman guaranteeing the right to free speech (40); eventually the daughter demands, in a further invocation of Christianity, "Who did my mother think she was? God?" (139). Frida's expulsion from the Communist Party in 1938, for criticizing Stalin's purges, is an "excommunication" (186).

These Christian tropes manage subtly to discredit Silvia's mother,[11] as if reversing the "matrilineal" inheritance of Judaism which the daughter discusses (35): the mother's allegiance is only to Communism, although her daughter manages to be a Jewish child. In a typically double-voiced observation, Silvia notes the incompatibility for women of traditional Judaism and political activity: "Jewish society is matrilineal as far as the principle of being Jewish is concerned, patrilineal in everything else, and wholly and totally patriarchal. A traditional Jewish woman's place was, and is, certainly not in politics" (35). While this observation suggests sympathy for Frida's plight, it also possesses an oedipal subtext: in adulthood, unlike her mother, the pink daughter *did* manage to take up a "place in politics" while retaining her Jewish identity. Silvia admits that "a fraction of my fervour [for the British Social Democratic Party] was probably based on having triumphed over the indoctrination against Social Democracy from an age when, according to the Jesuits, it should have stuck" (43). Once more, the pink Jewish daughter wins out over the red but also Jesuitical mother (later Silvia adds, to dis-

tinguish herself from this Christian taint, "I am not a Jesuit,"
123). What Silvia observes of her mother's discourse, however, is
just as true of her own: "For an atheist, saints and heaven featured large in her vocabulary" (45).

Despite its emphasis on marginality, Silvia's memoir culminates in her accession to the center of British establishment life.
As the wife of the MP and later peer Bill Rodgers, Silvia describes
attending such symbolically "central" (3) occasions as the State
Opening of Parliament and dinner at the House of Lords, and
launching a Royal Navy ship, yet, as she puts it of a friend, "the
nearer she got to the centre, the more marginal she felt" (282).
One might argue that, as one of the Gang of Four who left the
Labour Party to found the Social Democrats in 1981, Rodgers
himself courted marginality; but by this very act—voluntarily
becoming the splinter group of a main political party—the SDP
paradoxically asserted their centrality to British political life.
They even merged with the Liberal Party in 1988. In a sense, the
same argument could be made of Silvia's status as a Jewish
refugee in Britain; her difference emphasizes the fact that Englishness can be defined by its exclusion of Judaism, so that the
latter is an element necessary to that definition.[12]

The clearest overlap of the viewpoint of a refugee child and
that of a British peer's wife takes place in Silvia's accounts of the
British government's wartime record. She describes Lord Halifax
as the epitome of Munich, second only to Chamberlain: "He was
so typically English in appearance: his height, his leanness, his
hat, the way he wore his clothes, so elegant, casual, such disdain
for everyone and everything around him. Is it odd that I make
him sound attractive? Not really. Any small refugee child is
bound to be just as impressed as repelled by such a figure. However, if I hear any reference to him now I shudder because of his
stance over Munich" (156). Such passages reveal the full force of
the historical irony of Silvia's marriage to Bill Rodgers. It meant
that not only did the daughter of a revolutionary Communist
take part in the creation of the British Social Democratic Party,
but also that a Jewish refugee of Polish origin from Nazi Germany became a member of the very British establishment that
had tried to prevent the immigration of people like Silvia Szulman.[13] Silvia describes meeting in the 1960s a diplomat, Patrick
Reilly, who she later found out had assiduously tried to prevent

Jews from entering Palestine in 1939. Silvia's view of Reilly is temporally and politically split. She met him as a British adult, the wife of a Labour junior minister, and attributed his wife's hostility to their political differences; later she collapsed this temporal difference, and ascribed the hostility to her "origins" (172), shrinking back down to the German-Jewish child whose fate was in the hands of Reilly and his ilk.

Silvia's adulthood is a British one, her childhood Jewish-German.[14] This is clearest in her altered response to Blake's "Jerusalem," the hymn she first heard at school assembly in Britain in 1939. Her initial view of it was related to her own ethnicity—"I was amazed. No one gave any sign of being in the least interested in either Palestine or the Jews." This humorous childhood error gives way to an adult view of "Jerusalem" as a song about class betrayal. It reveals the fact that "satanic mills" and not the "pleasant land" cited in Blake's poem are the legacy of the "deprived," who have been neglected by the Labour Party, while Silvia reminds us that "in 1939 I knew nothing of . . . William Blake or Labour Councils" (197).[15] Although a tension between ethnicity and class has persisted throughout *Red Saint, Pink Daughter*, in Silvia's reaction to her mother's Marxism, the daughter attains this class awareness in the context of British history and politics.

Silvia's conclusion is to admit that she "enjoys" her marginal status and "making such a meal" of it (278). However, perhaps unexpectedly, it is her gender that persists most unambiguously as an "off-centre" identity ("every woman is born a marginal"), as her Communist German youth has been shed, and her Jewishness acknowledged as secular (the only time she fasted on Yom Kippur it turned out to be the wrong day). Jewishness is an external attribute, like a "coat" that is nonetheless "not so easy to cast off." Silvia compares her Britishness similarly to an accessory, part of a performance: "I like having a British passport . . . and like a child with its first watch often hold it so that other people queuing at passport controls can see it." Silvia even questions whether she still "belongs" to her mother. Although Silvia quotes Sartre's "if you go into exile, you lose your place in the world" (279), it is not clear that her journey has been so full of loss as one in which she has been enabled to step outside the usual fixed markers of religion and nationality.

"I HAVE MADE MY HOME HERE": ANITA LASKER-WALLFISCH, *INHERIT THE TRUTH, 1939–1945*

Anita Lasker-Wallfisch's memoir is distinct from Rodgers's in several ways, all arising from the fact that she and her sister Renate did not arrive in Britain until March 1946, nearly a year after their liberation from Bergen-Belsen. The memoir was originally written as a private document to allow Lasker-Wallfisch's children to "inherit the truth" of her experiences.[16] It gives an account of the childhood of the narrator, Anita, who was born in Breslau, then part of Germany (now Polish Wroclaw), in 1928; and the failed efforts of her parents, Alfons and Edith Lasker, to emigrate to Britain, where their eldest daughter Marianne was living. The elder Laskers were deported to Poland and killed in 1942. The memoir describes the deportation of Anita and Renate from a Gestapo prison to Auschwitz, where Anita, as the cellist in the camp orchestra, contrived to save her sister; they were then sent by cattle truck to Belsen in 1945, and a year later, after the liberation of the camp, joined their sister in Britain.

Although the postwar journey that the narrator Anita's younger self undergoes, from "marginal" alien to assimilated and acculturated Briton, is akin to Silvia's, Anita's experience of concentration camps constitutes a division between her experience and Silvia's—that of a Holocaust survivor versus an evader. While Silvia can entitle one of her chapters "What *Might Have* Happened to Me" (my italics), and is relieved to have only the scar of typhus on her neck and not a tattoo on her wrist (1996, 166), Anita's experience is highlighted in the very presentation of her memoir. A photograph of her forearm, its Auschwitz tattoo clearly visible, appears on the book's back cover, while extra subheadings emphasize the historical truth of Anita's experiences: "Survivor of Auschwitz and Belsen" appears under the author's name on the front cover, while "The Documented Experiences of a Survivor of Auschwitz and Belsen" features on the title page.[17] The "marginality" versus "centrality" that Silvia emphasized throughout her memoir is replaced by a different spatial metaphor in the foreword to *Inherit the Truth*: "Providing normality for my children meant that among other things they should not feel different or isolated [by hearing tales of atrocity about their grandparents]. Now, fifty years later, I know that this was all a pipedream. There is no place in normal life for stories which are so outrageously horrendous that they seem like fairy tales at best, and gross exaggerations at worst" (13). While Silvia felt marginal to life in Britain, Anita here hints at a more general or existential anxiety about the "place" of the Holocaust in everyday life. She suggests that excluding or marginalizing it is impossible, as it is situated within that very "normality." The Holocaust itself is only one manifestation of the disquieting fact that "the dividing line between human integrity and barbarism" is "precariously thin" (144). This is a different way of formulating the question Lawrence Douglas discusses in his article "The Shrunken Head of Buchenwald": were the Nazi atrocities "acts *against* civilization," or was the Holocaust, rather, "an act *of* civilization" (Douglas 2001, 287; Bauman 1989)? Anita clearly aligns herself with the latter.

The two distinctive formal features of *Inherit the Truth* lie in its origins as a private account of the war, and its reliance on contemporary letters and other documents. The memoir's address to specific readers—Anita's children—is matched by the letters' address to their recipients. Yet both have become transmuted by publication into a broader address to any reader ("you must remember" [29], "Do you fully understand?" [46]), and the letters and documents "substantiate" (14) the text's detail. The letters are not distinguished typographically from Anita's commentary on them, so the past and present are often hard to separate. Anita's editorial voice speaks with hindsight, while the letters describe an unfolding present; in Michael André Bernstein's terms, they represent respectively the potential for backshadowing—seeing the past in terms of the present—and the reality of sideshadowing—respecting all possible outcomes as equal (Bernstein 1994). However, Anita does not blame the victims, a logical effect of backshadowing narratives identified by Bernstein. Indeed, she uses her more complete knowledge of her family's fate to *disrupt* the possibility of blame by emphasizing a narrative structure not only without "normal" cause and effect, but within which death has destroyed the possibility of meaning. Of a failed emigration attempt, Anita writes, "All I remember today about that crisis is that we were sitting in an office, probably the Italian Embassy, all eager and full of nervous tension as the official kept turning our documents over and over, the rubber stamp in his hand, and almost ready to validate our passports, and then decided not to bring the stamp down on its intended target for reasons which I no longer recall, and which are of no importance now anyway" (32). This is the logic not of backshadowing but of fallible and exhausted memory, constructed out of scenes that do not link up. In an odd reversal, the letters of the time, despite their partial knowledge, reveal more about the exact chronology and emotional nature of the situation than hindsight could, as Anita suggests: "I gather now, as I re-read the letters, that even then [summer 1940] my father had not given up hope" (33). The letters act like a diary in preserving moments of present time and the voice of the writer, effecting for the reader an uncanny return to the past.

As in many retrospective Holocaust narratives, Anita tries to keep chronological control of her story but cannot help at times telling it out of order:[18] "But I am jumping ahead . . ." (45); "I will go back now" (46); "the reason for this will become plain" (58); "Back to 1945" (114). A letter from Eric Williams, written in 1974 about his "Wooden Horse" escape from Stalag Luft III in 1943, helped by documents forged by Anita and Renate in a paper factory in 1941, is reproduced as a flash-forward during Anita's account of October 1941. This overdetermination of the difference between story (Anita's narrative) and plot (the events in their historical order) becomes especially hard to unravel when the event at issue is the trauma of her parents' deportation in April 1942. Rather than narrate these events in the present time of writing, Anita resorts to a contemporary letter. However, Anita does not choose one from the very moment of deportation, and instead quotes from a letter written to Marianne from Belsen in June 1945, two months after the liberation of the camp, describing how the daughters, who were not on the deportation list, wanted to accompany their parents: "Vati—our clever Vati—wouldn't hear of it. 'It is better for you to stay. Where we are going, you get there soon enough.' We didn't exchange many words. There was a lot to do—packing—packing . . . (We were not aware then that everything was going to be taken off them anyway.) Vati concentrated on concluding his own—or rather everyone else's—affairs [among other things, he completed the Vermögenserklärung, or declaration of possessions: see Appendix 1]" (45).[19] The layers of retrospection here are from different temporal points. In 1945, Anita could corroborate her father's foresight—"clever Vati"—and her own lack of foreknowledge—("We were not aware then . . ."); while the present-time narrative voice also intrudes, using the square brackets of editorial intervention, to present yet another finding—the *Vermögenserklärung*, which is reproduced in the text (146). It is hard to identify the present-time voice in this extract; in effect, Anita comments as different incarnations of herself, each one irreparably disjointed from the other by the different historical perspectives of 1942, 1945, and 1996.[20]

Anita's attitude to her Germanness apparently resembles Silvia's in *Red Saint, Pink Daughter*, but unlike Silvia's response to external hostility, Anita experiences revulsion at her own nationality in the war's immediate aftermath, as she puts it in a letter written to Marianne in 1945: "The most difficult thing to stomach is that we are *German* Jews . . . But I have acquired a large stomach, and have managed to swallow even the fact that I am a German Jew, although it stuck in my throat" (115). The self-conscious imagery here calls upon a series of different introjective clichés and invests them with some literality, developing the first suggestion, that Germanness is hard to stomach, as if—to quote the *Oxford English Dictionary*—it were an "affront." Anita refers jokingly to the "large stomach" she has mentioned before to Marianne—Renate having to "watch her figure" (101) in Belsen due to the quantity of food available after the liberation strikes a note of resistance. It is not only food that Anita has digested, but her Germanness—the phrase "to swallow" this fact suggests, again in the words of the *OED*, both the "credulity" of accepting an outrageous truth, and once more "stomaching" an "affront." The unpalatable truth "stuck" in Anita's "throat": this is not food but the words required to acknowledge her nationality, and the German language itself (this letter appears in the context of Anita learning English in order to work as an interpreter). Germanness is a bitter pill, to be soothed away by Britishness.

Unlike Silvia, Anita insists that her "new life" and "home" in England are "another story" (144), not part of this one, and that she has no regrets. This calm tone, which persists throughout, is partly the result of its original address to Anita's children. But it also conveys Anita's conviction that "normality" contains within it irrationality and violence. Despite the rational and minimizing tone of narration ("our life as interpreters [in Belsen for war crimes trials] was quite congenial" [101]; "We were aware that we were a bit of a disappointment in some ways [as newly arrived survivors in Britain, because] we looked like reasonably normal people" by 1946 [15]), Anita's story is about abnormality and enormity. Anita does not do what Andrea Hammel laments about "the narrative drive" of Rodgers's *Red Saint, Pink Daughter*, which is to designate the past "as something which needs to be left behind" (2001, 184) for the sake of the more successful present. Rather, Anita's narrative techniques make the past into the present; and as her addressees are, if not her children, then British nonsurvivor readers more generally, their interest is at least as much in the past as in the present of which they are a part.

"ALL SHE MOST WANTED WAS BEYOND HER REACH": KAREN GERSHON, A LESSER CHILD

Karen Gershon's memoir *A Lesser Child* is subtitled *An Autobiography*, and its form is unusually mixed even for texts of this kind. It was originally written in German, Gershon's mother tongue, although she lived in Britain from 1938 until her death in 1993; and Gershon writes about her younger self in the third person. Gershon explains the latter technique in the foreword: "This is an autobiography, as truthful as I could make it; only, I was unable to write about myself in the first person. Kate was my childhood name" (1992, ix). Using the third person produces novelistic, although not fictional, effects in this factual work: while every member of Kate's family is described in the third person like Kate, it is the young Kate who is the focalizer. The adult narrator reconstructs certain events[21] in the present in a manner again familiar from the novel; in Gershon's autobiography, this habit of showing events through Kate's eyes confirms narratively the otherwise invisible link between young character and adult narrator. Use of the third person, on the other hand, conveys the abrupt severing of ties between the German-Jewish child Kate Loewenthal, and the adult British-Jewish poet and writer Karen Gershon. *A Lesser Child* is a nonfiction *Künstlerroman*, the portrait of an artist as a young girl, with an overwhelming historical inflection. Indeed, as was the case with Silvia Rodgers's and Anita Lasker-Wallfisch's works, rather than being a straightforward autobiography, in which historical events are subordinated to personal ones, *A Lesser Child* is the description of how overwhelming historical events played themselves out in the life of an individual woman.

Kate was born in Bielefeld, Germany, in 1923, the third daughter of Paul and Selma Loewenthal. The very title of her autobiography, *A Lesser Child*, reveals its imbrication of developmental with historical issues. The title's historical resonance is even clearer in its original German version, *Das Unterkind*, which makes ironic reference to the Nazis' racial designation of the non-Aryan as an *Untermensch*. But the narrator of Kate's story who gave it this title also has in mind the child's familial status, a thread that runs throughout the text. The adult narrator claims that Kate "could never catch up with her sisters. That this was impossible must have convinced her that she was a lesser child even before the Nazis came to power, when she was in her tenth year" (13). The adult narrator presents this "lesser" notion as an unhappy confluence of internal predisposition with external forces.[22] For instance, to explain Kate's brief flirtation with Christianity at a time of Judaism's denigration, the narrator notes that Kate "valued herself and what she had so little that Christianity must be better" (116). It is clear that *A Lesser Child* is not an autobiography of development and fulfilment so much as a memoir of potential not fully reached, an experience of inferiority, exile, and orphanhood (Paul and Selma Loewenthal were both killed during the war).

As is the case with the other two memoirs I have discussed, *A Lesser Child* has a distinctive view of the relation between past and present. The limited developmental view of a child is matched by the restricted historical view of someone living in Germany in the 1930s. At times, the historical view is shown to have priority, although such a perspective can only be supplied later by the adult narrator. For instance, the child interpreted her parents' behavior according only to the familial scenarios of paternal philandering and maternal hysteria. Kate's father often stayed out late, but "the cause of Selma's anxiety at such times *may not have been*, as Kate believed, his philandering, but his reckless tongue: he would tell political jokes without caring who might overhear him. When she observed her mother weeping in his arms, this *may not have been*, as she believed, evidence of a reconciliation after a quarrel. Paul may have been trying to comfort her when she was in despair over their worsening circumstances" (102, my italics).[23] Yet again we see that the apparently spatial distance between narrator and character is actually the temporal distance of adult from child. This temporal difference is even more strikingly conveyed by the odd tenses: "There was only Friedemann [to conduct synagogue services], though as far as Kate *was* concerned the 'only' *is* out of place" (161, my italics): it is as if the child were commenting on the adult's language about her.[24] Added to this is the symbolic coincidence that it is a child who has only prewar knowledge, an adult who possesses fuller understanding, as if before the Holocaust everyone lived in a childlike state of ignorance.

At other times, Kate reads everyday events exclusively in terms of their political or, particularly, racial significance, including school friendships, pupils' first impressions of her, altercations with teachers, Kate's view of her father ("Suddenly she was seeing the Jews as the Nazis saw them . . . The only thing about [her father] which still mattered was that he was a Jew, and Jewish men did not matter" [179]), and even the acquisition of a kitten. Kate is wary of irritating the mother cat's owner, a neighbor, by spending too much time with the kittens ("Seven months of the Hitler regime had taught her caution in her dealings with Aryans"), favors the one black kitten because "it was the outsider," and when offered a kitten for herself is "convinced" that this is to fob her off, because "the owner did not want a Jew coming into her garden." Yet in this case it seems that there is no such racial inflection to be had: "[Kate] tried, and failed, to relate it to her Jewishness when she was told that she could have [the kitten] for nothing" (43). In this way the child's internalization of Nazi codes is made clear in terms of the racialization of archetypal childhood incidents. The adult narrator also gives racial interpretations of events, in terms which do not always include Kate's voice: Selma asked to keep her daughter with her in hospital and the narrator explains, "Either moved by this Jewess, or unconcerned about Jews, they gave in to her" (48). This sounds like the cynical, knowing interpretation of an adult in the present, rather than the floundering, defamiliarizing efforts of a child to understand illogical laws.

Sometimes the Holocaust future intrudes backward, shockingly, into the child's world. But this is far from the backshadowing I mentioned earlier, according to which the present is seen and valued only in terms of the future. In *A Lesser Child* the narrator is in the habit of reporting the fate of characters in the midst of their life, for instance, about a visit by Tante Hete when Kate lay ill in bed:

> [Tante Hete] also said that Kate's having been so ill was really a bless-ing: though God had allowed them to come down in the world, he had with Kate's recovery provided them with something for which to praise him.
>
> Tante Hete and Onkel Max Sieger were sent to Theresienstadt: he died there; she was sent on to Auschwitz and did not survive.
>
> The present which she brought Kate was the book *Pinocchio*. (54)

The events here—Tante Hete's visit to Kate, her death in Ausch-witz—clearly took place at different times, but the past tense in which they are related do not distinguish them.[25] Although the future intrudes, its sickening closeness to a time of inno-cence is clearly signaled; the woman who thanked God and gave her niece a gift she "loved," is the same one who was killed in a death camp.

These sudden, incongruous flashes, although calmly (even understatedly—"did not survive") reported, symbolize both the eruption of intolerable and unassimilable violence and death into what Anita Lasker-Wallfisch calls "normality," and the work-ings of memory. When looking back on Kate's parents, the adult narrator is struck by the overlap of two incompatible temporal and spatial moments, as shown in this description of a day in 1938 just after Kristallnacht, when Kate and her mother are advised to take a detour to meet up with Kate's father: "The day had turned colder and greyer—or it may just have seemed so to Kate. She linked arms with her mother; they were now the same height and Kate was to grow no taller. They crossed the Kessel-brink. Selma and Paul were to be among the first eighty-eight Jews from the town [Bielefeld] deported eastwards; they were not among the six survivors from that transport" (180). It is as if describing the scene—acknowledging her own future ("was to grow no taller"), the acts of linking arms and crossing the road—forces the narrator to supplement the child's experience of phys-ical closeness and a purely geographical "brink" with knowledge of displacement and death. Only later do we learn more details of the elder Loewenthals' fate (they were deported to the Riga ghetto, where Paul died after a year's forced labor, Selma in 1944 after the ghetto's dissolution, either in a mass shooting or at Auschwitz [186]). Although this method—using prolepsis, while also keeping information back—appears to be exclusively Holocaust related, it is used in *A Lesser Child* as a way of conveying abrupt, untimely death of any kind. The narrator makes clear that Kate's beloved oldest sister Anne died young, but only later do we learn that she died after the war in Britain, in a Bristol hospital (125). Given the text's third-person, novelistic narration, these flash-forwards appear as much aesthetic as psychological; indeed, the two are one. Their presence confirms that we are reading a memorial, and a literary text. This is clear in the following description of Kate's mother, after the death of her father followed swiftly after that of her mother: "Selma once more put on mourning; she continued to wear black until made to exchange it for concentration camp uniform. She used to say that she was wearing mourning for the Jews of Germany" (39). The logic of this observation is similar to those I have already mentioned, but the detail about "concentration camp uniform" is a conceit rather than a fact, something which the adult narrator neither witnessed nor verified. Instead, it symbolizes the unutterable future, the passage from the garb associated with rites of individual mourning to the garb of mass death.

As with Lasker-Wallfisch's *Inherit the Truth*, Gershon's Britishness exists outside her memoir, as a context that forms the narrator's life after the text ends. In this manner it is different from other refugee narratives, such as Lore Segal's *Other People's Houses* or Judith Kerr's *When Hitler Stole Pink Rabbit*, which focus on the experience of uprootedness in Britain—and as does Karen Gershon's Kindertransport anthology *We Came as Children*. Yet it is plain throughout, even without detailed knowledge of the author's life, that *A Lesser Child* is a memoir of exile and unbelonging. Kate's national and "racial" identity is put into question during the 1930s. For instance, when Kate's schoolmate Ingrid would not sign her autograph book, on the grounds that, Ingrid claimed, "I am a *German* girl," Kate asked herself, "And am I *not* a German girl?" (143). Over the course of the memoir, however, Kate becomes more of a Jewish girl, developing from one whose earliest story, narrated in pictures because she could not write, featured a butterfly who was killed and "buried under a cross. Of course [Kate] knew how to draw a Star of David; she also knew that it was alien to her native environment" (20). The last phrase is ambiguous: Kate's "native environment" is partly assimilationist Germany, partly her home atmosphere and personal inclination. Nazi persecution turned Kate into a Jewish girl, and, later, into the British Karen narrating the German child's story. Just as preHolocaust knowledge coincided fittingly with Kate's youth, so Jewishness itself has an innocence only in the pre-war world: "For Kate, the Jewish religious rituals stood for that brief best time of her life, her early childhood" (160).

Conclusion

Each memoir I have discussed uses a different way of narrating the traumatic past, either by relating it forcefully to the present, or by relegating the present to the unseen moment of writing. Given the fact that these are all accounts of exile, the memoirs that do not describe the present have a European *énoncé*, a British *énonciation:* that is, what is represented is German, but the act of narration is British. This is particularly clear in Gershon's case, in which the British adult narrator tells the story of her childhood in German. Unlike traditional autobiographies, as we have seen, the notion of progressive self-realization does not take center stage in any of the three memoirs: Rodgers realizes the irony of her marked change of status taking place through marriage; Lasker-Wallfisch followed up the musical career begun before the war to become a founder member of the English Chamber Orchestra, in which she plays the cello, but barely mentions this; while Gershon's adult literary career is also predicted within the text, but not described.[26] Lasker-Wallfisch and Gershon do not give an account of their later avocation and success partly because of the temporal parameters they have chosen; but also because theirs are not accounts of triumph and transcendence—rather, they are partial, individual stories subordinated to greater historical forces. This accounts also for Rodgers's bemused realization that even her husband achieving a peerage cannot prevent her feeling an outsider.

The critic Andreas Lixl-Purcell sees autobiographies of exile by German-Jewish women writers published after 1960 as distinctive because, "rather than evoking the suffering during exile and the torments of expatriation, they juxtapose the present with what preceded it. The vignettes of life before exile are offered to situate the reader in a present which otherwise would have no historical continuity at all" (1988, 5). As we have seen, Rodgers's memoir is the only one that deals with anything that might be termed the "torments of expatriation"; Lasker-Wallfisch and Gershon go even further than the trend Lixl-Purcell describes in omitting "the present" altogether. Exile overwhelms all other experiences in the construction of these writers' identity; but the act of writing offers some "historical continuity."

Finally, we might suggest that, despite their clear differences, these three memoirs constitute a specifically Jewish part of what Charmian Brinson has described as the "collective autobiography" of women exiles from Nazism in Britain.[27] Not only do such works document similar experiences, they represent a different kind of autobiographical subject: one who, in Lixl-Purcell's words, discovered a new form of identity based upon "permanent uprootedness" and the destabilizing of what was "periphery," what center; (1988, 6–7) and whose texts document not chronological development and achievement, but the act of survival. Indeed, the notion of collectivity goes against traditional conceptions of autobiography, as the account of an exceptional and "unrepresentative" individual (Wirth-Nesher 1998, 113). In these texts even insistence on individuality, such as the experiences of marginality, or "lesser" status, simply reminds the reader that these memoirs are both representative—of others who underwent the same historical calamity—and memorial, of those who died.

NOTES

1. This is mentioned in the Crick Report of 2003, which advocates a controversial "citizenship test" for new arrivals to Britain. The report claims that to be British "does not mean assimilation into a common culture so that original identities are lost." It goes on to claim that such "loss" has not been incurred by the distinctive Irish and Jewish communities in Britain, but cautions that variety should not entail immigrants living "parallel lives" to the mainstream (quoted by Alan Travis, "Being a Good Brit: A User's Guide," the *Guardian*, Sept. 4, 2003, 9).

2. While Britishness could be described as a matter of formal nationality, Englishness is an informal cultural identity even harder to accede to.

3. See for instance the anthology of primary material edited by Carol Rittner and John K. Roth, *Different Voices: Women and the Holocaust* (New York:

Paragon House, 1993); and critical works *Women in the Holocaust*, ed. Dalia Ofer and Leonore J. Weitzman (New Haven: Yale University Press, 1998), and S. Lillian Kremer, *Women's Holocaust Writing: Memory and Imagination* (Lincoln: University of Nebraska Press, 2001), and Anna Hardmann "Women and the Holocaust", *Holocaust Educational Trust Research Papers* 1. No. 3 (1999/2000).

4. Examples include Helen Lewis's *A Time to Speak* (Belfast: Blackstaff Press, 1992), and Leon Greenman's *An Englishman at Auschwitz* (London: Vallentine Mitchell, 2001). Lasker-Wallfishch's memoir falls into this category.

5. The World Movement for the Care of Children (Kindertransport movement) brought around 7,400 unaccompanied Jewish children on specially commissioned trains from occupied Europe to Britain in 1938 and 1939; the parents of most were killed during the war, and many of the "Kinder" stayed on in Britain after the war. Individual accounts of this experience include Judith Kerr's *When Hitler Stole Pink Rabbit* (1971; repr., London: Collins 1974), Martha Blend, *A Child Alone* (London: Vallentine Mitchell, 1995), and Fanny Stang, *A New Beginning* (London: Minerva, 1997). Gershon's memoir falls into this category. Although she was a child who arrived in Britain at this time, Silvia Rodgers's memoir does not belong to this category, as she was not sponsored by the Kindertransport movement; in her anthology about the Kindertransport experience twenty-five years on, Gershon estimates that a further thousand children came to Britain as domestic servants or with their parents (Karen Gershon, ed., *We Came as Children: A Collective Autobiography* [New York: Harcourt, Brace and World, 1966], iv). Rodgers was one of these.

6. Some recent examples include Leila Berg, *Flickerbook: An Autobiography* (London: Granta, 1997); Linda Grant, *Remind Me Who I Am, Again* (London: Granta, 1998); Mona Golabek, *The Children of Willesden Lane* (London: Time Warner, 2002); Irene Gunther, *Only a Girl: Remembering My Syrian-Jewish World* (London: Xlibris, 2002); Gillian Rose, *Love's Work* (London: Chatto and Windus, 1995).

7. See Bella Brodzki (1988) for a discussion of the relation between femininity and displacement or exile, the mother and language. She argues that many women's autobiographies "are generated out of a compelling need to enter into discourse with the absent or distant mother" (246), which is the case with each of the memoirs, as is the "antinostalgic" (247) ambivalence each exhibits.

8. Mary Jean Corbett (1998) quoting Avrom Fleishman; he argues that the memoir's limited focus is the reason for "the lower generic status of this form" in contrast to autobiography (Corbett 1998, 261 n 5). See also Lee Quinby (1992). Quinby repeats the notion that while autobiography has been the "privileged aesthetic and ethical discourse of the modern era," the memoir has been "marginalized" (Quinby 1992, 299).

9. See also Sidonie Smith, who writes in similar vein that for a woman autobiographer "ideologies of race and class, sometimes even of nationality, intersect and confound those of gender . . . In her doubled, perhaps tripled, marginality, then, the autobiographer negotiates sometimes four sets of stories, all nonetheless written about her rather than by her" (Smith 1987, 51).

10. "I had never been the centre of my parents' universe," Silvia observes; "That place was held by the Party" (141). Silvia also describes her mother's

efforts to save her Marxist books from being burnt in 1933: "it's almost as if she loved them more than her children" (96). Later, Silvia gives different evidence of her own marginality: she claims that her younger brother André was the apple of her mother's eye, so much so that she did not hold it against him when he left Britain for South Africa, claiming that Ted Heath was not a sufficiently right-wing prime minister (143). By this means Silvia presents herself as marginalized even within the family, as a daughter, and a Social Democrat one at that (see also Hammel 2001, 182).

11. Or occasionally less subtly; Silvia describes an incident from mid-1930s Berlin when her mother evaded an ex-Communist trying to denounce her to the police: "It was how Judas betrayed Jesus, and my mother had no taste for crucifixion or martyrdom other than the occasional domestic one" (98).

12. See Colin Richmond, who notes the equation of "Englishness with non-Jewishness" in his "Englishness and Medieval Anglo-Jewry" (1992, 56).

13. Silvia notes that in 1939 Malcolm MacDonald, the Dominion and Colonial Secretary, "refused to save 20,000 Jewish children" (172), as if these children had included her younger self. Andrea Hammel sees the memoir's distinctive tone as the result of an uneven hybrid: "The discourse in Red Saint, Pink Daughter oscillates between private autobiographical reminiscing and accounts of public history, between marginality and centrality" (2001, 180). I would argue, rather, that the interdependence of the terms is highlighted in Rodgers's memoir by her particular circumstances, and by the apparently abrupt leap in her biography from private to public memory—a feature shared, as Hammel points out, by other (usually male) "exile" autobiographies such as George Weidenfeld's.

14. Silvia describes her postwar attitude to Jewishness itself as a fate 'escaped' (243).

15. One cannot help but see the latter view as an SPD one; in Tony Richardson's 1962 film The Loneliness of the Long-Distance Runner it is specifically Labour who has failed the working classes.

16. As Charmian Brinson points out, this is not uncommon, since many women who were not "experienced writers" felt impelled to write autobiographies for their children's sake; she mentions works by Anna Lambert and Margarete Grünfeld (Brinson 2001, 3).

17. This emphasis on documentation arises partly from a wish to refute Holocaust deniers, those who "maintain that the Holocaust is a serious distortion of the facts, or even a downright lie" (13).

18. See for instance Spiegelman's Maus I and II, and Ida Fink, The Journey, trans. Joanna Wechsler and Francine Prose (Harmondsworth: Penguin, 1992).

19. Only half of the letter is quoted here; the rest of it appears at the "right" time, when Anita reaches 1945 in her narrative (114).

20. Anita struggles with narrative time in a different way when describing her parents' final letters after deportation: she repeats the two messages (her mother was ill and could not add to Vati's note; and a quotation from a psalm: "I will lift up mine eyes unto the hills from whence cometh my help") twice, with slightly different details (46, 47), leaving the reader uncertain how many communications there were and which was the very last.

21. For instance, the arrest of the girls' grandfather is described using the

verbs of reconstruction: it *"must have been* meant as a warning to the Jewish community," and "[Opa] *must have known* he was about to be arrested" (37, my italics); and the viewpoints of other people are often described, for instance each of the sisters' in turn (24).

22. In this way, Gershon's *A Lesser Child* enacts the overlap between personal and historical catastrophe that Dominic LaCapra argues is next to impossible. In his *History and Memory after Auschwitz*, he claims that "it is deceptive to reduce, or transfer the qualities of, one dimension of trauma to the other" (1998, 47): but it seems to me that the child's-eye view of the war succeeds in a balanced or dialogic version of such a "transfer."

23. The adult narrator uses the provisional tenses of reconstruction again in this quotation; and the narrator sees this familial analysis as a screen for something worse: Kate's blaming her father "for what the Nazis were doing to the family" (101).

24. A more extreme and sustained version of this attempt by the younger self to rewrite the adult's narrative is Raymond Federman's novella *The Voice in the Closet/La Voix dans le Cabinet de Débarras* (Madison: Coda Press, 1979), an experimental narrative about an adult trying to write his memories of the day in July 1942 when all his family except himself were deported from Paris to Auschwitz. The child that the writer once was starts to comment on and try to rewrite the adult's necessarily inaccurate version.

25. The case here is different from, for instance, Lore Segal's technique of relating future events within parentheses throughout her memoir *Other People's Houses*; this is partly because the events Segal relates are usually not deaths, and thus can be clearly separated off from the present.

26. Gershon published six collections of poetry, three works of nonfiction, and three novels.

27. Brinson 200, 4; she includes under this heading what she terms the "more limited" Kindertransport accounts, which are generally by Jewish writers (5). The same assumption that there could be such a "collective" autobiography is made implicitly in the introduction to Lixl-Purcell 1988, 1–2.

Stages of Memory: Imagining Identities in the Holocaust Drama of Deborah Levy, Julia Pascal, and Diane Samuels

Susanne Greenhalgh

> What makes you shape and reshape yourself so
> brightly from so much pain and suffering?
> Who gave you the right?
> —Charlotte Salomon, *Life? or Theater?*

ALL THREE WRITERS I DISCUSS IN THIS ESSAY BELONG TO THE "SEC-ond generation" of Holocaust writers "who either imagine themselves into the Holocaust or recount their fate as children of survivors" (Bartov 2000, 226). Deborah Levy's "Imagining Germany," commissioned by Ruskin College, Oxford, is a response to the work of the German artist Joseph Beuys, and takes the form of an "audio installation" available online from 2001; Julia Pascal's *Holocaust Trilogy* (2000) is made up of three plays pro-duced over several years, which combine extensive historical research with the techniques of postmodern physical theater, whilst Diane Samuels's *Kindertransport*, based on the testi-monies of those who escaped from Germany to Britain under a scheme for children, employs both naturalistic and symbolist styles and has been frequently performed in Europe and America since its premiere in 1993. Although very different in form and content, these plays and performances are similar in that they not only provide ways for an audience to "imagine themselves into the Holocaust" but also interrogate both imagination and memory in relation to that process.

In using the term "stages of memory," therefore, I seek to set several different meanings of its keywords in play. Clearly I have in mind the Freudian "scene" of remembered or repressed trauma, recognizing how memory changes through time, over generations, giving rise to what can be perceived as distinct sequences, scenes, stages, in its processes. Additionally, I am deliberately echoing the title of Claude Schumacher's edited collection of essays, *Staging the Holocaust,* a collection that considers the performativities, as well as the performance, of the Shoah, the display of Holocaust memory in national as well as purely theatrical contexts.[1] All the works discussed, I argue, engage with memorialization as well as with memory, the public understanding of the Holocaust as well as its private experiences and griefs.

In their discussion of the historical and national processes by which the Holocaust became part of collective memory in Germany, Israel, and America, Daniel Levy and Natan Sznaider emphasize the significance of such generational shifts in the nature of memory, from the *social memory* of the experiencing group to the *historical memory* of those who come after, formed by media, books, education, public memorialization, and so on. The war generation, whose experience was based on autobiographic memories, was "gradually replaced by postwar generations whose understanding of the Holocaust was based on symbolic representations; and [there was] a growing historicization of the event . . . Characteristic of these changes was the temporal duality of memory: the memories of the Holocaust came to be regarded as unique with reference to the past and universal for the future. That is to say, the Holocaust past is something that happened predominantly to the Jews, while the Holocaust future might happen to anyone" (Levy and Sznaider 2000, 96). All my texts reflect to a greater or lesser degree on how far the theatrical medium, so strongly associated with the present and with presence—"liveness" as Philip Auslander terms it—is also equipped to represent the temporal duality of memory, looking back to the past and forward to the future. As Samuels says in the introduction to *Kindertransport:* "Past and present are wound around each other throughout the play. They are not distinct but inextricably connected. The re-running of what happened many years ago is not there to explain how things are now, but is a part of the inner life of the present" (1996, vii). However there are significant contrasts between Samuels's chosen mode of interiority and retrospection, Pascal's invocation of past theatrical conventions and performances, and Levy's exploration of invented memory.

Such variety of forms and emphases are to some extent the consequence of the process outlined by Levy and Sznaider. Former modes of collective memory, constitutive of the "imagined communities" of nation-states are giving way to forms of "transnational connections (such as 'dual citizenship' or 'bi-lingualism')." As such, Holocaust memory has become "cosmopolitanized," the distinctive form taken by collective memories in the age of globalization and mediation "providing new epistemological vantage points and emerging moral-political interdependencies" (2000, 87). Examples of this reshaping are the emergence of the Holocaust as focal point of a new European moral "shared memory" and as an evolving global icon, capable of mobilizing the human rights agenda, as in the announcements of Holocaust Memorial Days across the world: "The cosmopolitanization of Holocaust memories . . . refer[s] to concrete social spaces that are characterized by a high degree of reflexivity and the ongoing encounter with different cultures. . . . The cosmopolitanization of memory does not mean the end of national perspectives so much as their transformation into more complex entities" (92).

The stages and figures created by Levy, Pascal, and Samuels are "cosmopolitanized" in the sense that they are "characterized by a high degree of reflexivity and the ongoing encounter with different cultures" (93). They are also marked by what Levy and Sznaider view as a further constituent part of cosmopolitan memory, its "recognition of the history (and the memories) of the 'Other'":

> Half a century after the Holocaust, it is no longer the atrocities themselves that are at the center of attention (especially in light of the fact that the majority of surviving victims have died), but how the heirs of the victims, the perpetrators and bystanders are coping with these stories and the evolving memories. In other words, the recognition of the "Other" diffuses the distinction between memories of victims and perpetrators. What remains is the memory of a shared past. It is not shared due to some mythical desires and the belonging to some continuing community of fate, but as the product of a reflexive choice to incorporate the suffering of the "Other." (103)

This concern with the processes of "Othering" has been especially significant within the rereadings of female Jewish identity and of Holocaust history and representation made by feminist scholars and critics during the last few decades. Vivian M. Patraka proposes that the "problem" now is to "locate 'Jewish-ness' for women in regard both to the Holocaust and to the pos-sibility of a collective identity that relates to that history" (Patraka 1999, 55). However she admits that there is still a paucity of either critical or artistic work that confronts these gender issues in relation to drama and performance. I would argue that the texts I discuss do precisely this. In addition to the pioneering work on women playwrights of the Holocaust by Patraka herself and writers such as E. R. Isser (1990), research by scholars in other fields is helpful. Marlene Heinemann's work on the memoirs of women survivors, for instance, identifies female-specific themes of *anatomy* and *destiny, characterization,* the description of *intimate and/or sexual relations,* and the attempt by each writer to inscribe her work with *authenticity.* Such a model has applicability to works which attempt to imagine, rather than record, the identities constructed by the experience of the Holocaust (Heinemann 1986).

Also relevant to my discussion is what Deborah Levy has called the "space of address" of these texts (Levy, cited in Good-man 1993, 224). This can include the physical spaces and media for and in which these texts have been or will be performed, rang-ing from studio theaters to conventional auditoriums, from radio transmissions to online lectures, and performances across the world as well as in their originating culture. Rather than "ghet-toizing" these plays by their thematic concerns, I seek to situate them in the broader contexts of contemporary women's play-writing in Britain, especially as part of the new "international-ism" and "bilingualism" that Susan Bassnett has identified emergent in British theater and performance in recent years. Questions of territorial and national identification, of home and homelands, of learned languages and native tongues, what Bass-nett calls the "politics of location" (2000, xx) are a significant aspect of all the works I discuss. However this should not be read as a claim that these writers form any kind of "group" or "move-ment," let alone a specifically "British" one. Indeed I want to insist on their differences, in background, choice of themes and forms, in their understanding of what both stage and memory can be, perhaps finally of what the Holocaust was and is. If there is a connection to be found between these different works, it is chiefly in their creation of what Pascal has termed "the fractured

world of exile" (Pascal 2000, 5), and their variously explicit inter-
rogations of national, as well as religious or ethnic, identities.
Like the character of Rachel in Pascal's play *The Dybbuk*, these
writers are "haunted by faces, different accents, different bodies,
all the lost cousins and aunts and uncles who I want to have
known" (5) and by geographies that have been altered forever by
vanished lives. All my chosen texts can be characterized as stagings of this fractured world, peopled by dramatic figures who are
outsiders, travelers, refugees, driven by actions of departure, journeying, but seldom of arrival, captured in gestures of memory
and mourning, on stages echoing with the clashing voices of multilingualism, cluttered with the abandoned baggage of lost homes
and histories.

In this sense they are examples of what Una Chaudhuri has
termed "topographic theatre," dramatizations of the "conjunc-
ture of language and place" (Chaudhuri 1995, 166), positing "a
new kind of placement, not in any one circumscribed and clearly
defined place but in the crossroads, pathways, and junctions
between places. At the extreme it advocates a new kind of placelessness . . . placelessness not as the absence or erasure of place
but as the combination and layering, one on top of another, of
many different places, many distinct orders of spatiality" (138).
However, acknowledgment of these postmodern features must
be accompanied by recognition that, more significantly still,
these works are embodiments of what Omer Bartov has proposed
as the central and enduring experience of the Holocaust: "The
Holocaust is at the center of a crisis of identity, whose ramifica-
tions range far beyond its chronological boundaries and the life-
span of its survivors . . . It is a crisis that casts doubt on the very
definition of identity, on what it means to know who you are,
where you come from, what you are capable or incapable of doing,
experiencing, imagining" (Bartov 2000, 229). Levy, Samuels, and
Pascal not only confront the risks to be run in pursuing solidarity with the dead through acts of imagination but make their
interrogation of the contemporary politics of this difficult and
painful process a major aspect of their work.

☙

Diane Samuels's play *Kindertransport* is undoubtedly the most
successful of the works discussed here, reaching the widest pos-

sible audience by means of a West End transfer of the original
Soho Theatre production, as well as by many performances in
America, Germany, and other countries, and by adaptation for
BBC radio. Writing of American plays based on survivors' testimony, Alvin Goldfarb has criticized their "oversimplified" representations that "draw analogies that diminish the magnitude of
the Shoah, as well as strive to provide emotional reassurance to
their audience through simplistic plot resolutions," especially
when embedded in the melodramatic conventions of "familial
redemption" (1998, 120–21, 123). Samuels's play might appear
to fit into this category through its condensation of multiple survivors' testimonies into a family drama of secrets and lies.
Although Samuels, a former schoolteacher, appears to locate her
play firmly in the historicity of the memorial accounts on which
she draws, it is also possible to argue that the voices of her Kindertransport interviewees are assimilated as much as authenticated
through the creation of the representative figure, Eva/Evelyn.

Played by two actesses, this figure is irredeemably split in time
and identity between the refugee German Jewish child and the
naturalized, baptized English woman, and between two mothers,
the *haute bourgeoise* Helga and the working-class Lil. The location for the play is appropriately a storage room of memories and
the material objects that Evelyn has collected to assuage her
sense of dispossession: in a sense it is the madwoman's attic of
classic women's fiction, site of threatening secrets and doppel-
gangers. The play's surface naturalism, reliance on psychological
relationships, and apparent clarity of narrative structure is at
first reassuring, even sentimentalizing. The flashbacks to Eva's
childhood are chronological, clearly marking the stages of her
shedding of Jewish identity, from the eating of a ham sandwich
to the selling of her mother's gold jewelry, including the Star of
David.

These sequences are interspersed with the surreal atmosphere
of the tale of the Ratcatcher, who leads guilty greedy children
into the abyss. This thematic motif is made visual by means of
the illustrated storybook from which the tale is read, the lighting effects, and the metamorphoses of the single male actor into
a succession of uniformed men who intrude on the otherwise
entirely female stage space. The work is made aural through the
repeated musical theme that marks his appearances. The Ratcatcher is also psychologically symbolic, an emblem of terror for

the child Eva that evokes Bruno Bettelheim's theories about the role of fairy tales in the development of morality and maturity of the young.[2]

All these elements make it easy for the play to be read and received by audiences as simultaneously a familiar psychic drama of mother-daughter relations, a story of childhood trauma, and also a variation on the tragedy of the Jews, a "memory play" uncovering the hidden personal wounds still bleeding from those years, along the lines of, say, Tennessee Williams's *The Glass Menagerie,* in order to legitimate the departure of a child from the maternal home into maturity and the outside world. But I would argue that the play has even darker levels of memory, more bleak questions to ask of the nature of memory itself. Evelyn's obsession with cleanliness is not simply a symptom of the psychological damage of loss of her mother, or her later rejection of her. Rather it can be read as a sign of her internalization of the Nazi doctrine of the Jews as pollution, from which her baptism as a Christian has "cleansed" and "purified" her. The abyss which Evelyn fears is not, as she herself asserts, simply the past itself, or the pain of memory, it is her own self-loathing, which is focused, unacknowledged, on her Jewishness. It is this that makes the final exchange between mother and daughter so painful. This is the only sequence in which the Evelyn of the present, as opposed to the Eva of the past, interacts with Helga. Since the narrative makes it clear that, on the naturalistic level, they never met again after the dockside scene in which Eva refused to accompany her mother to a new life in America, the status of this scene is deliberately—and disturbingly—indeterminate. Does it dramatize an exchange of letters? Is it a replay of an actual conversation in which unforgivable things were said (similar in fact to the parallel scene in which Evelyn accused Lil of being a "child-stealer")? Or is Evelyn's internalized staging of an exchange that never happened, *invented* memory: her final descent into the abyss, the saying of the unsayable, which releases (banishes?), like an exorcism, the child Eva from the stage?

> EVELYN: I wish you had died.
> HELGA. I wish you had lived.
> EVELYN. I did my best.
> HELGA. Hitler started the job and you finished it.
> EVELYN. Why does it have to be my fault?

HELGA. You cut off my fingers and pulled out my hair one strand at a time.

EVELYN. You were the Ratcatcher. Those were his eyes, his face . . .

HELGA. You hung me out of the window by my ears and broke my soul into shreds.

EVELYN. You threw me into the sea with all your baggage on my shoulders.

HELGA. You can never excuse yourself.

EVELYN. How could I swim ashore with such heaviness on me? I was drowning in leagues and leagues of salty water.

HELGA. I have bled oceans out of my eyes.

EVELYN. I had to let go to float.

HELGA. Snake. Slithering out of yourself like it was an unwanted skin. Worm.

EVELYN. What right have you to accuse me? You kept saying something. What was it? Over and over? Yes. "No," you said. That was all. "No, I won't help you. You have to manage on your own. Take the needle. Sew the button and it's time to go. You don't need me. See it's good." Was it really so very good, Mutti? Was it really what you wanted? It wasn't what I wanted.

HELGA. My suffering is monumental. Yours is personal.
Eva exits.

EVELYN. What about what you did to me? You should have hung on to me and never let me go. Why did you send me away when you were in danger? No one made you. You chose to do it. Didn't it ever occur to you that I might have wanted to die with you? Because I did. I never wanted to live without you and you made me. What is more cruel than that? Except for coming back from the dead and punishing me for surviving on my own. (act 2, scene 1, page 87)

Eva/Evelyn is unable to forgive her mother for choosing survival of her people over survival of the bond between mother and daughter. Divesting herself of her Jewishness, "slithering out of yourself like it was a unwanted skin" as her mother (never?) says, leaves her with a "blank," which is preferable to the "abyss" of the past: "The older I get the less of myself I become" (act 2, scene 1, page 68). It is true that discovery of her mother's history fills the "blank space" for her aptly named daughter Faith; a background and context that is not just a "pile of ashes" but a surviving family, a "gift" as Helga told Eva, received by so few of the Jews of Europe. It is also true that Evelyn refrains from burning the two books that survive from her former life to hand them to her own child. But she still rejects her own Jewishness, a revenge for her mother's "abandonment," knowing this is the deepest way in which to punish her. She cannot forgive her for demanding that she be a carrier of the future, rather than a victim of the past. The claims of the "monumental" and the "personal," the fate of the millions, their need not simply to be remembered but to survive through their children, and the cost of this to those who come after can never be reconciled, it seems.

At the end of the play the shadow of the Ratcatcher again covers the stage. Samuels ultimately rejects the comforts of family reconciliation to which her narrative structure appeared to lead. In this play memory and the obligations of memorialization are staged as a living curse rather than as any kind of healing process that can be employed to exorcise, or at least close the door on, the past. However, since the "space of address" remains the home and family history, represented by the modified naturalism of modernist theater with its focus on individual subjectivity, the play ultimately constructs memory as primarily a personal, rather than political, process.

≈

Julia Pascal is an actor-director as well as playwright who has established her own theater company and is strongly influenced by the broader crosscurrents of contemporary European physical theatre, as well as by a more politicized conception of Holocaust history than Samuels. She has published a number of newspaper articles arguing for the significance of the Holocaust in relation to previous and subsequent genocides, such as those of the Armenians and the Rwandans at the beginning and end of the twentieth century. Writing of attempts to represent the Holocaust theatrically, she has admitted "you can never show people starving in concentration camps. But, on stage, you can make them mirror the audience; they are ordinary people ripped out of their lives. And, because theatre takes place in the present, it isn't relegated to history" (Pascal 1995, 40). Her concern with "presentness" as well as presence leads Pascal to daring experimentation with the "authenticity" that Heinemann regards as a crucial measure for the integrity of survivor memoirs.

For the theater production of her 1990 play *Theresa*, based on the true story of an Austrian Jewess stranded in the Channel Islands and deliberately detained by the Guernsey authorities to be handed over to the Nazis after occupation, Pascal had no qualms about rewriting her subject's personal history. Her heroine was changed from a young woman to a middle-aged one with a grown-up son so that she could be embodied by the actress and dancer Ruth Posner, herself a child survivor. Here Posner's potency as a living document, "someone who could transmit this memory of Nazi occupation, by her very presence," (5) offers a bodily "authenticity" that Pascal privileges above the documentary evidence that she painstakingly researched in archives and through interviews with eyewitnesses. Pascal's interest in different, more broadly cultural forms of "authenticity," is also apparent in her use of expressionist dance, a mode of "bodily remembering" that is both a homage to the dance tradition brought out of Germany by the exiled dancer Hilde Holger, and an example of "how the heirs of the victims, the perpetrators and bystanders are coping with these . . . evolving memories" (Levy and Sznaider 2000, 103). Arising out of collaboration with the German choreographer Thomas Kampe (who, as Pascal stresses in her introduction to the collected plays, is the son of a Wehrmacht officer), the *process* of devising a performance text, what the performance theorist Richard Schechner has termed the evocation of "restored memory," is as important to Pascal as is the production eventually created.

Pascal's openness to the possibilities of physical theater has other outcomes. In the dramaturgy of this contemporary Holocaust "memoryscape" (to use Levy and Sznaider's term 2000, 88) the visually inflected "landscape," which Helene Keyssar has argued is the special terrain of women's drama, often turns into a "soundscape": an interrogation from other sensory perspectives of the problematics of the visual, either to document or to imagine the past. Voice, not in the metaphorical sense of much literary analysis but in the precise sense of vocal expressivity, among other sounds, is thus as important as images and movement in these stagings of memory. Chaudhuri argues that this "auralization of dramatic meaning" and "renewed narrativity" are necessary developments in postmodern representation of "the painfully emergent history of our times," which demands not simply to be seen but also *heard* (1995, 148). It is no accident, I suggest, that Levy's "Imagining Germany" is an audiotext (though sometimes accompanied by images) and that both Samuel's *Kindertransport* and Pascal's *Theresa* have been successfully adapted for radio, a medium that requires a reconception of the body's signification.

Thus Pascal's play, rewritten for radio as *The Road to Paradise*, restores the facts of her life to Theresa, since neither expressionist dance nor Posner's personal history, evoked by the actor's visible presence, can play a role. However this does not mean the absence of the "living body" in a play about death. On the contrary, as Frances Gray (2001) suggests, "While an image has infinite potential to become a lifeless object on which meaning can be imposed, voice cannot exist without breath, without a living body to control the vibrations which the breath sets up in the vocal folds to make sounds. Voice signifies an independent, choice-making presence, not one that can be definitively constructed by a gaze. A voice is not a site, you cannot inscribe anything upon it: . . . voice is an action." In this sense Pascal's radio version develops further aspects of another kind of "authenticity" already integral to the play. As is frequently the case in rehearsal, the personal past of the actors also became part of the text. Posner's childhood recollections and remembered Polish nursery rhymes became part of, in James Young's phrase, the "texture of memory" in the play's soundscape, a texture made up of voices, in the form of accented narration and dialogue juxtaposed with expressionist screams of anguish, which are in turn blended with the montage of fragments of music and its cultural associations, from jazz to Mozart and Strauss; all culminating inevitably in the sound of the trains bound for Auschwitz.

Another key element of the "memoryscape," as in Pascal's other plays, is its multilingualism, an intermingling of German, Polish, and French with the dominantly English dialogue. Chaudhuri has drawn attention to the place of language and narrative in the "dramatizing of displacement" in contemporary drama, and identified translation, "the problem of interlinguistic communication in a world desperately in need of connection" as its major signifier (1995, 137–38). Although Pascal explains her play's multilingualism as homage to both a personal and historical past, "that pre-Holocaust European Jewish gift of seamlessly flowing from one language to another as my grandparents did" (2000, 6), it also, I suggest, locates the play in relation to contemporary "cosmopolitanized" Holocaust memory, broadly European rather than specifically national.[3] Even more crucially, language is delineated as an unstable and destabilizing terrain for identity in the post-Holocaust world.

This interrogation of post-Holocaust language becomes central in the second play of the trilogy, *A Dead Woman on Holiday*, whose protagonist, Sophia, a French Jew, is a translator at the Nuremberg war trials. Patraka has also emphasized the significance of the translation motif in representations of the Holocaust, particularly how it can bear witness to "the very limits of the process of translation (even as we absorb information) and to its inevitable deformations and inadequate equivalencies. The trope of translation reminds us not only of the limits of translation in reference to Holocaust history, but of the weight and labor of translation itself, foremost for the survivor, then of the performing interpreter, and, finally, for us in the position of spectators" (1999, 25). Although the major action of the play is Sophia's love affair with a married American interpreter, itself portrayed as a desperate attempt to survive her wartime memories or even come back to life sexually and psychically, the play is also concerned with the contamination of language by genocide. Even the supposedly rational processes of justice and the impartial discourse of the law are made senseless by the testimonies of the trials. Key scenes are those in which the cruel ironies of Sophia's situation as a "dead woman on holiday" (adapted from Primo Levi's recollection of a nazi guard's brutal witticism about the doomed status of those Jews still left alive) are brought home through the juxtaposition of languages.

Adultery;
Adulterer;
Adulterous;
... *adultère*
... *adultère;*
... *adultère*
Alien
... *étranger.*
Alimony:
... *pension alimentaire.*
Allegiance:
... *allégeance;*
... *fidelité.*
Annihilation:
... *annihilation.* (2000, 75)

Speaking the words of the witnesses and prisoners at the trial is experienced as a form of deathly possession, making Sophia both physically sick and unable to remember the words of the sabbath prayers.

Intercut with the attempts of Paul and Sophia to recover from the wounds of war through a discourse of romantic love infused by Platonic idealism are the vicious diatribes of the German Woman, terrifyingly alive with hatred as Sophia's grip on the will to live becomes more tenuous. The play's closing moments, in which the allies' national anthems overlay the threat to the future of the German Woman's undying hatred, and Sophia and Paul move from separate spots toward each other, allow no satisfaction in the judgments at Nuremberg, or the future of a "new Europe," and only a tenuous endorsement of the alliance of languages and cultures represented by their cross-cultural love affair.

It is the final play of the trilogy, incorporating the classic Yiddish play by Solomon Ansti, *The Dybbuk*, that is most self-reflexive of its own strategies of representation. In part this is a consequence of its employment of the "performance-within-a-performance." This is a device identified by Freddie Rokem as both a mode of epistemological experimentation and a means of creating a dialectic between the "real and the fantastic," that which can be comprehended and that which is beyond the grasp of ordinary experience (1998, 44). The play begins with a journey to Germany (echoing Pascal's own, on tour with her previous play *Theresa*) by a British Jewish girl of the present, uncertain of her identity and her relationship to her Jewishness:

> JUDITH: Am I ashamed to be a Jew? Is this my own self-hatred? My own anti-semitism? I don't even believe in God, so what makes me a Jew? They don't talk of such things in my family. Keep your head down. Be British, be cool, be part of the crowd. (2000, 106).

For Judith, as for Pascal, Germany is "a country filled with the ghosts of those who died too early," Europe a "gaping grave" (2000, 8): "I go to Germany and I think that Hitler won." (106) The "dream of assimilation" gives way to dreams of the dead "all the lost. . . . I want to have known" and a process of imaginative identification that culminates in the seamless merging of past and present as Rachel becomes one of a group of secular young Jews awaiting death in an unnamed ghetto. At the obvious level their improvised performance of *The Dybbuk*, an exercise in memorial reconstruction on both the narrative and metatheatrical levels, acts as a celebration of the survival of culture, language, and fellowship even as Pascal's previous play questioned the limits of that survival. The conclusion of the play, a *danse macabre*, representing the deaths of millions, is also a dance of rebirth: "You can kill a people but you cannot kill their culture" (127).

But the staging of the story of the dybbuk is more troubling than this celebratory gloss by Pascal herself suggests. In Ansti's original play the possessed Leah becomes a double entity, fused with her lover Hanan who clings to earthly life, she is a mystical figure, both male and female, a cabbalistic parallel to the Platonic doctrine of twin souls evoked by Sophia in *A Dead Woman on Holiday*. In Pascal's version, played by Rachel, the dramatic figure is now fourfold: Leah/Dybbuk/Rachel of the past who died/ Rachel of the present:

> RACHEL (as LEAH/DYBBUK) . . . Where would I go? All the roads are closed to me. There is heaven and earth, there are worlds without end.
>
> (*as herself*) England, America, Africa. But nowhere, nowhere is there a space for me. (126)

The dybbuk's resistance to the rabbi's command to leave the body and its final cries of denial dramatize the victims' struggle to live and their resistance to their planned fate, but the exorcism leaves the Rachel of the present either alone, and separated from the dead whose spirits she had invoked, or absorbed into the collective fate of millions represented by the endless procession of figures enacting both grotesque and affecting dying gestures. As a dramatic figure she is both multiple, a personification of collective memory, and nonexistent, emblem of that "terrifying, powerful absence" that Patraka situates at the center of the "Holocaust performative" (1999, 6–7):

> It is the goneness of the Holocaust that produces the simultaneous profusion of discourses and understandings; the goneness is what opens up, what spurs, what unleashes the perpetual desire to do, to make, to rethink the Holocaust . . . The Holocaust performative acknowledges that there is nothing to say to goneness and yet we continue to try and mark it, say it, identify it, memorialize the loss over

and over . . . the constant iteration against the pressures of a palpable loss and not merely a set of discursive conventions. With proliferation comes, inevitably it seems, denial, resistance, appropriation, trivialization, and misrecognition. (7)

Although Pascal's plays powerfully stage the desire for imagined identification with both the culture and the lives of those who are gone, they also acknowledge the impossibility, even for theater, of bringing the dead to life.

᠍ᡪ

Both Samuels and Pascal construct their memory plays from the evidence of the past; Deborah Levy's exploration of the Holocaust is firmly located in the present. Here her chosen mode of performance is significant. Patraka has examined some of the potentialities of performance art for the representation of the Holocaust, in particular its frequent employment of autobiographical experience from the perspective of the present tense (1999, 24). Claire Macdonald has called Deborah Levy's dramatic writing a " 'theatre of utterance'—the world is spoken into being in the gap between the real world and the imagination" (2000, 241). The child of political exiles from South Africa, trained in the performing arts at Dartington, "there is no home, no authenticity, no closure, and no finality in her works." Rather her work can be seen as stagings of identity as a constant process of imagined reinvention. This is evident in her use of Holocaust motifs in her early performance piece *Pax* commissioned by The Women's Theatre Group in 1984, notionally as an "anti-nuclear" play. This places four female "archetypes " in a "large desolate house in the Wilderness" to "take on the past, present and future of twentieth-century Europe." Although the women claim kinship with each other as daughters, mothers, aunts, and nieces, their relationships are less familial than generational. The KEEPER of the house is virtually an embodiment of cosmopolitan memory itself: according to Levy she is "The past, and Europe herself. A woman who carries the burden of history around with her" (2000, 4). Although she evokes the specifics of the Holocaust—"My family were abolished. I watched their smoke rage from the chimneys" (49)—she is a universal witness of wars, revolutions, and atrocities around the globe, from Manchuria, Ethiopia, China to Cuba, and Latin America, both stateless refugee and keeper of memory. The MOURNER who represents the present and the HIDDEN DAUGHTER, type of the future, along with the DOMESTICATED WOMAN, archetypal homemaker, are deliberately comic as well as suggestive of the effects of atrocity, replaying to the point of absurdity some of the accustomed tropes of feminine representation and parodying both the conventions of the well-made play and its narrative of family returns and departure, as well as the portentousness of overt theatrical symbolism. In this collage of European history the Holocaust takes its place as just one more fragment of memory, however haunting.

This elusiveness is also evident in Levy's 2001 audio lecture-cum-performance installation, consisting of three addresses, of varying lengths, of which only the last, "Imagining Germany," appears directly to address the Holocaust. "I dreamt of this" juxtaposes evocations of Oscar Wilde, artist, victim, and exile, with an unexplained image seen through the open front door of Levy's North London House of a slaughtered lamb. In "Migrations to Elsewhere and Other Places," "Alice the European" debates the geography of place with the White Rabbit in Wonderland. In "Imagining Germany," the longest piece, Levy stages an encounter with the work and personal history of Beuys, an artist who was a member of the Hitler Youth, and was shot down as a Luftwaffe pilot, and whose work makes frequent use of materials that emerge from autobiographical experience but also recall the millions of possessions and remains collected from the Jews in the camps, some of which are now preserved in museums and memorial sites. Parallel with this exploration of Beuys's work, and its place in the "evolving memory" of the Holocaust, Levy contemplates first visits to Israel and Germany, creating an imaginary itinerary out of recollected "photographs, postcards, fragments of black and white documentary." Throughout, her use of the present tense for her narrative gives a strong sense of at least an imagined performance that increases as the talk goes on with the accumulation of the visual detail of the journey, from the shiny chrome newness of the rebuilt German cities to the geranium-covered balconies of the Bavarian countryside.

Above all it evokes a sense of growing unease. From the searching for a flicker of response to her Jewish name at passport control Levy recounts her growing "fear in my body about being there at all. It feels like being stuck in the past and that is a place I don't wish to be in. . . . There is fear inside me and nightmare inside me—it could have been me." The culmination apparently comes in a meeting with an elderly couple whose friendliness vanishes when they hear her name, but crucially Levy's imagination takes her further, picturing her own children as Aryan little girls playing in the Alpine meadows amid the "Nazi grass, Nazi trees, Nazi sky," finally to the recognition of the other in herself, "I too am not civilized . . . I too am racist . . . the sinister thing is me." Levy's performed journey is not after all into the past, as was Rachel's in *The Dybbuk*, or Evelyn's in *Kindertransport*, but into her own present, her own politics of location, her own responsibilities as a writer.

Levy not only stages the invention of memory out of the mediatized echoes of the Holocaust that saturate contemporary culture, but also explores an invented identity as her own "Other," both Jewish and "Aryan." It is here that the significance of the "doubling" of Germany with Israel as potential destination becomes apparent. Implicitly the listener/viewer is invited to contemplate *why* Levy has twinned Munich and Tel Aviv, what contemporary Israel might have in common with Nazi Germany, what links the atrocities of the past with those of the present? This suggestion—it is certainly no more than this—of equivalence invites ethical interrogation rather than imposing interpretation. Here Levy"s autobiographical "presence' is vital. Although both Pascal's dramatic figures, Sophia and Judith/ Rachel, are in part autobiographical projections of the playwright's present as well as figures of self-identification with the victims of the past, they cannot encompass the suggestiveness and allusiveness that Levy's web self-performance of "confession" can achieve. Levy's work perhaps points to one possible response to the "crisis" identified by Rokem, "which is soon to become reality, when all the survivors will have died and it will be impossible to give a testimony" (1998, 51). Instead of seeking to give a voice to the dead perhaps performance must seek to explore the ways in which we are all not simply "born later" but are in a sense ourselves survivors, required to confront our own guilt and responsibility.

꙰

All these writers can be termed "cosmopolitan," in the sense that they reclaim and revision memory and history of the Holocaust in contexts both inside and outside national "imagined communities," whether those of their Jewish heritage or of their adopted British homes. In Samuels's case this is primarily achieved by putting these two identities in direct collision; for Pascal and Levy those identities are much more fluid and unfixed. I find all these performance texts, in their very different ways, both powerful and disturbing. This is not simply because they unflinchingly explore the continuing trauma of the Holocaust on successive generations. It is rather because of their characters' willingness to confront the otherness within their own identities, to acknowledge how memory is invented as well as recovered, to question the meanings of authenticity, to explore their own hidden guilts. The plays also, I think, deliberately refuse memorialization, even if both Pascal's trilogy and Samuels's *Kindertransport* have already been performed as part of Holocaust Day remembrance. In this their insistence on voice as well as image is significant. For as Gray suggests, "A voice is not a site, you cannot inscribe anything upon it . . . voice is an action."

Their dramatic figures are not simple representations of Jewish women, British or otherwise; they are multiple, or split figures, possessed, haunted, speaking in tongues, nowhere at home. Helge tells Eva in *Kindertransport*, "Home is inside you. Inside you and me. It is not a place," but Pascal's use of the dispossessed soul of the dybbuk embodies another experience: "England, America, Africa. But nowhere, nowhere is there a space for me." Though very different in style and specific subject matter Pascal, Levy, and Samuels all construct stages that are terrains of displacement, offering their audiences nightmare fairy tales as well as the preserved words of religious or cultural tradition. Claire Macdonald's view of Levy's work is equally applicable to Pascal's and Samuel's plays: "There is . . . no authenticity, no closure, and no finality" in their view of Holocaust memory. All the works, too, can be viewed as directed as much toward the future as to the past, sharing that "temporal duality of memory" identified by Levy and Sznaider, and asking with Samuels, "What future grows out of a traumatized past?" (Macdonald 2000, 236). Jenny Bourne has depicted the feminist Jewish "hauntology" of the Holocaust as a constant psychic consciousness of living in an "imagined world" of "impending destruction" (Bourne 1987, 16; cited in Patraka 1999, 56). Through their recognition of the Holocaust as "a crisis that casts doubt on the very definition of identity, on what it means to know who you are, where you come from, what you are capable or incapable of doing, experiencing, imagining" (Bartov 2000, 246), these three writers have helped map the evolving geography of that imagined world.

NOTES

1. See E. R. Isser, "Toward a Feminist Perspective in American Holocaust Drama," *Studies in the Humanities* 17 (December 1990): 139–48.

2. Bruno Bettelheim's *The Uses of Enchantment: The Meaning and Importance of Fairy Tales,* first published in 1975, as well as his other child-focused psychoanalytic theories and practice, had great influence worldwide during the latter part of the twentieth century not least because of the moral authority accorded him for his own experiences as a concentration camp detainee. In recent years, however, his reputation has been called into serious question. There has been significant criticism of his authoritarian views and therapeutic practices, which have been labeled child abuse by some, as well as of his dishonesty in claiming academic qualifications he had not been awarded and plagiarizing the ideas of others, including in *The Uses of Enchantment,* and exaggerating the extent of his Holocaust ordeal. In view of Samuels's focus on "good" and "bad" mothering in her play it is interesting that much of Bettelheim's work laid the blame for children's illness (including autism) at the mother's door.

3. It should be noted that one of Pascal's stated aims in the play was to show how British complicity in the Holocaust went beyond reluctance to take in refugees or act against the extermination camps, to include acts of actual collaboration with Nazi genocidal policies.

"The pressure of what has been felt": The Poetry of Elaine Feinstein

Rose Atfield

Eʟᴀɪɴᴇ ꜰᴇɪɴsᴛᴇɪɴ ᴡᴀs ʙᴏʀɴ ɪɴ 1930, ɪɴ ʙᴏᴏᴛʟᴇ, ʟᴀɴᴄᴀsʜɪʀᴇ, ᴏꜰ second-generation Jewish-Russian immigrants. Well aware of the persecution her great-grandparents had suffered, she celebrates the fortuitous chance of being a Jewish woman writer in twentieth- and twenty-first-century British culture. Fortuitous, as she "escaped" the fate of many Jewish children of her generation and grew up in this knowledge, embracing risk in poetic, personal, and political practice. An awareness of residual guilt, at being "saved" while others perished, lies at the margins of her poetic expression but it explains her marked challenge to accepted authority, social expectations and conventional style.

She found herself constrained by the inwardly reticent tone of poetry current in the austere English society of the 1950s; her own celebratory response is conveyed in the rich sensuousness of her imagery, which emphasizes her delight in natural and human simplicities and their underlying profundity. In her work she turns the potentially negative circumstances of feeling and being seen as an "alien," due to her Russian-Jewish background, to positive advantage in extending her own poetic range to embrace and reflect a wider diversity of British culture.

The element of "alienation" in her work makes the critical perspective of Julia Kristeva a fruitful aid to exploring the psychological and feminist motivation of her poetry. Kristeva's own experience of exile and thus her sympathy and understanding of ethnic diversity offer an illuminating interpretation of Feinstein's overall concerns for family, motherhood, social history and poetics, as presented in the collections of her poetry published between 1966 and 2002.

In "Song of Power" (1966; Lawson 2001, 78) her Jewish heritage is evident in her defensive maternal stance toward "baiting children in my / son's school class," who repeat the insulting demon-stration of abjection, the disturbing aspect of human nature that Kristeva suggests finds foreigners "unclean." The deliberate choice of diction echoes "Jew-baiting" down the centuries, as does: "say I am a witch: black is the / mirror you give me"; this takes the poem beyond simple recording of the specific incident into "herethics," challenging binary oppositions of culture and nature in the mother-child relationship. The experience explored in the poem is that which Adrienne Baker refers to, "of being an immigrant . . . one which continues to have reverberations for the children, grandchildren and even great grand children of the immigrants" (1993, 9).

In the poem Feinstein counteracts the challenge of the boys' insults, which are intended to reject the unfamiliar, by invoking "any supernatural power / my strangeness earns me." At the same time she resists orthodoxy by claiming, "all Gods are // anarchic even the Jews' / outside his own laws"; the enjambment skillfully emphasizes the reach and extent of her risk taking. Feinstein further ambiguously calls on "strange ones with wild hair / all the earth over"—gods and/or Jews—to "make . . . a fire their children / may learn to bear at last / and not burn in," cre-ating a potent, interconnected image of inherited suffering and phoenix-like resurgence. The poem thus effectively reflects Kris-teva's ethics, that a mother does the best for her children out of love, not just duty (law), and it is a love not only for the individ-ual but for the human race, the universal "other."

As well as the children's insults, the poem implies abjection in societal disapproval of the fertile Jewish mother: "criminal, to bear three / children like fruit / cannot be guarded" The demand, "Should I have lived sterile?" dramatically separate on an indi-vidual line, conveys a tension between the poet's own uncer-tainties about protecting her children and establishing their inde-pendence and the scorn of others whose abjection takes the form of jealousy. This confirms Baker's further comment, 'How easily the second and third generations adapt to their host culture . . . depends on . . . the sense of acceptance or of rejection which they feel in the society to which they have come" (1993, 9).

This question of adaptation Feinstein applies to the poetic as well as to the personal community, having noted that "when I began to write I was very well aware I didn't have the right *voice* for current English poetry" (Schmidt 1997, 36–40). "Song of

Power," from her first collection, *In a Green Eye*, eschews conventional syntax and punctuation, to produce a more ambiguous, emotive response to experience than the contemporary "Movement" poets, whom she found "were often embarrassed at the idea of expressing emotion" (Schmidt 1997, 41–44).

This emotive signification of feeling, the semiotic expression, is clearly evident in "New Sadness / Old City" (1971; Lawson 2001, 85), which sensuously encapsulates an inevitably affecting visit to Jerusalem. The Jewish historical experience is subtly evoked through a personal recollection, initially simply stated: "I saw Jerusalem from the Magog hills last night," then evocatively elaborated in deliberately open form. The tumble of adjectives, "hot . . . shaking . . . white . . . scrubby . . . waterless . . ." creates a "breathless" catalogue that is literally echoed later in the poem as the tension of the visit is conveyed through skillfully balanced gaps and enjambment, together with tersely appropriate diction: "sadly . . . whispers . . . invisibly . . . listened . . . uneasily . . . elicit. . . ." This is the potent effect created through repudiation of the orderly, constrained, symbolic language of the "Movement" poets, with whose "dislike of personal exposure . . . defensive caution," Feinstein was "very impatient" (Schmidt 1997, 36–44). Even J. H. Prynne, "the surface" of whose poems she "admired," exhibited a logical construction she resisted: "He was . . . more intellectual than emotional. He looks at the world in conceptual terms" (Schmidt 1997, 36–42).

It was Marina Tsvetaeva, whose work Feinstein has made it a mission to translate, who "proved to be the most important single influence on my poetry," and "taught me to be unafraid of exposing my least dignified emotions" (Feinstein 2002, xiii), as she comments in a retrospective introduction to her 2002 *Collected Poems and Translations*. She also emphasizes learning from the Russian poet "the technical discipline of a rhythm flowing down a page even when held in stanzas" and in this volume and beyond, the influence is clear. In the introduction to an earlier selection of her poems in 1985, she called Tsvetaeva "my teacher of courage. She opened the way to a wholeness of self-exposure which my English training would otherwise have made impossible" (Couzyn 1985b, 116).

Feinstein's writing embodies Kristeva's concept of a "speaking being," subject to and subject of both semiotic and symbolic processes. In "New Sadness / Old City" (1971; Lawson 2001, 85), she challenges the established dichotomy of mind / body, confronting both the intellectual and emotional enormity of mass extermination through the tender image of the "gentle city" juxtaposed with the harsh desert landscape. The forceful oxymoron of "the death song of triumph" extends the historical perspective of the Holocaust and brings it into shattering immediacy, yet it is also offering a tantalizingly ambiguous perspective to the reader: is this the song of the desert, the conquering armies, the enemies of the Jews, or an allusion to the Shema?[1]

The "saints of the Lublin ghetto" seem present in this poetic recreation of the place but again the suggestion is in the form of a tentative query, "will . . . [they] enter . . . marvel at last or fear to. . . ." There is no actual question mark; only a gap to indicate a hesitant quandary. The open-endedness of the form is ideal for conveying the precarious uncertainties of a modern Jewish woman's experience of a historical "homeland."

The poem simultaneously dramatises Kristeva's theory of human beings as "open systems," created and recreated though relationships with others and cultural and artistic expression; undoing the dualism of word / flesh. The last verse is a particularly fine example, with its hushed yet hoarse, grating sibilance and alliteration: "listened like ghosts . . . breathless . . . taken tasting on our teeth . . . strange / illicit salts of elation." The "s" and "t" sounds recreate physically and mentally the unstable equilibrium of past and present, personal, political, and poetic experience. As Michael Woolf has commented, "The past is a painful burden that the [Jewish] writer inevitably carries into the present, into the future" (Woolf 1995, 133).

This "burden" is carried into the vivid representation of place that Feinstein creates in her poem "Survivors" (1973; Feinstein 2002, 69). Catalan Rome is home in the present to "new Romans" but also the "poorest Jews of Rome . . . those that remain. . . ." The title refers to these people but more to the resilience of their religious practice, which transfigures the poet's view of the "urine-scented" streets and renders them "miraculous." Their poverty evokes her pity, whom "the centuries have / left moneyless"; as explained by Baker, "many of the Oriental Jews remain poor . . . there remains a cultural gulf between their understandings and those of their host country" (1993, 18). This gulf is portrayed by the callous "blank polaroid stare" of those who reject them, and by the unpleasant connotations of ugly diction in describing the poor as "at every orifice." That rejection of such people is the more effectively dramatized since it mirrors Feinstein's own suffering of others' abjection in her childhood and young adulthood in England.[2]

Once again the difficulties of adapting to a new and different culture are recalled; the poet shows her historical understanding of the different waves of immigration into Europe from a wide variety of backgrounds, as she comments that these Jews' "service / goes on separately in a cellar / because they came through Fez once, not directly // out of Spain." The enjambment clearly reflects the gap between the different sections of the Jewish community and the lack of respect afforded them, due to their less "pure" origins, ironically recalling Nazi exclusiveness.

In poetic mode Feinstein is compressing a considerable amount of Jewish social history and through her reference to "Fez," distinguishing between her own "Ashkenazim" tradition and that of the Sephardim.[3] Despite these historical differences, Feinstein emphasises the more important connections, "their latest dead sit in gold letters / with the rest," offering further insight into the literary and doctrinal aspects of this Jewish community and showing her own interest and sympathy with them, as "Sephardim are seen as more exotic than the Ashkenazim . . . In their synagogues they have a liturgy enriched by the poets of the Spanish golden age" (Baker 1993, 16). The image of "gold letters" conveys simultaneously the rich gold leaf of the actual lettering, the sonorous resonance of the language and the cultural connection with the poets and survivors of the past.

The title of the earlier poem, "Song of Power," (Lawson 2001, 78) is echoed in the last verse, in which Feinstein celebrates the endurance and resistance to prejudice of these people, trying to fathom "the power . . . that brings them out / on Friday night . . . / to laugh in garrulous Sabbath on this pavement?" The refusal to hide, to conceal, to diminish their religious and social practice by denying their culture and heritage, gives the poet inspiration and through the poem she offers this to her readers.

Jules Smith has noted that Feinstein "can be fairly regarded as a feminist, early on bringing the female body and its experiences into the territory of fable and myth." This is illustrated in "Sybil" (1973; Couzyn 1985, 124), in which she transposes the mythical soothsayer to the twentieth century, when she shows, "it is all happening again." The "terror smiles through the screen"; brought into the apparently innocent context by modern technology but redolent of generations of human internecine strife, persecution, and destruction, the insidious process is compressed in the sinister oxymoron.

In this representation, the poet suggests both the distancing effect the "barrier" of the screen can provide yet also the disruptive and insistent intrusion of worldwide political upheaval, through "the modern / crystal set in the wall," of the anonymous "derelict warehouse," in the unnamed "neglected cit[y]" in which she has positioned her deliberately controversial mouthpiece. Feinstein's Sybil is no tantalizingly feminine oracle but "androgynous, black-skulled, and ricket-boned", "with a squint eye and a slant hand," more appropriate to the devastatingly inexorable continuation of violence than the romanticized vision of some early Hollywood screen goddess.

Mark Schechner has commented that the extermination of Jews during World War II "was a hidden wound, shrouded in darkness and suffered in silence, felt everywhere but confronted virtually nowhere" in Jewish-American literature (1990, 4); Kenyon suggests, "The holocaust casts a stronger shadow on Jewish writers than on British ones . . . Feinstein . . . represents those who write directly about Jewish experience . . . This horror, which her Russian-Jewish parentage has rooted deeply in her mind, provides her with a topic few British novelists have dared to tackle" (1991, 33, 39). In her poetry there is a more oblique approach but it is certainly confronted and tackled in the persona of the Sybil who "writes: beware this generation's prophecies"; the "handsome peasant with his violin" might be more than an image of apparent appeal hiding murderous intent, it could be a tangential reference to the musical skills of Heydrich, one of the main architects of the "Final Solution," or reflect the guards' sadistic insistence that concentration camp musicians played while their compatriots were taken to the gas chambers.

The "horror" is never far away from the wealth of family poems Feinstein has written, celebrating the generations of her grandparents, parents, husband, children, and grandchildren, of which "New Year" (1986; Lawson 2001, 92) is typical. This quintessentially Jewish, family gathering is observed in Cambridge, where Feinstein and her husband raised their three sons and are "once again . . . summoned . . . into the shabby synagogue." The diction of the poem shows she is particularly aware of "children

... relations ... lost relations ... brothers ... sons," confirming Baker's suggestion that "the very real ingrained expectation which women have in all societies to bear children is doubly reinforced in the Jewish woman in terms of the continuation of the people and the reparation of the Holocaust" (1993, 20).

The reference to the traditional repentance of Jewish New Year, "to consider mistakes and failures," thus has greater resonance in the poem as Feinstein creates a complicated tone of both regret and achievement in her recollection of personal, poetic and political allegiances at this significant time. She reassures herself with the comforting image of "my sons . . . happily seated round a family table"; but she also notes what her own mother would have considered a failure, they "never took to festivals." Looking back to her undergraduate and early married life, in an interview she remarked that "at first her close friends were men 'because they had the most interesting jobs.' . . . Feminism has given the strength to re-define oneself as not being a failure" (Kenyon 1991, 40). Another debt to Tsvetaeva is recorded in this context, as "she was a dangerous example, since in both of us domestic impracticality meant the usual tensions of wife, mother and poet were written horrifyingly large" (Feinstein 2002, xiii). This confirms Woolf's view, "The Jewish writer in Britain has . . . made material out of tension between the individual and those other pressures outside of themselves, frequently family or community" (1995, 133).

Her own mother would have rigorously upheld her children's attendance at all religious festivals, as in Feinstein's childhood, "We were very much part of the Jewish community . . . father was president of the synagogue. Largely through my mother, who did all the background administrative work, while he sat in his seat with his top hat and enjoyed being president" (Schmidt 1997, 36–39). As Baker records of Jewish women, "Historically, they worked and earned, they ran the home and raised and educated the children. In this way, they freed their husbands and sons from practical day-to-day responsibilities, enabling them to pray and study and involve themselves in the needs of the community" (1993, 127).

Feinstein thus demonstrates in her domestic and poetic practice the "third way" that Kristeva suggested feminism should develop, a way for women to feel at liberty to create both family and culture, to be of the body and the mind. This exemplifies Burman's comment, relating to the Russian-Jewish tradition from which Feinstein's family came, "The immigrants from Eastern Europe drew upon a different tradition: whilst they also perceived the woman's domestic role as of primary importance, this did not necessarily entail exclusion from the economic sphere" (1990, 62).

Thus in the poem "New Year," Feinstein describes the domestic setting yet explores the intellectual and economic questions of Judaism. She deliberately uses the Jewish terminology for the Jewish New Year festival, "Rosh Hashonah," and reports that "we have all come in out of the Cambridge streets"; this leads to the unnerving, perpetually underlying question, "How are we Jewish, and what brings us together / in this most puritan of Protestant centres?" David Brauner has summed up the vexed question of Jewish identity in this way: "According to orthodox Judaism . . . Jewishness is simply a matter of genetics: a Jew is anyone born of a Jewish mother . . . those who inherit, rather than choose, their Jewishness . . . For some . . . Jewishness is an innate, inalienable property, for others a learned tradition . . . for some, a nationality, for others a sensibility" (2001, 2–3). Feinstein is totally clear on her own personal establishment of her Jewishness: her "sense of security was exploded, once and for all, at the war's end, when I read exactly what had been done to so many children, as young as I was, in the Hell of Hitler's camps. You could say that in that year I became Jewish for the first time" (Couzyn 1985b, 115).

The destruction of childhood security is still clearly evident in the adult poet: at New Year she "look[s] back on too many surprises / and face[s] up to next year's uncertainties," showing her concern for her own family's security and her delight in "their laughter rising up to my bedroom." This exemplifies Kristeva's perspective on human psychology, that one's own sense of oneself is never completely established and undisturbed. Feinstein extends that to the wider Jewish community, "are they puzzled / themselves at the nature of being displaced?", still seeing themselves as "foreigners," like Kristeva did too, as the "threat" to order and the status quo, and commenting, in her 2002 retrospection, on the "sense of being an outsider . . . being at the periphery" (2002, xiii). She has also referred to her early childhood security having created "my own sense of resilience in later years spent in a world that felt altogether alien" (Couzyn 1985b,

114). The poem ends with an image of compromise, wisdom gained through past disappointments yet also a note of optimism, reflecting this "resilience," in the effective contrast of "scrubby hedge" and "birds of paradise."

In the title of "Annus Mirabilis 1989" (1990; Schiff 1995, 176), Feinstein acknowledges the excitement and relief at the destruction of the hated Berlin Wall, but with a reminiscence of "Ten years ago," in Budapest rather than Berlin. She confirms Kenyon's comment, "Feinstein displays a female talent for suggesting the political arena through the personal" (Kenyon 1991). Her sense of risk is evident here as she recalls, "we watched a dissident cabaret" and the poem is unusual in being in compact, rhymed quatrains, possibly implying the constraints of the Communist regime, the need for outwardly "respectable" and "controlled" activities, while harboring dissent and resistance.

The cabaret is played out "beneath the Hotel Astoria," further emphasizing the "underground" nature of both performance and audience. Interestingly, it is the content of the drama which provides the central tension of the poem, the presentation of "Einstein as a Jewish tailor." Feinstein presents her emotional response to this insensitive guying, "I was chilled by the audience euphoria." This is consciously rhymed with "laughter," which enhances the stark opposition of reactions to the scene: the Hungarians' "indignation was all about nuclear science," whereas Feinstein is horrified by the insidious persistence of prejudice and persecution, apparently flippantly ignored, as she "pondered the resilience of an old monster."

The choice of the term, "monster," recalls childish fears yet also makes clear the hideous tenacity of something literally monstrous, out of proportion, out of control, which has dominated the writer's life. Recalling her first awareness of the monstrous nature of the concentration camps of the Second World War, she explained how "that appalling revelation of human cruelty towards ordinary people did me incalculable emotional damage. For a long time afterwards, I could feel no ordinary human emotion without testing it against that imagined experience, and either suspecting it or dismissing it" (Couzyn 1985b, 115). This recollection offers clear reasoning behind the celebration of "ordinary emotions" in the poems that relish family life and the continuance of the race, as in "Eclipse" (1997; 2002, 144), when after a sensuous and ethereal depiction of the darkened garden, the poet's perspective is drawn inward to the comfort of "three generations / sit together." The powerful combination of senses evoked seems an expression of *jouissance*—Kristeva's term conveying physical, mental, and spiritual pleasure.

Feinstein's grandchildren provide her with this intense pleasure, especially as they continue the Jewish rituals: "This year, Katriona read the questions from the Haggadah; / Lara knew the ancient stories . . ." She remarked in a memoir "My mother could carry none of the children she conceived after me—she had rhesus negative blood—and my survival seemed miraculous" (Feinstein 1983, 160). This awareness has clearly been carried into her wonder and awe at the wider world and her family's place in it, as the last part of "Eclipse" once again broadens the perspective and looks out beyond the specific window and the particular family to the vastness of human experience of the planet, "imagining ourselves on the globe / of the earth, and trying to believe it is our own / brown shadow moving over the moon." The contentment of the family unit, providing protection against the incomprehensible unknown, is potently conveyed in the simple language and soft tones of the poem's conclusion, quelling the underlying uncertainty explained by Baker: "Historically—and still in the unconscious of many women—there is the feeling that 'self-development' is contrary to a religious-cultural ethos which emphasises not autonomy but reciprocity of roles" (1993, 205).

Another intensely emotional experience is recalled in "Lisson Grove" (1997; 2002, 144), in which Feinstein recreates the sense of impotence at a deathbed in a sweltering summer. The atmosphere is vividly depicted in apposite details of "sycamore wings . . . fan whirring . . . ," and the desperation of being unable to respond to the terrifying demand to "make sense of your life" leads once again to the central historical fact against which all experience is weighed:

> At your bedside, I feel like someone
> who has escaped too lightly
> from the great hell of the camps.

The choice of the word "escaped" is frequently employed by Feinstein, reminding her readers once again of her overall sense of fortuitousness, as referred to in an interview: "If you've escaped the holocaust entirely by the serendipitous chance of your family deciding not to settle in Germany . . ." (Schmidt 1997, 36). The poem is extended beyond the actual circumstances, much as "Eclipse" was, and the resonance of such specific terms used by the poet make fascinating connections with her fictional, prose, and critical works.

She has commented that "the war, when it began, hardly reached us; even the arrival of a timid young refugee girl from Germany (who was adopted by my parents for six or seven years), did nothing to dispel the absolute conviction of safety in which I moved" (Couzyn 1985b, 114).[4] The sense of safety, soon to be so cruelly shattered by the realization of the "hell" of the camps, is continually sought by Feinstein, consciously and unconsciously, throughout her work; the impossibility of its recapture is the underlying motivation for her poetry.

This is evident in another poem, "Allegiance," (Lawson 2001, 96) in which the personal experience of a holiday with a friend is the context for a similar consideration of opposing perspectives as was explored in "Annus Mirabilis 1989." The opening verse, as so often, is vivid with sensuous imagery and depicts the mood and atmosphere of the setting; the lyrical quality of the repetition of "l" sounds, "whole . . . alight . . . glow . . . local . . . floats," creates a deceptively peaceful sense of place, which belies the tension below the surface of companionship. The "English friend" with whom the poet dines has inherited the confidence of the colonizer, from "intrepid forebears"; by contrast, Feinstein's "inheritance / Kovno, Odessa, packing and running away—"is another of the writer's typically compressed and laconic summaries of her personal and political history.

In conversation with Michael Schmidt, Feinstein was quick to add "Russian Jewish blood" when asked if she had some Russian blood in her family, and to explain, "all four grandparents were Russian Jews, who came over from Odessa" (Schmidt 1997, 37). As Baker has commented, "It was, in fact, the large-scale immigration between 1881 and 1905 of Ashkenazim from Eastern Europe which dramatically changed the character of British Jewry. During this period, hundreds of thousands of Jews poured into Britain, fleeing increasing economic restrictions, persecution and pogroms in Russia, Poland, Lithuania, Galicia and Roumania" (1993, 10). In Feinstein's conversation she continues, "The grandfather on my mother's side was well-read in Rabbinic literature . . . could speak five languages . . . My mother's brothers were socialists. . . . My father spoke Yiddish which he enjoyed." All these snippets of background information tie in with Baker's historical overview: "They spoke in Yiddish and they brought with them the Orthodoxy and the customs of their shtetls (small Jewish towns). The majority were impoverished and unsophisticated; some were religiously learned; the non-religious amongst them were intellectual and socialist" (1993, 10).

This inheritance is clearly a vital element in the poem "Allegiance," which is superficially about a convivial meal but extends to a conversation with darkly political undertones: "over Yemenite eggplant and fried dough / We talk about the Roman exploitation." The easy, conversational tone hardens as the poet compares this ancient history, which is "easy to agree," with "Politics here and now are another matter." The colloquial language employed in the poem draws the reader into a pleasant, nonthreatening scene, which becomes polarized; the variant responses are potently dramatized by the skillful use of enjambment: "the soldiers // Look like oppressors to her . . . my inheritance . . . Makes me fear for them."

The last stanza explodes the surface courtesies with an acknowledgment of inherent difference, each individual exposing their own abjection, reacting to the "outsider" who threatens to dissipate the carefully constructed borders of self. Once again Feinstein incorporates a bewildering variety of tones in her final lines—resentment, regret, compassion, distrust, pity, as she concludes ironically, "I can't share the privilege of guilt . . . Nor could she taste the Hebrew of Adam." The final breakdown of communication is evoked in stark, essential imagery of dissipated elements: "iron, salt and blood."

The setting of a meal is a frequent starting point for Feinstein's recapturing of experience and recreating the emotion involved to expose this to the reader. The ubiquitous human activity renders the personal reminiscence universal. As the poet has herself remarked, "People have always been the centre of my concerns . . . my poems usually spring from some experience in my own life" (Feinstein 2002, xiii). Thus "Galway" (2000; 2002, 194), opens "At the Breton restaurant" with an ordinary, humane concern for "huge brown lobsters [that] will boil slowly into restaurant red." This is quickly developed into philosophical musing, "Do we lie to ourselves about everything?"

The poet's continual quest for the "truth" of experience, the meaning of a life that might not have been lived had circumstances been different, is encapsulated in the understandable shudder of resistance to the reality of the lobsters' fate, merely to provide a luxury item for the human palate. This is a reflection of Kristeva's fascinating examination of "food loathing," though clearly not as intense as that experience, nevertheless part of rejecting what is considered "other" to oneself, linked with the later concern in the poem to "eat and drink well away from the jostle." The writer recalls the need to protect herself and her integrity at a literary festival where she has evidently been subject to an excessive "shuffle of book-signings." This effectively sibilant description is used as a mctonym for the dilemma of any writer who needs to expose themselves in their work to attain validity, yet fears the pressure of societal demands and expectations. As she has commented, "I have worked most of all for directness and lucidity, because I distrust any music that drowns the pressure of what has been felt" (Feinstein 2002, xiii). In the poem she celebrates the fact that "These days we say what we like."

She sees this as a luxury in poetical terms in the same way as the lobsters are a culinary luxury, remembering the fate of many Russian writers, some of whose work she has lovingly translated, "none of us will need to burn our lines. . . ." The poem ends on a less complacent note however, with a hint of sectarian violence over the border, in the pun "Ireland is eerily booming." The surface meaning of the prosperity of the south of Ireland is savagely undercut by the adverb "eerily," a suggestion that this "good life," symbolized by the lobsters, may be at the expense of others' suffering in bomb attacks and terrorist activity. The question posed at the beginning of the poem is potently echoed here, the implication being that as at all times in human history, one person's peace and contentment can seemingly only be enjoyed at the risk of another's destruction. Although the poet remarked, in "Allegiance," that she could not "share the privilege of guilt," this was clearly ironic as she carries a sense of guilt at her good fortune throughout her work.

It is present also in "Hotel Maimonides" (2002, 204), when a memory of a visit to a "Jewish quarter" and considerations of "Hebrew ancestor" are combined with "relish [of] heaped fruits, a sleep post lunch . . . in this hotel." The contrast sparks off the poet's continual concern, "What will become of you now, my people . . . The history is not encouraging."

The second section of the poem opens "At home in Belsize Park," where the poet contemplates the guilt-inducing contrast further and traces her initial resistance, "What has the fanatic Middle East / to do with me?", to its acceptance. The deliberate gap created by the enjambment dramatizes this response, extended to the irritated tone of the defense, "My grandparents / are buried in British earth, my children / are married out," which of course is in fact the very reason that is being denied.[5] Continuing the progression of her reaction to her insistent feeling of guilt, Feinstein again makes effective use of colloquial language to demand, "Why are my dreams disturbed," and concludes, "because / I have lived in a rare island of peace," both the literal island of England and the metaphorical island of her writing world and her imagination. She castigates herself that "it is far too easy to be liberal," and although referring directly to the Jews in her comment on the "dispossessed," the implication must also be for her own family and those Russian writers whose works she has saved from obscurity. Finally she contemplates the inexorable continuance of "battle . . . negotiations sadly no longer the issue" and accepts that, as she said in an interview, "we must face the fact that 'springs of spite' which lead people to kill (as referred to by her character, Tobias, in her novel *The Children of the Rose*) continue, even after the horror of mass extermination . . . The enormities of the human psyche are in us all. The responsible writer must face up to this" (Kenyon 1991, 44).

To counteract this constant awareness of the evil in human nature, Feinstein nevertheless also continues to celebrate "what Lawrence called the 'great privilege of being alive.'" The poems chosen above foreground her Jewish heritage and its attendant discomforts in the context of British society, but the majority explore, with her own particular female, Russian, Jewish perspective, the experience of "being an outsider," the "tensions of wife, mother and poet." (2002, xiii)

The concept of "escape" could be seen as "escapist," in that Feinstein avoids direct confrontation of the holocaust in her poetry whereas it is more directly explored through the characters in her novels. This implies that the distancing effect of third person, fictionalized narrative gives the writer "permission" to create an imaginative empathy with those who suffered. Theodor Adorno notoriously admonished that "To write lyric poetry after Auschwitz is barbaric."[6] The first-person, semiautobiographical qualities of the poetry demand a greater "honesty" than the attempt to recreate an experience that could only ever be "second-hand" and thus in some way an insult to those who did actually suffer it. As Clendinnen has suggested, reflecting Kristeva's concept of the abject and the impossibility of "speaking" horror, the use of Holocaust imagery can lead to an "inversion effect," art can be "rendered vacuous and drained of authority" (Clendinnen 1999, 164–65).

What might thus be seen as Feinstein's evasion avoids hackneyed cliché—her ebullient, expansive readings reflect her personality that has been generously exposed in her work, yet unfairly neglected in critical response. The personality is extended to "universality," the individual microcosmic experience is in no way self-indulgent but the springboard for poems continuing to escape—yet also ironically encouraging the reader to insert the actual words in their experience of the poems. Feinstein's particular talent for rendering the physicality of the psychological offers the reader illumination and reassurance.

NOTES

1. The *Shema* is the central statement of Jewish belief: "Hear, O Israel: the Lord is your God; the Lord is One" (Deuteronomy 6:4) joyfully recited at the moment of death.

2. "Survivors" is also a title of one of Feinstein's novels, which have received more attention than her unfairly neglected poetry. Kenyon suggests that "Jewish writers working in Britain share a culture, but not a history . . . In Jewish . . . novels the figure of the survivor occurs more than in [other] British fiction" (1991, 40).

3. "'Ashkenaz' is the Hebrew for Germany, just as 'Sepharad' is the Hebrew word for Spain . . . Sephardim, originally meaning Jews of Spanish and Portuguese origin, also include Jews from the Mediterranean basin and from the orient . . . They came from Spain . . . Turkey . . . following the collapse of the Ottoman Empire, they came from the Balkans and from the Levant. These newcomers were very different from the descendants of the earlier Sephardim of Spanish and Portuguese origin and they often chose to found their own separate congregations" (Baker 1993, 16).

4. This memory of generosity relates to the wider British *kindertransport* rescue-scheme: "particularly in response to the brutalities of Kristallnacht in 1938—brutalities which were orchestrated by the Nazi government—the

British offered hospitality to the 10,000 children brought by the Children's Transport Programme from Germany, Austria and Czechoslovakia" (Baker 1993, 10). Also see works edited by Karen Gershon, *We Came as Children* (London: Macmillan, 1966); edited by Bertha Leverton and Schmuel Lowensohn, *I Came Alone: The Stories of the Kindertransports* (Sussex: Book Guild, 1990); edited by Jonathan Mark Harris and Deborah Oppenheimer, *Into the Arms of Strangers* (London: Bloomsbury, 2000).

5. "The vast majority of American and British Jews are Ashkenazim; descendants of those who fled from persecution. They are the children and grandchildren or great-grandchildren of two large waves of immigration. The first major influx followed the murder of Alexander II in Russia in 1881—an event which unleashed state-instigated pogroms throughout anti-Semitic countries of Eastern Europe. Refugees came in their thousands to Britain until stopped by the 1905 Aliens Act" (Baker 1993, 20).

6. See Theodor Adorno "Commitment," reprinted in *Aesthetics and Politics* ed. Rodney Livingstone, Perry Anderson and Francis Mulhern, 177–95 (London: New Left Books, 1977).

Checklist of Jewish Women Writers in 20th Century Britain

BROOKNER, Anita (b. London 1928–) German/Polish-Jewish parents;
Family and Friends (1986) *Latecomers* (1988); *A Family Romance* (1993).

FEINSTEIN, Elaine (b. Bootle 1930–) Russian Jewish grandparents;
The Survivors (1982); *Collected Poems* (2002).

FIGES, Eva (b. Berlin 1932–) London 1939 with German Jewish parents;
Little Eden: a Child at War (1978) memoir; *Konek Landing* (1969); *Tales of Innocence & Experience* (2002)—memoir.

GALFORD, Ellen (b. New Jersey 1947–) came to UK 1971;
The Dyke and the Dybbuk (1991).

GERSHON, Karen (b. Germany 1924, d. Cornwall 1993)—London 1938 alone;
ed. *We Came as Children: A Collective Biography* (1966); *A Lesser Child* (1992).

GRANT, Linda (b. Liverpool 1951–) grandparents Russian-Jewish immigrants;
When I Lived in Modern Times (1999) *Remind Me Who I Am, Again* (1998) *Still Here* (2002).

JACOB, Naomi (b. Ripon 1884, d. Italy 1964) Grandparents German Jewish / Yorkshire;
Gollantz Saga (1930–)—7 volumes; *Barren Metal* (1935).

KARPF, Anne (b. London 1950–) – parents postWar Jewish refugees from Germany;
The War After: Living with the Holocaust (1996).

LASKER-WALLFISCH, Anita (b. Breslau 1925–) London 1946. Parents German-Jewish;
Inherit the Truth, 1939-1945: The Documented Experiences of a Survivor of Auschwitz and Belsen (1996).

LEVERTOV, Denise (b. Ilford 1923–) mother Welsh / father Russian-Jew. To USA 1946;
Collected Poems (1979).

LEVY, Deborah (b. South Africa 1956–) London 1963; parents South African Jews;
Pax (2000).

LOY, Mina (b. London 1882, d. USA 1966). Father Jewish-Hungarian/ mother English;
Anglo-Mongrels and the Rose (1925).

MILLER, Betty (b. Cork 1910, d. London 1965) Father Lithuanian-Jewish / mother Swedish-Jewish;
Farewell Leicester Square (1941; reprinted 2000).

MITCHELL, Yvonne (b. London 1925, d. 1979)—father Jewish;
The Same Sky (1952)—play.

NEUBURGER, Julia (b. London 1950–)—rabbi; mother German-Jewish refugee;
On Being Jewish (1995).

PASCAL, Julia (b. Blackpool 1950–)—parents Jewish;
'Teresa' in *Holocaust Trilogy* (2000).

REID BANKS, Lynne (b. London 1929–) parents Scottish; married Jew in Israel;
Defy the Wilderness (1983); *Letters to my Israeli Sons* (1976).

RODGERS, Silvia (b. Berlin 1928–) London 1938 with Polish-Jewish parents;
Red Saint, Pink Daughter: A Communist Childhood in Berlin and London (1996).

RUBENS, Bernice (b. Cardiff 1923, d. London 2004) Welsh-Jewish mother/ Russian-Jewish father;
Madame Sousatzka (1962); *The Spring Sonata* (1983); *The Elected Member* (1969); *The Sergeants' Tale* (2003).

SAMUELS, Diane (b. Liverpool 1960–)—parents Liverpool-Jewish;
Kindertransport (1992).

SEGAL, Lore (b. Vienna 1928–) London 1938 with Austrian-Jewish parents— USA 1951;
Other People's Houses (1964).

SPARK, Muriel (b. Edinburgh 1918–)—one grandparent Russian Jew;
The Mandelbaum Gate (1965).

STERN, G[ladys] B[ronwen] (b. London 1890, d. 1973) Grandparents middle-European Jewish origin;
The Tents of Israel (1924); *The Rakonitz Chronicle* (1924–32).

TOBIAS, Lily (b. Swansea 1887, d. Haifa 1984). Parents Polish-Jewish;
The Samaritan (1939).

WANDOR, Michelene (b. London 1940–) Russian-Jewish parents;
Guests in the Body (1986); *The Wandering Jew* (1987).

Bibliography

Primary Texts

Bellow, Saul. 1954. *The Adventures of Angie March.* London: Weidenfeld and Nicolson.

Berg, Leila. 1997. *Flickerbook: An Autobiography.* London: Granta.

Blend, Martha. 1995. *A Child Alone.* London: Vallentine Mitchell.

Brookner, Anita. 1981. *A Start in Life.* London: Penguin Books.

———. 1982. *Providence.* London: Penguin Books.

———. 1985. *Family and Friends.* London: Penguin Books.

———. 1988. *Latecomers.* London: Grafton.

———. 1991. *A Closed Eye.* London: Penguin Books.

———. 1992. *Fraud.* London: Penguin Books.

———. 1993. *A Family Romance.* London: Penguin Books.

———. 2001. *The Bay of Angels.* London: Penguin Books.

———. 2002. *The Next Big Thing.* London: Penguin Books.

Federman, Raymond. 1979. *The Voice in the Closet/ La Voix dans le Cabinet de Débarras.* Madison: Coda Press.

Feinstein, Elaine. 1966. *In a Green Eye.* London: Goliard Press.

———. 1971. *The Magic Apple Tree.* London: Hutchinson.

———. 1973. *The Celebrants and Other Poems.* London: Hutchinson.

———. 1977. *Some Unease and Angels: Selected Poems.* London: Hutchinson.

———. 1983. "A Legendary Hero." In *Fathers: Reflections by Daughters,* ed. Ursula Owen, 159–68. London: Virago.

———. 1985. "Elaine Feinstein Writes." In *The Bloodaxe Book of Contemporary Women Poets: Eleven British Writers,* ed. Jeni Couzyn, 112–17. Newcastle upon Tyne: Bloodaxe.

———. 1986. *Badlands.* London: Hutchinson.

———. 1990. *City Music.* London: Hutchinson.

———. 1997. *Daylight.* Manchester: Carcanet.

———. 2000. *Gold.* Manchester: Carcanet.

———. 2002. *Collected Poems and Translations.* Manchester: Carcanet.

Fink, Ida. 1992. *The Journey.* Trans. Joanna Wechsler and Francine Prose. Harmondsworth: Penguin.

Galford, Ellen. 1984. *Moll Cutpurse: Her True History.* Edinburgh: Stramullion.

———. 1986. *The Fires of Bride*. London: Women's Press.

———. 1990. *Queendom Come*. London: Virago.

———. 1993. *The Dyke and the Dybbuk*. London: Virago.

Gershon, Karen, ed. 1966. *We Came as Children: A Collective Autobiography*. New York: Harcourt, Brace and World.

———. 1992. *A Lesser Child: An Autobiography*. Translator unnamed. London: Peter Owen.

Golabek, Mona. 2002. *The Children of Willesden Lane*. London: Time Warner.

Grant, Linda. 1998a. *The Cast Iron Shore*. London: Granta Books. (Orig. pub. 1996.)

———. 1998b. *Remind Me Who I Am, Again*. London: Granta.

———. 2000. *When I Lived In Modern Times*. London: Granta Books.

———. 2002a. "Defenders of the Faith." *Guardian Review*, July 6, 2002, 4–6.

———. 2002b. *Still Here*. London: Little, Brown.

Greenman, Leon. 2001. *An Englishman at Auschwitz*. London: Vallentine Mitchell.

Gunther, Irene. 2002. *Only a Girl: Remembering My Syrian-Jewish World*. London: Xlibris.

Jacob, Naomi. 1925. *Jacob Ussher*. London: Butterworth.

———. 1932. *Young Emmanuel*. London: Hutchinson.

———. 1933. *Me: A Chronicle about Other People* London: Hutchinson.

———. 1936a. *Barren Metal*. London: Hutchinson.

———. 1936b. *Our Marie*. London: Hutchinson.

———. 1952a. *The Gollantz Saga*. Vols. 1 and 2. London: Hutchinson.

———. 1952b. *Robert, Nana and—Me: A Family Chronicle*. London: Hutchinson.

Karpf, Anne. 1996. *The War After: Living with the Holocaust*. London: Heinemann. Reprinted in 1997 as *The War After: Living with the Holocaust*. London: Minerva.

Kerr, Judith. [1971] 1974. *When Hitler Stole Pink Rabbit*. London: Collins.

Lasker-Wallfisch, Anita. 1996. *Inherit the Truth, 1939–1945: The Documented Experiences of a Survivor of Auschwitz and Belsen*. London: Giles de la Mare.

Levertov, Denise. 1946a. "Denise Levertov Writes." In *The Bloodaxe Book of Contemporary Women Poets: Eleven British Writers*, ed. Jeni Couzyn, 75–79. Newcastle upon Tyne: Bloodaxe.

———. 1946b. *The Double Image*. London: Cresset.

———. 1960. "Statement on Poetics," "Biographical Note." In *The New American Poetry*, ed. Donald M. Allen, 411–12, 440–41. New York: Grove.

———. 1964. *O Taste and See*. New York: New Directions.

———. 1965. *The Jacob's Ladder*. London: Cape. (New York: New Directions, 1961.)

———. 1967. *The Sorrow Dance*. New York: New Directions. (London: Cape, 1968.)

———. 1970. *Relearning the Alphabet*. London: Cape. (New York: New Directions, 1970.)

———. 1972. *Footprints*. New York: New Directions.

———. 1973. *The Poet in the World*. New York: New Directions.

———. 1975. *The Freeing of the Dust*. New York: New Directions.

———. 1978. *Life in the Forest*. New York: New Directions.

———. 1979a. *Collected Earlier Poems 1940–60*. New York: New Directions.

———. 1979b. "Poems by Women." In *Denise Levertov: In Her Own Province*, ed. Linda Wagner, 98–100. New York: New Directions.

———. 1981. *Light Up the Cave*. New York: New Directions.

———. 1982. *Candles in Babylon*. New York: New Directions.

———. 1986. *Oblique Prayers: New Poems with 14 Translations from Jean Joubert*. Newcastle upon Tyne: Bloodaxe. (New York: New Directions, 1984.)

———. 1988. *Breathing the Water*. Newcastle upon Tyne: Bloodaxe. (New York: New Directions, 1987.)

———. 1993. *The Door in the Hive; Evening Train*. Newcastle upon Tyne: Bloodaxe, 1993. (New York: New Directions, 1989, 1992.)

———. 1996. *Sands of the Well*. New York: New Directions.

———. 1997. *Tesserae*. Newcastle upon Tyne: Bloodaxe. (New York: New Directions, 1995.)

———. 2001. *The Great Unknowing*. Tarset: Bloodaxe. (New York: New Directions, 1999.)

Levy, Deborah. 1991. "Placing Ourselves." In *So Very English*, ed. Marsha Rowe, 228–37. London: Serpent's Tail.

———. 2000. *Plays: 1*. London: Methuen.

———. 2001. "Imagining Germany." Joseph Beuys Lecture 2001, Ruskin College, Oxford, http://www.ruskin-sch.ox.ac.uk/lab/02/jbl2001/.

Lewis, Helen. 1992. *A Time to Speak*. Belfast: Blackstaff Press.

Loy, Mina, 1916. "To You." *Others* 3, no. 1 (July): 27–28.

———. 1923. *Anglo-Mongrels and the Rose* ["Exodus"]. *Little Review* 9 (Spring): 10–18.

———. 1923/24. *Anglo-Mongrels and the Rose* "continued"; "English Rose" and "Ada Gives Birth To Ova." *Little Review* 9 (Autumn and Winter): 41–51.

———. 1925. *Anglo-Mongrels and the Rose*. In *Contact Collection of Contemporary Writers*, 137–94. Paris: Three Mountains Press.

———. 1958. *Lunar Baedeker and Time-Tables*. Ed. Jonathan Williams. Highlands, NC: Jargon.

———. 1997. *The Lost Lunar Baedeker*. Ed. Roger Conover. Manchester: Carcanet.

Miller, Betty. 1933. *The Mere Living*. London: Victor Gollancz.

———. 1935. *Sunday*. London: Victor Gollancz.

———. 1945a. "Notes for an Unwritten Autobiography." *Modern Reading* 13:39–46.

———. 1945b. *On the Side of the Angels.* London: Robert Hale.

———. 1948. *The Death of the Nightingale.* London: Robert Hale.

———. 2000. *Farewell Leicester Square.* London: Persephone Books. (London: Robert Hale, 1941.)

Pascal, Julia. 1985. "Prima Ballerina Assoluta." In *Truth, Dare or Promise: Girls Growing Up in the Fifties,* ed. Liz Heron, 27–43. London: Virago.

———. 1995. "On Creativity and Anger." In *Women in Theatre: Contemporary Theatre Review* 2, no. 3: 39–48.

———. 2000. *The Holocaust Trilogy.* London: Oberon Books.

Reid Banks, Lynne. 1962a. *An End to Running.* Harmondsworth: Penguin.

———. 1962b. *The L-Shaped Room.* Harmondsworth: Penguin.

———. 1968. *Children at the Gate.* London: Chatto and Windus.

———. 1972. *The Backward Shadow.* Harmondsworth: Penguin.

———. 1975. *Sarah and After, the Matriarchs.* London: Bodley Head.

———. 1976. *Letters to My Israeli Sons.* London: W. H. Allen.

———. 1976. *Two Is Lonely.* Harmondsworth: Penguin.

———. 1982. *Torn Country: An Oral History of the Israeli War of Independence.* New York: Franklin Watts.

———. 1983. *Defy the Wilderness.* Harmondsworth: Penguin.

Rittner, Carol, and John K. Roth, eds. 1993. *Different Voices: Women and the Holocaust.* New York: Paragon House.

Rodgers, Silvia. 1996. *Red Saint, Pink Daughter: A Communist Childhood in Berlin and London.* London: André Deutsch.

Rose, Gillian. 1995. *Love's Work.* London: Chatto and Windus.

Roth, Philip. 1969. *Portnoy's Complaint.* London: Jonathan Cape.

Rubens, Bernice. 1962. *Madame Sousatzka.* London: Eyre & Spottiswoode.

———. 1986. *The Elected Member.* London: Abacus. (Orig. pub. 1969.)

———. 2002. Interview in *Guardian* G2, May 23, 2002, 3.

Samuels, Diane. 1995. *Kindertransport.* London: Nick Hern Books. (Rev. ed. 1996.)

Segal, Lore. 1974. *Other People's Houses: A Refugee in England 1938–48.* London: Bodley Head. (Orig. pub. 1965.)

Spiegelman, Art. 1986. *Maus I, A Survivor's Tale: My Father Bleeds History.* Harmondsworth: Penguin.

———. 1991. *Maus II, A Survivor's Tale: And Here My Troubles Began.* Harmondsworth: Penguin.

Stang, Fanny. 1997. *A New Beginning.* London: Minerva.

Tobias, Lily. 1919. "Jewish Women and Palestine." *Socialist Review* 88:61–67.

———. 1920. "Zionism and Militarism: Some Other Considerations." *Zionist Review* 4 (5): 89–90.

———. 1921. *The Nationalists and Other Goluth Studies.* London: C. W. Daniel.

———. 1931. *My Mother's House.* London: George Allen & Unwin.

———. [1933] 2004. *Eunice Fleet*. Ed. J. Donahaye. Dinas Powys: Honno Press.

———. 1935. *Tube*. London: Hutchinson.

———. 1939. *The Samaritan. An Anglo-Palestinian Novel*. London: Robert Hale.

———. 1945. Letter to Leo Abse. October 11, 1945. Leo Abse Archive, National Library of Wales G/a/168.

———.1975. "Daniel Deronda, a Play." *Jewish Quarterly* 23 (3): 8–12.

SECONDARY TEXTS

Aaron, Jane. 1999. *A View across the Valley: Short Stories by Women from Wales c. 1850–1950*. Glamorgan: Honno Classics.

Abse, Leo. 1993. "A Tale of Collaboration Not Conflict with the 'People of the Book.'" *New Welsh Review* 6 (2): 16–21.

———. 2000. Letter to Jasmine Donahaye.

———. 2002. Unpublished interview with Jasmine Donahaye.

———. 2003. Cultivating Irreverence. *Planet: The Welsh Internationalist* 160:7–17.

Allen, Donald M., ed. 1960. In *The New American Poetry*. New York: Grove.

Améry, Jean. 1966. "On the Necessity and Impossibility of Being a Jew." In *At the Mind's Limits: Contemplations by a Survivor on Auschwitz and Its Realities*. Translated from the German *Jenseits von Schuld und Sühne* by Sidney and Stella B. Rosenfeld. Indiana: Indiana University Press, 1980; London: Granta, 1999.

Anderson, George K. 1991. *The Legend of the Wandering Jew*. Hanover, NH: Brown University Press. (Orig. pub. 1965.)

Arditti, Michael. 1995. "Interview with Julia Pascal." *Guardian*, November 22.

Arnold, Elizabeth, 1989. "Mina Loy and the Futurists." *Sagetrieb* 8, no. 1–2 (Spring/Fall): 83–117.

Ashby, Margaret. 1989. "Naomi Jacob." In *Dictionary of British Women Writers*, ed. Janet Todd, 348–49. London: Routledge.

Aston, Elaine, and Janelle Reinelt, eds. 2000. *The Cambridge Companion to Modern British Women Playwrights*. Cambridge: Cambridge University Press.

Augustine, Jane, 1989. "Mina Loy: A Feminist Modernist Americanizes the Language of Futurism." *Mid-Hudson Language Studies* 12 (1): 89–101.

Bailey, Paul. 2001. *Three Queer Lives: An Alternative Biography of Fred Barnes, Naomi Jacob and Arthur Marshall*. London: Hamilton.

Baker, Adrienne. 1993. *The Jewish Woman in Contemporary Society: Transitions and Traditions*. London: Macmillan.

Bard, Julia. 1988. "Face to Face with the Community." In *A Word in Edgeways*. London: J. F. Publications.

Bartov, Omer, ed. 2000. *The Holocaust: Origins, Implementation, Aftermath.* London: Routledge.

Bassnett, Susan. 2000. "The Politics of Location." In *The Cambridge Companion to Modern British Women Playwrights,* ed. Elaine Aston and Janelle Reinelt. Cambridge: Cambridge University Press.

Bataille, Georges, 1991. *The Accursed Share: Volume 1.* Trans. Robert Hurley. New York: Zone Books.

Batsleer, Janet, et al. 1985. *Rewriting English: Cultural Politics of Gender and Class.* London: Methuen.

Bauman, Zygmunt. 1989. *Modernity and the Holocaust.* Oxford: Polity.

———. 1991. *Modernity and Ambivalence.* Ithaca, NY: Cornell University Press.

Beauman, Nicola. 1983. *A Very Great Profession: The Women's Novel 1914–39* London: Virago.

Beddoe, Deirdre. 2002. *Out of the Shadows: A History of Women in Twentieth-Century Wales.* Cardiff: University of Wales Press.

Bernard, Catherine A. 2000. "Tell Him That I: Women Writing the Holocaust." *Other Voices* 2, no. 1 (February).

Bernstein, Michael André. 1994. *Forgone Conclusions: Against Apocalyptic History.* Berkeley and Los Angeles: University of California Press.

Bettelheim, Bruno. 1975. *The Uses of Enchantment: The Meaning and Importance of Fairy Tales.* New York: Knopf.

Bhabha, Homi K. 1995. *The Location of Culture.* London: Routledge.

Bottome, Phyllis. 1937. *The Mortal Storm.* London: Faber. (Boston: Little Brown, 1938.)

Bourne, Jenny. 1987. "Homelands of the Mind: Jewish Feminism and Identity Politics." *Race and Class: A Journal of Black and Third World Liberation* 29, no. 1 (Summer): 1–24.

Bracco, Rosa Maria. 1993. *Merchants of Hope: British Middlebrow Writers and the First World War, 1919–39.* Oxford: Berg.

Braidotti, Rosi, 1994. *Nomadic Subjects: Embodiment and Sexual Difference in Contemporary Feminist Theory.* New York: Columbia University Press.

Brauner, David. 2001. *Post-War Jewish Fiction: Ambivalence, Self-Explanation and Transatlantic Connections.* London: Palgrave.

Bridgwood, Christine. 1986. "Family Romances: The Contemporary Popular Family Saga." In *The Progress of Romance: The Politics of Popular Fiction,* ed. Jean Radford. London: Routledge.

Brinson, Charmian. 2001. "Autobiography in Exile: The Reflections of Women Refugees." In *German-Speaking Exiles in Great Britain,* ed. J. M. Ritchie. Amsterdam: Rodopi.

Brodzki, Bella. 1988. "Mothers, Displacement, and Language." In *Life/Lines: Theorizing Women's Autobiography,* ed. Bella Brodzki and Celeste Schenck. Ithaca, NY: Cornell University Press.

Brothers, Barbara. 1993. "British Women Write the Story of the Nazis: A Conspiracy of Silence." In *Rediscovering Forgotten Radicals: British Women*

Writers 1889–1934, ed. Angela Ingram and Daphne Patai, 244–64. Chapel Hill: University of North Carolina Press.

Bruner, Jerome. 1990. *Acts of Meaning.* Cambridge, MA: Harvard University Press.

Burke, Carolyn, 1985. "The New Poetry and the New Woman." In *Coming to Light,* ed. Diane Wood Middlebrook and Marilyn Yalom. Ann Arbor: University of Michigan Press.

———. 1987. "Getting Spliced: Modernism and Sexual Difference." *American Quarterly* 39:98–121.

———. 1996. *Becoming Modern: The Life of Mina Loy.* New York: Farrar, Straus & Giroux.

Burman, Rickie. 1990. "Jewish Women and the Household Economy in Manchester, c. 1890–1920." In *The Making of Modern Anglo-Jewry,* ed. David Cesarani, 55–75. London: Blackwell.

Cawelti, John G. 1976. *Adventure, Mystery, and Romance: Formula Stories and Popular Culture.* Chicago: University of Chicago Press.

Cesarani, David. 1985/6. "The Alternative Jewish Community." *European Judaism* 50–54.

———. 1998. "Reporting Antisemitism: The *Jewish Chronicle* 1879–1979." In *Cultures of Ambivalence. Studies in Jewish–Non-Jewish Relations,* ed. Sian James, Tony Kushner, and Sarah Pierce, 247–82. London: Vallentine and Mitchell.

Charitou, Irini. 1983. "Questions of Survival: Towards a Postmodern Feminist Theatre." Interview with Deborah Levy. *New Theatre Quarterly* 9, no. 35 (August): 225–32.

Chaudhuri, Una. 1995. *Staging Place: The Geography of Modern Drama.* Ann Arbor: University of Michigan Press.

Cheyette, Bryan. 1993. *Constructions of "the Jew" in English Literature and Society: Racial Representations 1875–1945.* Cambridge: Cambridge University Press.

———. 1998. *Contemporary Jewish Writing in Britain and Ireland.* London: Peter Halban.

———. 2000. *Muriel Spark.* Devon: Northcote House.

Chothia, Jean, ed. 1998. *The New Woman and Other Emancipated Woman Plays.* London: Oxford University Press.

Clark, Jon, Margot Heinemann, David Margolis, and Carol Snee, eds. 1979. *Culture and Crisis in Britain in the Thirties.* London: Lawrence and Wishart.

Clendinnen, Inga. 1999. *Reading the Holocaust.* Cambridge: Cambridge University Press.

Coleman, Vera. 1989. "Lily Tobias." In *The Blackwell Companion to Jewish Culture from the Eighteenth Century to the Present,* ed. Glenda Abramson, 759–60. Oxford: Blackwell Reference.

Corbett, Mary Jean. 1998. "Literary Domesticity and Women Writers' Subjectivities." In *Women, Autobiography, Theory: A Reader,* ed. Sidonie Smith and Julia Watson. Madison: University of Wisconsin Press.

Couzyn, Jeni, ed., 1985. *The Bloodaxe Book of Contemporary Women Poets: Eleven British Writers*. Newcastle upon Tyne: Bloodaxe.

Croft, Andy. 1990. *Red Letter Days: British Fiction in the 1930s*. London: Lawrence and Wishart.

———. 1993. "Ethel Mannin: The Red Rose of Love and the Red Flower of Liberty." In *Rediscovering Forgotten Radicals: British Women Writers 1889–1934*. ed. Angela Ingram and Daphne Patai. Chapel Hill: University of North Carolina Press.

Cunningham, Valentine. 1988. *British Writers of the Thirties*. Oxford: Oxford University Press.

Davies, Grahame. 2002. *Chosen People: Wales and the Jews*. Bridgend: Seren Books.

Deeney, John. 2000. "Workshop to Mainstream: Women's Playwriting in the Contemporary British Theatre." In *Women, Theatre and Performance: New Histories, New Historiographies*, ed. Maggie B. Gale and Viv Gardner. Manchester: Manchester University Press.

Donahaye, Jasmine. 2001. "Hurrah for the Freedom of the Nations." *Planet: The Welsh Internationalist* 147:28–36.

———. 2002. " 'A dislocation called a blessing': Three Welsh Jewish Perspectives." In *Welsh Writing in English: A Yearbook of Critical Essays* 7, ed. Tony Brown, 154–73. Bridgend: New Welsh Review.

———. 2004. Introduction to *Eunice Fleet*, by Lily Tobias. Dinas Powys: Honno Press.

Douglas, Lawrence. 2001. "The Shrunken Head of Buchenwald: Icons of Atrocity at Nuremberg." In *Visual Culture and the Holocaust*, ed. Barbie Zelizer. London: Athlone Press.

DuPlessis, Rachel Blau. 1985. *Writing Beyond the Ending: Narrative Strategies of Twentieth-Century Women Writers*. Bloomington: Indiana University Press.

Eliot, T. S., ed. [1918] 1954. "A Retrospect." In *Literary Essays of Ezra Pound*, 3–14. London: Faber.

Endelman, Todd. 1990. *Radical Assimilation in English-Jewish History 1656–1945*. Bloomington: Indiana University Press.

Frankel, Sara. 1987. "Interview with Muriel Spark." *Partisan Review* 54, no. 3 (1987): 448–49.

Fuss, Diana, 1991. *Inside Out: Lesbian Theories, Gay Theories*. London: Routledge.

Galchinsky, Michael. 1996. *The Origin of the Modern Jewish Woman Writer: Romance and Reform in Victorian England*. Detroit: Wayne State University.

Gilman, Sander, 1986. *Jewish Self-Hatred: Anti-Semitism and the Hidden Language of the Jews*. Baltimore, MD: Johns Hopkins University Press.

Goldfarb, Alvin. 1998. "Inadequate Memories: The Survivor in Plays by Mann, Kesselman, Lebow and Baitz." In *Staging the Holocaust: The Shoah in Drama and Performance*, ed. Claude Schumacher, 111–29. Cambridge: Cambridge University Press.

Goldsmith, Martin. 2000. *The Inextinguishable Symphony: A True Story of Music and Love in Nazi Germany.* New York: J. Wiley.

Goodman, Lizbeth. 1993. *Contemporary Feminist Stages: To Each Her Own.* London: Routledge.

Goodman, Paul. 1922. Jewish and Welsh Nationalism. *Zionist Review* 5 (10): 161.

Goodman, Romana. 1920. *Zionist Women's Work: The Jewish League for Cultural Work in Palestine.* London: Federation of Women Zionists of the United Kingdom.

Goody, Alex. 2000. "Autobiography/Auto-mythology: Mina Loy's *Anglo-Mongrels and the Rose.*" In *Representing Lives: Women and Autobiography,* ed. Alison Donnell and Pauline Polkey. London: Macmillan.

———. 2001. "To Who?: Gender, Authority and the Speaking Subject in Loy's Love Lyrics." *How2* 1, no. 5 (March). http://www.departments.bucknell.edu/.stadler_center/how2.

Graham, David. 2003. "So How Many Jews Are There in the UK?: The 2001 UK Census and the Size of the Jewish Population." *J(ewish) P(olicy) R(esearch) News* Spring 2003.

Gray, Frances. 2001. "Carry On, Echo: The Dissident Sound Body." http://www.ukc.ac.uk/sdfva/sound-journal/gray001.html.

Gubar, Susan. 1983. "The Birth of the Artist as Heroine: (Re)production, the Künstlerroman Tradition, and the Fiction of Katherine Mansfield." In *The Representation of Women in Fiction,* ed. Carolyn Heilbrun. Baltimore, MD: Johns Hopkins University Press.

Habermas, Jürgen. 1985. "Between Eroticism and General Economics: Georges Bataille." In *The Philosophical Discourse of Modernity.* Cambridge: Polity Press.

———. 1986. "Vom äffentlichen Gebrauch der Historie." *Die Zeit,* November 7.

Haffenden, John. 1985. *Writers in Interview.* London: Faber.

Halio, Jay L., and Ben Siegel, eds. 1997. *Daughters of Valor: Contemporary Jewish American Women Writers.* Newark: University of Delaware Press.

Hammel, Andrea. 2001. " 'Still on Edge'?: Marginality and Centrality in Silvia Rodgers' *Red Saint, Pink Daughter.*" In *German-Speaking Exiles in Great Britain,* ed. J. M. Ritchie. Amsterdam: Rodopi.

Hanson, Clare. 2000. *Hysterical Fictions: The "Woman's Novel" in the Twentieth Century.* Basingstoke: Macmillan.

Hardmann, Anna. 1999/2000. *Women and the Holocaust, Holocaust Educational Trust Research Papers* 1, no. 3.

Harris, Jonathan Mark, and Deborah Oppenheimer. 2000. *Into the Arms of Strangers: Stories of the Kindertransport.* London: Bloomsbury.

Hartill, Rosemary. 1989. "Bernice Rubens: Our Father." In *Writers Revealed.* London: BBC.

Hartley, Jenny. 2001. "Warriors and Healers, Imposters and Mothers: Betty Miller's *On the Side of the Angels.*" In *Dressing up for War: Transformations of Gender and Genre in the Discourse and Literature of War,* eds. Aránzazu Usandizaga and Andrew Momuckendam, 173–88. Amsterdam: Rodopi.

Heinemann, Marlene. 1986. *Gender and Destiny: Women Writers and the Holocaust.* New York: Greenwood.

Henriques, Ursula R. Q. 1993. "The Jewish Community of Cardiff 1813–1914." In *The Jews of South Wales: Historical Studies,* ed. Ursula Henriques, 9–43. Cardiff: University of Wales Press.

Hochstadt, Steve, ed. 2004. *Sources of the Holocaust.* Basingstoke: Palgrave.

Homans, Margaret. 1998. "Representation, Reproduction, and Women's Place in Language." In *Literary Theory: An Anthology,* ed. Julie Rivkin and Michael Ryan, 650–55. Malden, MA: Blackwell, 1998.

Hosmer. Robert E., Jr. 1993. "Paradigm and Passage: The Fictions of Anita Brookner." In *Contemporary British Women Writers: Narrative Strategies,* ed. Robert E. Hosmer Jr., 26–54. New York: St. Martin's.

Hynes, Samuel. 1976. *The Auden Generation: Literature and Politics in England in the 1930s.* New York: Viking.

Isser, E. R. 1990. "Toward a Feminist Perspective in American Holocaust Drama." *Studies in the Humanities* 17 (December): 139–48.

James, Sian, Tony Kushner, and Sarah Pierce, eds. 1998. *Cultures of Ambivalence. Studies in Jewish–Non-Jewish Relations.* London: Vallentine and Mitchell.

Jaskoski, Helen, 1994. "Mina Loy Outsider Artist." *Journal of Modern Literature* 18, no. 4 (Fall): 349–68.

Johnson, Marigold. 1981. "Pillow Talk and Politics." *Times Literary Supplement,* October 2, 1118.

Johnson, Paul. 1987. *A History of the Jews.* London: Weidenfeld and Nicolson.

Jones, Lewis. [1937] 1978. *Cwmardy.* London: Lawrence and Wishart.

———. [1939] 1978. *We Live.* London: Lawrence and Wishart.

Judt, Tony. 2002. "Israel: The Road to Nowhere." *New York Review of Books* 49, no. 8, May 9, 4.

Juhasz, Suzanne. 1976. *Naked and Fiery Forms: Modern American Poetry by Women: A New Tradition.* New York: Harper.

Keenoy, Roy, and Saskia Brown, eds. 1998. *The Babel Guide to Jewish Fiction.* London: Boulevard.

Kenyon, Olga. 1988. *Women Novelists Today: A Survey of English Writing in the Seventies and Eighties.* Brighton: Harvester.

———. 1989. *Women Writers Talk.* Oxford: Lennard.

———. 1991. *Writing Women: Contemporary Women Novelists.* London: Pluto.

———. 1992. *The Woman Writer's Imagination.* Bradford: University of Bradford.

Keyssar, Helen, ed. 1996. *Feminist Theatre and Theory.* Basingstoke: Macmillan.

Kinnahan, Linda. 1994. *Poetics of the Feminine: Authority and Literary Tradition in William Carlos Williams, Mina Loy, Denise Levertov, and Kathleen Fraser.* New York: Cambridge University Press.

Kobler, Dora. 1947. *Four Rachels.* London: Education Department of the Federation of Women Zionists.

Kremer, S. Lillian. 2001. *Women's Holocaust Writing: Memory and Imagination.* Lincoln: University of Nebraska Press.

Kristeva, Julia. 1980. *Desire in Language.* Trans. Leon S. Roudiez. New York: Columbia University Press.

———. 1982. *Powers of Horror: An Essay on Abjection.* Trans. Leon S. Roudiez. New York: Columbia University Press. (Republished Hemel Hempstead: Harvester, 1991.)

———. 1991. *Strangers to Ourselves.* Trans. Leon S. Roudiez. Hemel Hempstead: Harvester.

Kushner, Tony, ed. 1992. *The Jewish Heritage in British History: Englishness and Jewishness.* London: Frank Cass.

———. 1994. *The Holocaust and the Liberal Imagination: A Social and Cultural History.* Oxford: Blackwell.

LaCapra, Dominic. 1998. *History and Memory after Auschwitz.* Ithaca, NY: Cornell University Press.

Lacey, Paul A. 1972. *The Inner War: Forms and Themes in Recent American Poetry.* Philadelphia: Fortress.

Lassner, Phyllis. 1998. *British Women Writers of World War II: Battlegrounds of Their Own.* London: Macmillan.

Lawson, Peter, ed. 2001. *Passionate Renewal: Jewish Poetry in Britain since 1945.* Nottingham: Five Leaves.

———. 2001b. "Way Out in the Centre: Elaine Feinstein in Conversation with Peter Lawson." *Jewish Quarterly* 181 (Spring): 65–69.

Leverton, Bertha, and Schmuel Lowensohn, eds. 1990. *I Came Alone: The Stories of the Kindertransports.* Sussex: Book Guild.

Levy, Daniel, and Natan Sznaider. 2000. "Memory Unbound: The Holocaust and the Formation of Cosmopolitan Memory." *European Journal of Social Theory* 5 (1): 87–106.

Lichtenstein, Rachel, and Iain Sinclair. 1999. *Rodinsky's Room.* London: Granta.

Light, Alison. 1991. *Forever England: Femininity, Literature and Conservatism between the Wars.* London: Routledge.

Litvinoff, Emanuel, ed. 1979. *The Penguin Book of Jewish Short Stories.* Harmondsworth: Penguin.

Lixl-Purcell, Andreas, ed. 1988. *Women of Exile: German-Jewish Autobiographies since 1933.* New York: Greenwood Press.

Llwyd Morgan, Derec. 1994. *"Canys Bechan Yw": Y genedl etholedig yn ein llenyddiaeth/"For she is small": The Chosen Nation in Our Literature.* Aberystwyth: Pryfysgol Cymru.

Llywelyn, Dorian. 1999. *Sacred Place: Chosen People.* Cardiff: University of Wales Press.

Lyndon, Sonja, and Sylvia Paskin, eds. 1996. *The Slow Mirror and Other Stories: New Fiction by Jewish Writers.* Nottingham: Five Leaves.

Macdonald, Claire. 2000. "Writing outside the Mainstream." In *Cambridge Companion to Modern British Women Playwrights,* ed. Elaine Aston and Janelle Reinelt, 235–52. Cambridge: Cambridge University Press.

MacGowan, Christopher, ed. 1998. *The Letters of Denise Levertov and William Carlos Williams.* New York: New Directions.

Malcolm, Cheryl Alexander. 2002. *Understanding Anita Brookner.* Columbia: University of South Carolina Press.

Martin, Harry. 1988. *Understanding Denise Levertov.* Columbia: University of South Carolina Press.

Maslen, Elizabeth. 2001. *Political and Social Issues in British Women's Fiction, 1928–1968.* London: Palgrave.

Moi, Toril. 1986. *The Kristeva Reader.* Oxford: Blackwell.

Monroe, Harriet. 1923. "The Editor in France." *Poetry* 23.

Montefiore, Hugh. 1998. *On Being Jewish Christian: Its Blessings and Problems.* London: Hodder and Stoughton.

Munt, Sally. 1995. "The Lesbian Flâneur." In *Mapping Desire,* ed. David Bell and Gill Valentine, 114–25. London: Routledge.

Newman, Louis I., ed. 1987. *The Hasidic Anthology.* Northvale, NJ: Aronson.

Nochlin, Linda, and Tamar Garb, eds. 1995. *The Jew in the Text.* New York: Thames and Hudson.

Ofer, Dalia, and Leonore J. Weitzman, eds. 1998. *Women in the Holocaust.* New Haven, CT: Yale University Press.

Orbach, Susie. 1993. Preface to *The Jewish Woman in Contemporary Society: Transitions and Traditions,* by Adrienne Baker. London, Macmillan.

Palmer, Paulina. 1993. *Lesbian Gothic: Transgressive Fictions.* London: Cassell.

Parker, Roszika. 1974. "Being Jewish: Anti-Semitism and Jewish Women." *Spare Rib* 79 (February).

Parnell, Michael. 1990. Interview [with Bernice Rubens]. *New Welsh Review* 9:46–54.

Patraka, Vivian M. 1999. *Spectacular Suffering: Theatre, Fascism and the Holocaust.* Bloomington: Indiana University Press.

Peate, Iorwerthe C. 1976. *Rhwng Dau Fyd.* Dynbych: Gwasg Gee.

Phillips, Caryl. 1997. *Extravagant Strangers: A Literature of Belonging.* London: Faber.

Phillips, Laura, and Marion Baraitser, eds. 2004. *Mordechai's First Brush with Love: Stories by Jewish Women in Britain.* London: Loki.

Plaskow, Judith. 1990. *Standing Again at Sinai: Judaism from a Feminist Perspective.* San Francisco: HarperCollins.

Pope, Juliet J. 1986. "Anti-racism, Anti-Zionism and Anti-Semitism: Debates in the British Women's Movement." *Patterns of Prejudice* 20, no. 3 (July).

Quinby, Lee. 1992. "The Subject of Memoirs: *The Woman Warrior*'s Technique of Ideographic Selfhood." In *De/Colonizing the Subject: The Politics of Gender in Women's Autobiography,* ed. Sidonie Smith and Julia Watson. Minneapolis: Minnesota University Press.

Radford. Jean. 1999. "Late Modernism and the Poetry of History." In *Women Writers of the 1930's: Gender, Politics and History,* ed. Maroula Joannou, 33–45. Edinburgh: Edinburgh University Press.

Rich, Adrienne. 1986. "Compusory Heterosexuality and Lesbian Existence (1980)." In *Blood, Bread and Poetry: Selected Prose 1979–1985,* 23–75. New York: Norton.

Richmond, Colin. 1992. "Englishness and Medieval Anglo-Jewry." In *The Jewish Heritage in British History: Englishness and Jewishness*, ed. Tony Kushner. London: Frank Cass.

Ringelheim, Joan. 1985. "Women and the Holocaust: A Reconsideration of Research." *Signs: A Journal of Women in Culture and Society* 10, no. 4 (Summer): 741–61.

Ritchie, J. M., ed. 2001. *German-Speaking Exiles in Great Britain*. Amsterdam: Rodopi.

Rokem, Freddie. 1998. "On the Fantastic in Holocaust Performance." In *Staging the Holocaust: The Shoah in Drama and Performance*, ed. Claude Schumacher, 40–52. Cambridge: Cambridge University Press.

Rose, Gillian. 1995. *Love's Work*. London: Chatto and Windus.

Rose, Jacqueline. 1996. *States of Fantasy*. Oxford: Oxford University Press.

———. 2005. *The Question of Zion*. Princeton: Princeton University Press.

Rubinstein, W. D., and Hilary L. Rubinstein. 1998. "Philosemitism in Britain and in the English-speaking World, 1840–1939: Patterns and Typology." *Jewish Journal of Sociology* 40 (1–2): 5–47.

Sachar, Howard M. 1994. *Farewell España: The World of the Sephardim Remembered*. New York: Vintage Books.

Samuel, Henry E. 1958. "A Welsh Missionary in Israel." *CAJEX* 8 (2): 50–52.

Schaum, Melita. 1986. " 'Moon-flowers out of muck': Mina Loy and the Female Autobiographical Epic." *Massachusetts Studies in English* 10, no. 4 (Fall): 4–276.

Schechner, Mark. 1990. *The Conversion of the Jews and Other Essays*. Basingstoke: Macmillan.

Schiff, Hilda, ed. 1995. *Holocaust Poetry*. New York: St. Martin's.

Schmidt, M. 1997. "Elaine Feinstein in Conversation." *PN Review*, Manchester, 24 (2): 36–44.

Schonfield, Hugh Joseph. 1933. *The History of Jewish Christianity*. London.

Schumacher, Claude, ed. 1998. *Staging the Holocaust: The Shoah in Drama and Performance*. Cambridge: Cambridge University Press.

Sedgwick, Eve Kosofsky. 1994. *Tendencies*. London: Routledge.

Şenay, Bülend. 2002. The Making of Jewish Christianity in Britain: Hybridity, Identity and Tradition. Lancaster University PhD thesis, 2002.

Shreiber, Meera, and Keith Tuma, eds. 1998. *Mina Loy: Woman and Poet*. Orono, ME: National Poetry Foundation.

Simon, Leon. 1921. Introduction to *The Nationalists and Other Goluth Studies*, by Lily Tobias. London: C. W. Daniel.

Skinner, John. 1992. *The Fictions of Anita Brookner: Illusions of Romance*. London: Macmillan.

Smith, Jules. n.d., http://www.contemporarywriters.com/authors.

Smith, Sidonie. 1987. *A Poetics of Women's Autobiography: Marginality and the Fictions of Self-Representation*. Bloomington: Indiana University Press.

Stephens, Meic, ed. 1998. *The New Companion to the Literature of Wales.* Cardiff: University of Wales Press.

Straub, Ervin. 1989. *The Roots of Evil.* Cambridge: Cambridge University Press.

Sylvester, Louise. 2001. "Troping the Other: Anita Brookner's Jews." *English* 50, no. 196 (Spring): 47–58.

Tuma, Keith. 1998. "Mina Loy's 'Anglo-Mongrels and the Rose.'" In *Mina Loy: Woman and Poet,* ed. Meera Shreiber and Keith Tuma. Orono, ME: National Poetry Foundation.

Tylee, Claire M. 2005. "Hyphenated Identity in the Woman's Novel." In *British Women Write the 1930's,* ed. Jane Marcus et al. Gainsville: University of Florida Press.

Usandizaga, Aránzazu. 1998. "The Female Buildungsroman at the Fin du Siècle: The 'Utopian Imperative' in Anita Brookner's *A Closed Eye* and *Fraud.*" *Critique: Studies in Contemporary Fiction* 39, no. 4 (Summer): 325–41.

Valentine, Gill. 1996. "(Re)negotiating the 'Heterosexual Street': Lesbian Productions of Space." In *Body Space: Destabilizing Geographies of Gender and Sexuality,* ed. Nancy Duncan, 146–55. London: Routledge.

Vincentelli, Maria. 1994. "Artefact and Identity: The Welsh Dresser as Domestic Display and Cultural Symbol." In *Our Sister's Land: The Changing Identities of Women in Wales,* ed. J. Aaron, S. Betts, T. Rees, and M. Vincentelli, 228–41. Cardiff: University of Wales Press.

Wandor, Michelene, ed. 1990. *Once a Feminist: Stories of the 1970's Generation.* London: Virago.

Williams, Raymond. 1977. *Marxism and Literature.* Oxford: Oxford University Press.

Williams, William Carlos. 1967. *The Autobiography of William Carlos Williams.* New York: New Directions.

Wilson, Elizabeth. 1986. *Hidden Agendas: Theory, Politics and Experience in the Women's Movement.* London: Tavistock.

Wirth-Nesher, Hana. 1998. "Introduction: Jewish-American Autobiography." *Prooftexts* 18:113–20.

Worpole, Ken. 1983. *Dockers and Detectives: Popular Reading, Popular Writing.* London: Verso.

Woolf, Michael. 1995. "Negotiating the Self: Jewish Fiction in Britain since 1945." In *Other Britain, Other British: Contemporary Multicultural Fiction,* ed. A. Robert Lee. London: Pluto.

Young, Robert J. C. 1995. *Colonial Desire: Hybridity in Theory, Culture and Race.* London: Routledge.

Zatlin, Linda Gertner. 1981. *The Nineteenth Century Anglo-Jewish Novel.* Boston: Twayne.

Zelizer, Barbie, ed. 2001. *Visual Culture and the Holocaust.* London: Athlone Press.

Zipes, Jack. 1992. *The Operated Jew: Two Tales of Anti-Semitism.* London: Routledge.

Contributors

ROSE ATFIELD lectures in English and Creative Writing at Brunel University, where she organizes the MA in Creative Writing. Her research interests lie in the fields of Irish literature and women poets; she has published articles on Eavan Boland and Jennifer Johnson and has a book forthcoming on Seamus Heaney.

DAVID BRAUNER is Director of American Studies at The University of Reading. His first book was *Post-War Jewish Fiction: Ambivalence, Self-Explanation and Transatlantic Connections* (2001). He has also published widely in the fields of contemporary American and Jewish fiction.

JASMINE DONAHAYE is completing her doctoral dissertation on the Jewish Literature of Wales at the University of Wales, Swansea. She edited Lily Tobias's pacifist novel *Eunice Fleet* for republication by Honno Press in 2004, and has published articles in the *Yearbook of Welsh Writing in English*, *The New Welsh Review*, and *Planet*.

DAVID FULTON is Lecturer in English at Brunel University. He has published essays on contemporary British and American poets.

ALEX GOODY is Senior Lecturer in Twentieth-Century Literature, and Deputy Director for the Research Centre in Modern and Contemporary Poetry at Oxford Brookes University. Her book *Mina Loy and the Cultures of Modernism* is forthcoming. As well as articles on Mina Loy, she has published work on Amy Levy, the New Woman, and New York Dada.

SUSANNE GREENHALGH is principal lecturer in the Drama Department at Roehampton Institute, University of Surrey, and has published articles on Shakespeare, contemporary women dramatists, and the politics of mourning for Princess Diana. She is

261

currently editing a collection of essays, *Shakespeare's Children/ Children's Shakespeare.*

PAULINA PALMER lectures in the English Department at Birkbeck College, University of London. Her publications include *Contemporary Women's Fiction: Narrative Practice and Feminist Theory* (1989); *Contemporary Lesbian Writing: Dreams, Desire, Difference* (1993); and *Lesbian Gothic: Transgressive Fictions* (1999).

DEBORAH PHILIPS lectures in the School of Arts at Brunel University. She has written extensively on popular culture and popular fiction and is the co-author (with Ian Haywood) of *Brave New Causes* (1998), (with Liz Linington and Debra Penman) of *Writing Well* (1998), and co-editor of *Tourism and Tourist Attractions* (1999).

SARAH SCEATS is head of English Literature at Kingston University, London. She specializes in twentieth-century fiction, especially women's writing. Her publications include articles on the work of contemporary women authors. She co-edited with Gail Cunningham *Image and Power: Women in Fiction in the Twentieth Century* (1996) and has published a monograph, *Food, Consumption and the Body in Contemporary Women's Fiction* (2000).

CLAIRE TYLEE is Senior Lecturer in English at Brunel University. Her publications include *The Great War and Women's Consciousness* (1990), *War Plays by Women* (1999), *Women, the First World War and Dramatic Imagination* (2000), and articles on twentieth-century literature and war. She has recently published on Holocaust writing and is at present researching work by Jewish women writers.

ARÁNZAZU USANDIZAGA holds the Chair of English Literature at the Autonomous University of Barcelona and is leader of a research group investigating war literature, financed by the Spanish Ministry of Education and Culture. She has co-edited two volumes of essays as a result: *Dressing Up for War* (2001) and *Back to Peace* (2004), and an anthology of Spanish war literature, and published articles in the field of women's writing.

SUE VICE is Professor of English Literature at the University of Sheffield. Her recent publications include *Introducing Bakhtin* (1997), *Holocaust Fiction* (2000), and *Children Writing the Holocaust* (2004).

Index

Names in bold are of authors discussed at length